WITHDRAWN
WRIGHT STATE UNIVERSITY LIBRARIES

Learning Across the Lifespan
Theories, Research, Policies

Other titles of interest

T. Husén, A.C. Tuijnman & W.D. Halls (eds.)
Schooling in Modern European Society: A Report of the *Academia Europaea*

C. J. Titmus (ed.)
Lifelong Education for Adults: An International Handbook

R. M. Thomas (ed.)
Encyclopedia of Human Development and Education: Theory, Research, and Studies

Pergamon journals of related interest

INTERNATIONAL JOURNAL OF EDUCATIONAL RESEARCH

LEARNING AND INSTRUCTION

Learning Across the Lifespan
Theories, Research, Policies

Edited by

A. C. TUIJNMAN
Department of Education,
University of Twente,
Enschede, The Netherlands

and

M. VAN DER KAMP
Department of Pedagogy, Andragogy
and Education,
University of Groningen,
Groningen, The Netherlands

PERGAMON PRESS

OXFORD · NEW YORK · SEOUL · TOKYO

U.K.	Pergamon Press Ltd, Headington Hill Hall, Oxford OX3 0BW, England
U.S.A	Pergamon Press, Inc., 660 White Plains Road, Tarrytown, New York 10591-5153, U.S.A.
KOREA	Pergamon Press Korea, KPO Box 315, Seoul 110-603, Korea
JAPAN	Pergamon Press Japan, Tsunashima Building Annex, 3-20-12 Yushima, Bunkyo-ku, Tokyo 113, Japan

Copyright © 1992 Pergamon Press Ltd

All Rights Reserved. No part of this publication may be reproduced, stored in a retrieval system or transmited in any form or by any means: electronic, electrostatic, magnetic tape, mechanical, photocopying, recording or otherwise, without permission in writing from the publishers.

First edition 1992

Library of Congress Cataloging-in-Publication Data
Learning across the lifespan: theories, research, policies/edited by A. C. Tuijnman and M. Van Der Kamp. – 1st ed.
p. cm.
Includes bibliographical references and index.
1. Adult learning – Netherlands. 2. Learning, Psychology of. 3. Adult education – Netherlands. I. Tuijnman, Albert. II. Kamp, Max van der.
LC5225.L42L43 1992   374'.9492 – dc20   92-31196

British Library Cataloguing in Publication Data
A catalogue record for this book is available from the British Library

ISBN 0-08-041926-7

Printed in Great Britain by BPCC Wheatons Ltd, Exeter

FOREWORD

We live in an era of turbulent economic, technological, demographic and social change. There can be no doubt that these changes represent opportunities and challenges for both initial and adult education, and that it is necessary for people to keep abreast of these changes in order to be able to function adequately in society and work. This argument is frequently used by educationalists, policy makers, and the media. Yet I believe that the real meaning of this challenge for education — for its financing, organisation, content, and didactic approach — is not fully recognized.

Initial and adult education should respond effectively to emerging trends and developments, since these create new demands. In initial education, pupils should be prepared for a life of active and conscious learning. A favourable attitude to learning as an adult should be imparted to the students in primary and secondary education. This can only be achieved if, in the curriculum, increased attention is paid to the development of learning strategies and skills for autonomous, efficient and effective learning.

When considering the education of adults, we need to understand the specific characteristics of their learning styles and what this means for the provision of adult education. In what way is adult learning distinctive from learning in childhood? How does adult learning relate to work, and to social and cultural activities? These are important questions because the educational process should be directed at and adjusted to the unique features of adult learning and the specific circumstances of adults in complex, changing societies.

This volume deals with both concerns. The importance of learning for life is addressed by all contributors. It not only presents a systematic overview of trends relevant to lifelong learning, but also offers an in-depth analysis of the state of the art concerning adult learning in the relevant social science disciplines. Its broad multidisciplinary orientation, and the focus on many practical issues of policy, in my opinion make this volume an important source for those concerned with the development of educational policy, practice, and research programmes. I therefore recommend this study to those politically, investigatively, or

v

otherwise involved in questions that have a bearing on the challenge of developing learning across the lifespan.

As a Minister of Education and Science I recognize a responsibility for the active stimulation of learning across the lifespan. First, I will be alert to developments in initial and adult education. Where necessary, I will undertake proper action to encourage the inclusion of "lifelong learning" elements in the school curriculum. This may even apply to teacher training, since teachers must be aware of the importance of instilling in all their students a capacity for learning how to learn efficiently and independently. In addition, I would like to emphasize the importance of a favourable research and development policy to promote the design and application of advanced educational technology suited to the special needs and interests of adults. Support for this publication might well be seen as an example of my intention in this respect.

J.J.M. RITZEN
Minister
Zoetermeer
May 1992
Netherlands, Ministry of Education and Science

EDITORS' PREFACE

There is a widespread consensus today that adult education and continuing vocational training are central elements in a strategy aimed at achieving economic growth and high life quality. The economic significance of postinitial education has increased in recent years as a consequence of demographic change, international trade competition, and new technology. For example, the fact that new technology so far seems to have had only a modest impact on productivity is explained as a result of a failure to match technology with the appropriate skills and an adequate organization of work. But the stakes are not only economic.

Adult education has also become a structural determinant of the employment opportunities, earnings and the quality of life of individuals. Hence questions of access and opportunity to learn are gaining in importance. In line with the above is the argument that adults who lack motivation, opportunity or the information they need in order to make an informed decision about how to participate in a lifelong learning society will increasingly find themselves at a disadvantage. This has a cost not only to the individual but also to employers and society. Thus there is a need to pay attention not only to the economic, but also to the social and political dimensions of adult education. Another implication is that educational systems obviously must prepare people for a life of active learning. But how can this be achieved?

In order to make skills formation a reality for all people regardless of prior experience of learning, sex, age, and life career, some degree of coherence amongst the highly diversified and ad hoc approaches to initial and adult education that characterize current provision must be promoted. Here a dilemma arises. Since the learning needs of adults are highly differentiated, the strategies to be followed will have to be diversified as well. How can a flexible yet comprehensive approach to skills formation be developed? In this volume the case is argued that the principles of lifelong learning should be at the heart of the new approach to skills development. Lifelong learning is advocated not as a theoretical and utopian idea but as the inevitable reality for the future of education in affluent, technologically advanced, and pluralistic societies.

Lifelong learning begins at home and in school, but beyond that and for a large part of the lifespan work is paramount. Hence the goal of transforming the work organization into a learning organization must feature prominently in a future-oriented policy for skills formation. An understanding of how learning in the work place occurs, whether in the form of structured training on or off the job or by means of informal and self-planned learning, may reveal ways of linking learning to business needs, determining priorities, and discovering incentives for learning. Interest in the factors that influence the demand for adult learning across the whole lifespan, and in the way adults choose among learning options and manage their personal development, has mounted as a result of this reorientation towards a lifelong learning strategy. The question of why and how adults learn at different moments in the lifespan has also come to the fore. A new interest in learning to learn and the teaching of adults is also apparent.

While lifelong learning is gaining momentum, governments have so far opted for a strategy to increase provision by relying on the strength of private initiative. Informal learning at the work place is given particular attention. This situation raises questions concerning the determinants of the nature and distribution of opportunity to learn at the work place. The increased reliance on nonformal and informal approaches to adult learning calls the role of public policy in influencing opportunity to learn into focus. A framework for a comprehensive strategy to promote life-long learning may be needed. What should be the role of the government in stimulating, coordinating and monitoring the development of adult learning?

***

It is clear from the above that lifelong learning critically depends not only on access and opportunity to learn but especially on the willingness and capacity of adults to learn effectively. The adult learner and the ways in which adult learning can be encouraged and improved are the focus of this volume. Although the organization of the book is described in detail in Chapter 1, a brief comment on the themes of the various contributions is in order. Each chapter addresses one or several of the questions raised previously in this preface, which many agree are at the forefront of the discussion today. In particular they concern theories and research on the following five themes: lifespan development and education; intelligence, transfer, and capacity to learn; informal learning in the work place; learning to learn; and the implications for policy.

Some of the chapters included in this volume are revisions of papers read at an international symposium on *Learning across the Lifespan:*

Implications for Initial and Adult Education, held at the University of Groningen from June 20 to 21, 1991.

This symposium required a lot of preparatory work. We would like to thank our colleagues on the planning committee, especially Peter Van Den Dool, the representative of the Dutch Ministry of Education and Science, which financed the symposium, and Willem Houtkoop of the Dutch Advisory Council for Adult Education and Training, who was the conference chair. Special thanks are also due to Jarl Bengtsson and Donald Hirsch of the Organization for Economic Co-operation and Development (OECD), who helped in identifying some of the issues that were discussed at the symposium. Chapters 2, 12, 13 and 14 are based on papers originally written for the Centre for Educational Innovation and Research (CERI) at the OECD. These papers were central to CERI's 1991 activity on the adult learner, which investigated the factors determining effective participation by adults in education and training. That work is being followed up in the new CERI mandate starting in 1992, under a project entitled Human Resources and Lifelong Learning.

Finally, but not least, heartfelt thanks are due to the participants and to Sandra Schele of the Centre for Applied Research on Education, University of Twente, The Netherlands, for her assistance in the many tasks required to get this manuscript ready for publication.

Enschede and Groningen   ALBERT TUIJNMAN
April 1992   MAX VAN DER KAMP

CONTENTS

Part 2: Capacity to Learn in the Lifespan

Part 3: Skills Formation in the Work Place

Part 4: Learning to Learn in the Lifespan

Part 5: Implications for Policy and Practice

Part 1

Lifespan Development and Education

Chapter 1

LEARNING FOR LIFE: NEW IDEAS, NEW SIGNIFICANCE

ALBERT TUIJNMAN
University of Twente, The Netherlands

MAX VAN DER KAMP
University of Groningen, The Netherlands

This first chapter introduces the issues that were discussed by some 50 experts and policy makers in the field of learning and education during the two days the participants convened at the University of Groningen in the Netherlands. The theme of the symposium relates to the quotation from Seneca: *Non scholae, sed vitae discimus.* "You do not learn only for examinations, but for your life after school", is a common interpretation. Inherent in this statement is the notion that initial education can provide sufficient skills and qualifications to last individuals for their entire "life after school". The same can be said of the Dutch saying: "What little Hans does not learn, big Hans will never know".

However, several of the chapters in this volume present arguments and insights that challenge the message contained in this saying. The research studies on lifespan development and education, which are discussed in the next chapters, especially call the validity of Seneca's observation into doubt. The purpose of the papers collected in this volume is not only to investigate the need for adult learning in different situations and contexts, but also to examine questions such as how and where adults learn and which approaches can be successful in making adult learning attractive and effective.

The chapters are organized into five parts, each of which addresses a common theme. Part 1 is concerned with theories and research on lifespan development and education. The studies in Part 2 give an overview of recent research in areas such as capacity to learn, aspects of fluid, crystallized and practical intelligence, and transfer of intellectual skills.

Part 3 deals with the skills adults need in different situations and how skills may be acquired through informal learning on the job. The studies reported in Part 4 investigate the principles of learning to learn in the lifespan, and how implementation can be facilitated. Part 5 deals with overall trends in adult education policy and practice, and spells out some of the implications for the organization of lifelong learning in industrialized societies.

Lifespan Development and Education

The attention of developmental psychologists was for a long time focussed on children, but extended in several directions during the 1970s and 1980s (see Thomas, 1990). By the early 1990s the field embraced the entire lifespan from conception to death, and educational psychologists have become interested in the contribution of informal and nonformal learning in addition to formal education. However, despite the fact that a vast body of writings on the theme of lifespan development and education has cumulated over a period spanning several decades of intensive research effort, there still is a dearth of empirical evidence for the various theories of lifespan development. Even consensus on the precise meaning of the term "lifespan development" is still lacking.

Seminal conceptual contributions were made early in the development of the field by Bühler (1933), Maslow (1968), Havighurst (1953) and Erikson (1980). Important also is the work of Baltes (1987) and colleagues, who conducted a series of investigations into the general principles of lifelong development and the degree and conditions of plasticity or modifiability in individual development. Havighurst (1953) introduced the concept of developmental tasks. He describes this as follows:

> a task which arises at or about a certain period in the life of the individual, successful achievement of which leads to his happiness and to success with later tasks, while failure leads to unhappiness in the individual, disapproval by the society, and difficulty with later tasks. (Havighurst, 1953, p. 2)

The developmental tasks of a particular group of people are seen as arising from three sources: physical maturation, cultural pressure resulting from the expectations of the community and the society at large, and aspirations in relation to individual values. Havighurst (1953) considers personality, or the self, as the outcome of interaction between organic and environmental factors. He studied the characteristics of developmental tasks by means of observation and introspection. In this way he identified a number of developmental tasks in relation to certain phases in the lifespan, for example, infancy and early childhood, middle childhood, adolescence, early adulthood, middle age, and later maturity. The related developmental tasks are, for example: learning to walk in infancy, achieving personal independence in middle childhood, successful entry into the labour market in early adulthood, and searching and maintaining satisfactory performance in occupational careers during middle age.

Age is a ubiquitous concept in developmental psychology. It is used either as the main or as a subsidiary criterion in anchoring virtually all accounts of change over the lifespan. Such a categorization of the developmental processes of people in accordance with age is useful in certain ways. For example, it can provide a reference framework in relation to which individuals can put into perspective the expectations of others, thus helping them in accomodating social and cultural demands into their daily activities. However, the problems and dangers of using age as a general criterion for identifying the developmental tasks people are likely to face at certain phases in their lifespan are well worth noting, "since age itself is not a cause of change or an explanation of behaviour" (Sugerman, 1986, p. 51). A major problem is that lifespan phases are to an extent culture-specific. The pattern of expectations in an advanced industrialized country in Europe may well be different from those existing in poor developing countries. This critical note has to be borne in mind when examining models of lifespan development, such as the one proposed by Fales (1989).

Fales (1989) provides an interesting description of the various phases of the lifespan. For each, some of the keyproblems which individuals in modern Western societies face are indicated:

1. Separating from family (late teens to early twenties). Tasks include becoming self-supporting, forming attachment with peers, separating emotionally from parents, and forming an identity.
2. Provisional adulthood (early to late twenties). Tasks include selection of a mate and intimacy, forming a family, deciding on life-style, forming an occupational identity, mastery of what one is 'supposed' to be in life.
3. Thirties transition (late twenties and early thirties). Tasks include evaluating and exploring alternatives to choices in phase (2), and establishing an adult relationship with parents.
4. Thirties stabilization (early to late thirties). Tasks include succeeding at phase (3) choices, solidifying a sense of self, increasing the attachment to the family and procreation, and giving up mentors.
5. Forties (mid-life) transition (late thirties and early forties). Tasks include re-evaluating the "dream" of the first half of life, restructuring the time perspective, establishing a sense of meaning, establishing generativity, and expanding emotional repertoire.

6. Restabilization (middle forties to middle fifties). Tasks include succeeding at phase (5) choices, developing self-acceptance, maintaining growth and flexibility emotionally and intellectually, and grandparenthood.
7. Preparation for retirement (late fifties to middle sixties). Tasks include developing adult relationships with children, preparing for the end of an occupational role, and developing alternative sources of self-esteem.
8. Young old period (middle sixties to late seventies). Tasks include exploring uses of leisure, consolidating a sense of self as continuous, maintaining health, income, social relations, and emotional attachments, re-evaluating meaning, and development spirituality.
9. Old old period (late seventies to death). Tasks include establishing self-acceptance, a life review, maintaining emotional attachments, adjusting to declines in health, relationships, and mental functions, facing death, and providing for generational continuity.

The above description of the lifespan by Fales is by necessity very general; each individual leads his or her own unique life within this framework. The two chapters on lifespan development in this volume, one by Tom Schuller and the other by Peter G. Heymans address questions concerning the empirical status of lifespan theories and whether such theories can be used as a basis for developing educational programmes.

Because of the changed demographic, socioeconomic and technological conditions, the capacity to solve problems in different contexts has become increasingly important. The skills people need across the lifespan have also become more complex, varied and demanding. It is therefore not realistic to expect that initial education can succeed in conferring all the necessary qualifications young people need in order to cope adequately with problems that may arise at different stages of the lifespan. Obviously, learning is also necessary later in life. Moreover, the popular belief that "time will tell ..." is only partly true; individuals will always have to make an effort themselves. Learning does not necessarily occur in educational institutions. A great deal of learning is self-directed, or it may take place in cultural institutions, or informally at the workplace. Many people also enrol in the adult education system. Despite the recent increase in the number of adults in the Netherlands who receive continuing vocational education, industrial training, and who take part in educational activities relating to social and cultural aims, Jo Ritzen, the Dutch Minister for Education and Science, is of the opinion that there is still underinvestment in postinitial education in The Netherlands (Ritzen, 1989).

It can be inferred from the research on the educational needs of the elderly (see Hiemstra, this volume) that a sharp increase in the demand and enrolment of older people can be expected in future. Also from these studies one can conclude that initial education does not offer sufficient qualifications for the entire lifespan. Yet this conclusion also masks a problem, since the data show that participation in adult education tends to be unidirectional: at least in the Netherlands, more men than women enrol, more young than older people, relatively few people from minority populations, and mainly initially well-educated people (Houtkoop and Van Der Kamp, 1992).

There is good reason to assume that the barriers to the participation of initially poorly educated adults are caused not primarily by financial constraints but by the interaction between what educational psychologists refer to as expectancy and valence. "Valence" expresses an affective attitude to the result of an action and "expectancy" expresses the individual's expectations of being able to participate in and complete the activity. Jointly these exert a "force" determining whether an adult is likely to participate in an educational activity (Bergsten, 1977; Rubenson, 1987). Because the poorly educated often have a negative experience of initial education they are, as a group, less inclined to enrol in adult education compared with the well-educated population. In Chapter 4 Roger Hiemstra concludes that the individualized and self-directed learning needs of adults need to be taken into account in the design of powerful learning environments.

Capacity to Learn in the Lifespan

Whereas in lifespan developmental psychology a number of general stage and process models have been proposed, for example those of Havighurst and Fales mentioned above, in studies on cognitive development no generic models have so far been presented. The general model of cognitive development in children and young adults developed by Jean Piaget forms no exception.

Two decades ago it was very common among researchers to believe that the intelligence of people increases until the early twenties, after which there would be a decrease during the remainder of the lifespan. There are different, often hypothesized explanations for this decrease; for example, the speed of peripheral sensory or motor processes would decline with increasing age, or cognitive performance would decline because certain cognitive activities would be less used with increasing age. Although these is much evidence supporting the view that the performance of cognition declines with increasing age, a number of recent studies indicate that intelligence is not an obstacle to learning at an old age (Peterson, 1987). David Lohman, one of the acknowledged experts in this field, qualifies Peterson's argument in the chapter on fluid and epistemic thinking, which is co-authored by Geoffrey Scheurman.

In an earlier article, Lohman (1989) summarizes the advances in three research traditions on intelligence: trait theories of intelligence, information-processing theories of intelligence, and general theories of thinking. An interesting trait theory is the theory of fluid and crystallized abilities. Crystallized intelligence depends on sociocultural influences; it involves the ability to perceive relations, to engage in formal reasoning, and to understand one's intellectual and cultural heritage. In general, crystallized intelligence continues to grow slowly throughout adulthood as individuals acquire increased information and develop an under-standing of the relation of various facts and constructs. Fluid intelligence, in contrast, is not closely associated with acculturation. It is generally considered to be independent of instruction or environment and depends more on genetic endowment. It consists of the ability to perceive complex relations, use short-term memory, create concepts, and under-take abstract reasoning. Fluid intelligence involves those abilities that are the most neurophysiological in nature. These are generally assumed to decline after people reach maturity. Lohman and Scheurman present seven thought-provoking conclusions concerning the implications for adult education.

Also important are the theories developed by Gardner (1984) and Wagner and Sternberg (1985). Gardner developed the theory of multiple intelligence, in which he proposes a taxonomy of relative independent systems of human symbols. Apart from linguistic and logical-mathematical symbol systems, Gardner distinguishes other dimensions such as musical intelligence, bodily-kinesthetical, spatial and visual intelligence. "Practical intelligence" is a promising concept coined by Sternberg and Wagner (1986), in which the concept of intelligence is broadened to include coping with problems in the context of private life and in the work situation. Scribner (1986) shows the importance of practical thinking on the job. Richard Wagner contributed a chapter to this volume which explains the concept of practical intelligence and the transfer of problem-solving skills.

Eric De Corte addresses similar questions that are at the forefront of the discussion concerning the implications of recent advances in intelligence research for the acquisition and transfer of intellectual skills: (a) what does skilled thinking, learning, and problem solving involve; (b) how can the acquisition of those skills be fostered through systematic instruction; and (c) what are the conditions for obtaining the transfer of cognitive skills to learning situations that differ from the original learning context? De Corte observes that in order to achieve cognitive transfer in learners, it is necessary to teach explicitly and intentionally for transfer. Whereas De Corte specifically addresses the question of how powerful learning environments can be designed in order to enhance the transfer of cognitive skills in children, Wagner's paper deals with the transfer of practical, problem-solving skills in adults. The focus is on tacit knowledge as an indicator of competence at work. The skills adults need in different contexts including the workplace are the subject of two chapters in Part 3.

Skills Formation in the Work Place

Many, often prescriptive arguments, support the idea that the level of investment in postinitial education needs to be increased. An overview of such arguments as well as data on the development of training expenditures in industrialized countries is given in OECD (1991). The growth of investment in postinitial education and training during the 1980s, which can be noted in many industrialized countries, can be understood against a new appreciation of its economic significance. However, increased investment can of course also be triggered by a decrease in the direct costs of education, low or reduced quality and efficiency in initial education, an extension of working life, and increases in wealth.

Neoclassical theory is at the heart of most studies of the relationship between education and macro-economic growth. These studies have often used simple production functions, which hold that the output of an economy depends, firstly, on the amount of capital and labour employed and, secondly, on the flow of new technology. Increases in capital and labour typically account for nearly half of the growth in output. The residual variance is attributed to technology. Education is usually not entered explicitly but it is assumed to influence both labour quality and technological progress. Hence studies estimating simple production functions with aggregate data support the view that education and macro-economic growth are related (Cohn and Geske, 1990).

A new theory of economic growth has been gaining in importance since the mid-1980s. Extended production functions take not only capital and labour but also knowledge into account. Knowledge, which is usually measured in terms of the level of education in a population, is therefore considered as a primary rather than a secondary production factor. Recent studies comparing growth rates in many different countries found that lack of human capital and education, not lack of labour or investment in physical capital, is what prevents economic growth in poor countries. Since there is ample evidence that adult education "adds to" the "stock" of human capital in a population (Husén and Tuijnman, 1991), it may be concluded that not only formal schooling but also adult education and training contribute to the growth of output in an economy.

Studies of the relationship between adult education and productivity growth in industry have usually concentrated on firm-specific job training. Blakemore and Hoffman (1989) and Bishop (1990), among others, report a positive correlation between training investment and output. Yet the direction of this relationship is often unclear. Profitable companies and firms with high turnover tend to invest more in training than small firms. But studies unequivocally showing that this investment also raises output are scarce. Exceptions are Bishop (1987), Barron et al. (1989), and Mendes de Oliviera et al. (1989). These authors show in well-designed studies that adult education has a significant effect on labour productivity. Barron et al. (1989) find that a 10 per cent increase in training investment leads to a growth of three per cent in labour productivity. If training raises the productivity of workers, then it is also likely to have an effect on the aggregate output of firms.

As noted above, studies in which measures of initial and adult education are specified in extended production functions show that education has a direct effect on productivity. But there is also evidence that adult education may have important indirect effects as well, since it influences the efficiency of employing other relevant factors of production such as capital and new technology (Levin, 1987; Eliasson, 1988; Romer, 1990). This insight is behind the rapidly rising interest in the economics of skills formation since the mid-1980s.

Technology is conventionally seen as a primary factor in production. The huge investment in new technology since the 1970s should have raised output, at least in theory. But the results in the industrialized countries were generally disappointing. This apparent contradiction gave rise to the formulation of the new theory of growth mentioned previously. According to the current position, the effect of technology on productivity is not linear and direct but dependent on interaction with other variables, of which skills formation and the organization of work are particularly important. Adult education is thus seen as a sine qua non for realizing the economic benefits that are, potentially at least, associated with an investment in new technology.

The new approach to growth theory is shown in Figure 1.1, which depicts skills formation at the heart of the economic production function. With the human factor assuming preeminence as a factor of production, concern with the consequences of underinvestment in adult education, and with inefficient and unequal participation, has come to the foreground of the debate at present. The new theory of economic growth discussed above leaves no room for doubt that people will have to learn during their entire lifespan. But what should they learn, exactly?

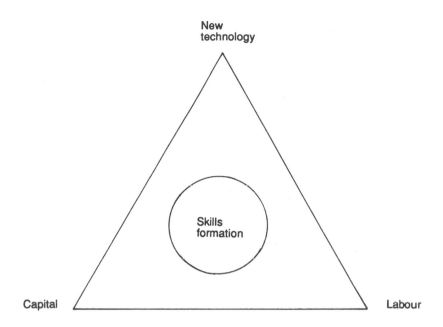

Figure 1.1. A theory of productivity and skills formation.

Basic skills certainly are at the forefront of attention. One of the authors' graduate students (Wolf, 1990) wrote a doctoral thesis on chronic, psychiatric patients and revealed deficiencies in basic literacy skills. Research in the Netherlands reveals that up to seven per cent of the adult population may be considered "functionally illiterate" (Doets et al., 1991). About four per cent of the autochthon Dutch population has difficulty writing, reading tables and completing standard forms. The percentage among the allochthonous immigrant population is several times as high. Estimates of illiteracy in other countries, notably Canada, confirm that a significant group of adults in the population lack the basic skills they need for effective functioning in the community, despite the fact that many of them have completed a full cycle of primary and even lower secondary education (Neice and Lessard, 1990).

Carnevale et al. (1990) carried out a nation-wide study in the United States on the "essential skills employers want". The researchers show that along with the most rudimentary skills of reading, writing, and computation, there is a whole other set of skills that workers must have appropriated in order to perform effectively. The researchers argue that for many American employers the basic skills repertoire has expanded substantially so as to include skills such as adaptability, creative thinking, group effectiveness, and the most fundamental of all, learning how to learn. Two chapters in this volume address the question as to which skills are needed in the modern workplace. Jeroen Onstenk concludes that learning skills, practical competence, situational skills, and transferable skills have more become important in the modern compared with the traditional workplace. The importance of informal learning on the job as an integral component of a strategy for skill formation is discussed by Ben Van Onna. He also contributes views on the skills employers need, and discusses the implications for skill formation.

Learning to Learn in the Lifespan

What does learning to learn mean? In the body of writing on this topic various descriptors exist: metacognitive learning, metalearning, and learning how to learn. Metacognitive training focuses on improving the strategies people use in planning, monitoring, and revising instructional experience, whereas concepts such as learning how to learn and learning to learn span a much wider territory. Robert Smith (1990), one of the contributors to this volume, notes that the latter terms are often used interchangeably to refer to knowledge, processes, and procedures by which people come to and are assisted to make appropriate educational decisions and carry out instrumental tasks associated with successful lifelong learning. These decisions and tasks include school learning, self-directed learning and small group learning, as well as deliberate efforts to enhance one's own or others' capacities and skills in these domains.

Smith (1990) prefers to use the term, learning to learn, "because it implies a continuing process as opposed to an attainment and conveys the meaning without implying that *how* to learn is necessarily more important than what, why, when, where, and whether to learn" (ibid. p. 4). The following learning to learn activities are mentioned:

1. Increasing the individual's self-awareness and the capacity for self-monitoring and reflection when engaged in educational activities;
2. Helping people to become more active learners and to assume an appropriate amount of control of learning-related activity;
3. Broadening the individual's repertoire of learning strategies;
4. Preparing people to accomodate the requirements of different delivery systems, methods, and subject areas;
5. Enhancing learner confidence and motivation;

6. Compensating for metacognitive deficiencies (for example, improving adolescents' ability to think conceptually and analytically);
7. Improving group inquiry and problem solving skills;
8. Helping people to make sound choices among the educational programmes and resources available to them;
9. Fostering organizational learning.

The list proposed by Smith can be extended: for example, one could add the competence needed to cope with shocking events in life. Learning to learn is not only a concept, but also an educational aim. As mentioned above, the notion is not new and relates to other concepts such as metacognitive skills, problem solving skills, learning strategies, and transfer. Transfer skills are studied by Robert-Jan Simons in Chapter 10. Whereas Simons approaches the principles that undergird learning to learn mainly from the perspective of the implications for school education, Smith concentrates on the implications for adult education.

Implications for Policy and Practice

So far only the theories and the research perspectives have been discussed. But what are the implications for initial and adult education? As was pointed out above, current initial education can not provide people with the qualifications they need for the entire lifespan. Lengthening the period of initial schooling does not seem to be an appropriate remedy. Yet extending the period of education has been the most common response to difficulties encountered in the transition of youth from school to work. According to Coleman and Husén (1985) this response has been effective in keeping youth out of the labour force, reducing the supply of labour, and thus reducing youth unemployment. However, whether it has been effective in creating a more able labour force is less clear. Some of the problems created by extended schooling such as the creation of unrealistic educational and occupational expectations, poor work discipline and unfavourable attitudes toward work, may nullify the benefits that can arise from such an investment. In addition, the benefits of extended schooling may well be distributed unequally among the youth who do well or poorly in school. The end result is that insofar as there are benefits from extended schooling, these are differentially distributed in favour of advantaged youth (Coleman and Husén, 1985).

A case can accordingly be made for reconsidering the relation between initial and adult education. The division of tasks between them may well have to become more balanced (see Clement et al., 1991, for a discussion of the position at present in different countries). This is one reason why adults ought to be stimulated to take part in adult education and continuing vocational training. However, one thing is clear: without a positive attitude to education and self-confidence, adults are not likely to actively engage in the lifelong learning society, whether it concerns vocational training or social-cultural activities. This underscores the argument that learning to learn is important and that it needs to be implemented at all levels of education. However, the introduction of learning to learn as an extra subject in the curriculum of initial education and adult education is not appropriate. Not only are the curricula already overburdened at present, it is also apparent that learning to learn implies a broad as well as deep entity of knowledge, attitudes and skills, which relate to all subjects and apply in different contexts.

Self-directed learning demands a self-responsible school climate. Coleman and Husén (1985) write that the principle of creating a largely self-directed and self-responsible community has never come to play a large part in educational philosophy and theory, even as the school moves ever further from the adult world. Special attention should be paid to certain groups at risk, who will probably never touch a book after leaving school because they lack metacognitive skills and confidence in their own learning strategies. Recently, in the Netherlands, the term 'start qualification' has been used as an indication of the minimum level of skills young people need before they can enter the labour market. If learning to learn is not a major element of such a start qualification, then the start of many young adults could turn out to be a false start.

It will be clear that the recent developments in cognitive science, human development theories, instructional science, and educational theory, and the advances in the analysis of skills and occupational requirements which are examined in various chapters in this volume, have many additional implications for the goals, structure, and content of both initial and adult education. These implications are discussed in the concluding chapters, which are contributed by John Lowe, Peter Van Den Dool and Willem Houtkoop, and the editors of this report. However, one problem is not taken up in these chapters, namely that of overschooling. Although the individual tends to derive a positive return on overschooling — research studies suggests that the rate of return may be as high as three to five per cent for each year of schooling over and above the level required for the job — there are critical economists who doubt whether the returns outweigh the costs. The problem of overschooling is often eschewed by research workers in adult education. This report forms no exception, even though it is acknowledged that the issue must be addressed, especially in the context of what is seen as the imperative of developing a lifelong learning society, which is the central conclusion arrived at in this volume.

References

Baltes, P. (1987). Theoretical propositions of lifespan developmental psychology. *Developmental Psychology, 23*, 611-626.

Baltes, P.B., & Brim, O.G. (Eds.) (1979-83). *Life-span development and behavior, Vols. 1-5.* New York: Academic Press.

Barron, J.M., Black, D.A., & Loewenstein, M.A. (1989). Job matching and on the job training. *Journal of Labor Economics 7* (1), 1-19.

Bergsten, U. (1977) *Adult education in relation to work and leisure.* Stockholm: Almqvist & Wiksell.

Bishop, J. (1987). The recognition and reward of employee performance. *Journal of Labor Economics 5*, S36-S56.

Bishop, J. (1990). Job performance, turnover and wage growth. *Journal of Labor Economics 8* (3), 363-386.

Blakemore, A., & Hoffman, D. (1989). Seniority rules and productivity: An empirical test. *Econometrica 56*, 359-371.

Bühler, C. (1933). *Der menschlichen Lebenslauf als Psychologisches Problem.* Leipzig: Hirzel.

Carnevale, A.P., Gainer, L.J., & Meltzer, A.S. (1990). *Workplace basics.* San Francisco: Jossey-Bass.

Clement, W., Drake, K., Eng Fong, P., & Wurzburg, G. (1991). *Further education and training of the labour force: A comparative analysis of national strategies for industry training: Australia, Sweden and the United States.* Paris: OECD.

Cohn, E., & Geske, T.G. (1990). *The economics of education. 3rd edition.* Oxford: Pergamon Press.

Coleman, J., & Husén, T. (1985). *Becoming adult in modern society.* Paris: OECD.

Doets, C., Groen, P., Huisman, T, & Neuvel, I. (1991). *Functionele ongeletterdheid in Nederland.* Amersfoort: SVE.

Eliasson, G. (1988). *The human factor in economic and technical change.* Paris: OECD Educational Monographs.

Erikson, E.H. (1980). *Identity and the life cycle: A reissue.* New York: Norton.

Fales, A.W. (1989). Lifespan learning development. In C.J. Titmus (Ed.), *Lifelong education for adults: An international handbook* (pp. 183-187). Oxford: Pergamon Press.

Gardner, H. (1984). *Frames of mind: The theory of multiple intelligence.* London: Heinemann.

Havighurst, R.J. (1953). *Developmental tasks and education. 2nd edition.* New York: David Mackay.

Houtkoop, W., & Van Der Kamp, M. (1992). Factors influencing participation in continuing education. *International Journal of Educational Research, 17* (6), 537-548.

Husén, T., & Tuijnman, A.C. (1991). The contribution of formal schooling to the increase in intellectual capital. *Educational Researcher 17* (7), 17-25.

Levin, H.M. (1987). Improving productivity through education and technology. In G. Burke & R.M. Rumberger (Eds.), *The future impact of technology on work and education* (pp. 194-214). London: The Falmer Press.

Lohman, D.F. (1989). Human intelligence: An introduction in theory and research. *Review of Educational Research 59* (4), 333-375.

Maslow, A.H. (1968). *Toward a psychology of being. 2nd revised edition.* New York: Reinhold.

Mendes de Oliviera, M.E., Cohn, E., & Kiker, B. (1989). Tenure, earnings, and productivity. *Oxford Bulletin of Economics and Statistics 51*, 1-14.

Neice, D., & Lessard, C. (1990). Definitions, estimates and profiles of literacy and illiteracy (Working paper). Ottawa: National Literacy Secretariat, and Social Trends Analysis Directorate, Department of the Secretary of State of Canada.

OECD (1991). Enterprise-related training. *OECD Employment Outlook,* July 1991, 135-175.

Peterson, D.A. (1987). *Facilitating education for older learners.* San Francisco: Jossey-Bass.

Ritzen, J.M.M. (1989). Government and job training. The Eric John Hanson memorial lecture series, Vol. IV (fall). Alberta: University of Alberta, Department of Economics.

Romer, P. (1990). Endogenous technical change. *Journal of Political Economy, 98.*

Rubenson, K. (1987). Participation in recurrent education: A research review. In H.G. Schütze & D. Istance (Eds.), *Recurrent education revisited* (pp. 39-67). Stockholm: Almqvist & Wiksell.

Schaie, K.W. (Ed.) (1983). *Longitudinal studies of adult psychological development.* New York: Guilford.

Scribner, S. (1986). Thinking in action: Some characteristics of practical thought. In R.J. Sternberg & R.K. Wagner (Eds.), *Practical intelligence: Nature and origins of competence in the everyday world.* London: Cambridge University Press.

Smith, R.M. (Ed.) (1990). *Learning to learn across the lifespan.* San Francisco: Jossey-Bass.

Sternberg, R.J., & Wagner, R.K. (Eds.) (1986). *Practical intelligence: Nature and origins of competence in the everyday world.* London: Cambridge University Press.

Sugarman, L. (1986). *Life-span development: Concepts, theories and interventions.* London: Methuen.

Thomas, R.M. (1990). *Encyclopedia of human development and education.* Oxford: Pergamon Press.

Wagner, R.K. (1987). Tacit knowledge in everyday intelligent behavior. *Journal of Personality and Social Psychology 52,* 1236-1247.

Wagner, R.K., & Sternberg, R.J. (1985). Practical intelligence in real-world pursuits: The role of tacit knowledge. *Journal of Personality and Social Psychology 50,* 436-458.

Wolf, J. (1990). *Oude bekenden van de psychiatrie.* Utrecht: SWP.

Chapter 2

AGE, GENDER, AND LEARNING IN THE LIFESPAN

TOM SCHULLER
University of Edinburgh, Scotland

This chapter presents a summary of major criticisms of conventional lifespan development theories, especially stage models, and considers the way in which the interaction between two major social variables, age and gender, suggests a need for a reappraisal of orthodox perspectives on the lifespan. [1] The conclusion points to, first, the inadequacy of provision in educational systems serving a population stratified by age and gender, and second, to the potential for people to learn from each other: for older people to learn from younger generations, and for younger people to profit from the experience of their predecessors. The challenge, in short, is to develop a lifespan development theory as well as a model of lifelong learning that can promote an integration between the learning patterns of different generations of men and women.

Change and Interaction in Lifespan Development

The understanding of adult development lags well behind the understanding of child development. There are, of course, studies galore of learning by different groups of adults, and some progress has been made in identifying particular learning styles and needs. There is a consensus at the policy level on lifelong learning as a prerequisite for economic success and social competence. But cultural diversity and the complexity of adult life has meant that there is no agreed paradigm within which evidence can be readily compiled and tested, nor a set of

---

[1] This chapter is a revised version of a paper originally prepared for the Centre for Educational Research and Innovation (CERI) at the Organisation for Economic Co-operation and Development (OECD), under its 1991 activity on The Adult Learner.

concepts such as those which Piaget and others have supplied for the early parts of the lifespan. The weighting of attention towards the early years has resulted in schemata which allocate more phases to the period up to adolescence than to the rest of the lifespan, the implication being that development tails off after early adulthood. Theories of human development thus reflect the deep-rooted ageism which prevails in social practice, for example in the educational system itself, still weighted heavily towards the front end. As McLeish (1976) observes, referring to one of the major figures in development theory:

> Although Erikson has made important contributions to the conception of the adult life drama as an arena of continuing potentiality of development arising out of major psychosocial encounters, his references to late adult life are like an artist's rough sketches of a proposes design, compared with his great canvas of psychosexual and psychosocial development in infancy, childhood and adolescence. (McLeish, 1976, p. 80)

Stage and Sequence

One of the key themes in the debate concerns the adequacy of the stage model. This has traditionally been the dominant model, from the earliest times and in many different cultural contexts. Aristotle proposed a three-stage model, Bede a four-stage model, and Shakespeare most famously a seven-stage one. Ecclesiastical murals even employ 10 stages (Burrow, 1986; see also Turnbull, 1984).

New stages emerge from time to time as socially recognized phenomena. An interesting example of this is G. Stanley Hall's successful popularization of the word "adolescence" in the second half of the 19th century. Decades later he attempted similarly to popularize the term "senescence", but it never achieved acceptance in the same way. This example demonstrates the way in which the "success" of a concept is determined by its political context. A phenomenon is not recognized until it in some way becomes a "problem".

Stage models have their value, intrinsically and heuristically, but they have been strongly criticized on a number of counts. Particularly open to attack have been those models which use a calibration of chronological age, allocating the beginning and end of successive stages to precise numerical years. Levinson (1978) claims that the period of self re-evaluation, which came to be known as the midlife crisis, never occurs before the age of 38 or later than 43. Cross (1981) follows this with a defined period of 37-42, during which career identity is settled. Such precision diverts attention from more important issues. It is a powerful illustration of the hold which chronology has over lifespan development theory.

In contradistinction to stage models are approaches which stress the socially constructed character of the lifespan. Indeed, the opposition begins with terminology, since, as Rossi (1980, p. 7) points out, "lifespan" tends to be favoured by developmental psychologists whilst sociologists favour "life course" or "life cycle". These approaches point to the way in which the entry and exit points of the different stages are determined by various social factors. Alterations in social circumstances can lead to a shifting of boundaries, calling fixed-stage models into doubt. Physically people become adult earlier, but are made to wait longer before achieving adult status. As Tucker (1977) observes:

> Adults in authority can to some extent impose their conceptions of childishness both on children and sometimes on other adults too. In this sense the whole concept of childhood can be said to be a man-made phenomenon. Thus childhood may be lengthened and prolonged at some periods of history, and abbreviated at others, according to adult perceptions, needs and expectations. (Tucker, 1977, p. 26)

The imposition is of course not often a conscious one. Yet the power which is exercised by assumptions about the appropriateness of actions to individuals' ages is such that age prejudice must be called into question. One could begin to look for challenges which may not be self-evident. It is easier to accept that the definition of childhood is socially imposed than it is to inquire into ways in which adulthood and its characteristics are socially constituted.

A more subtle challenge is posed by those who argue that it is not the matter of timing which is at issue, but the whole notion of sequence. In this line of thinking not only is the passage into and out of a given stage highly variable, but the stages themselves do not follow each other in preordained order, as is the assumption implicit in basic stage models. Not all individuals pass through the same set of stages; more fundamentally, they do not simply pass through one stage and leave it behind as they proceed to the next, but may loop back, blurring the boundaries and confounding the sequence. Gilligan (1982) makes a powerful case for this view, contrasting male and female patterns of development and their differing central concerns. Women's greater preoccupation with care and personal relationships, she argues, means that

> the middle years of women's lives readily appear as a time of return to the unfinished business of adolescence. This interpretation has been particularly compelling since life-cyle descriptions, derived primarily from studies of men, have generated a perspective from which women, insofar as they differ, appear deficient in their development. The deviance of female development has been especially marked in the adolescent years when girls appear to confuse identity with intimacy by defining themselves through relationships with others. The legacy left from this mode of identity definition is

considered to be a self that is vulnerable to the issues of separation that arise at mid-life. (Gilligan, 1982, p. 170)

Naturally no-one seriously supports the stages model in a pure form, but a crude historical analogy can be drawn with the notion of intelligence. Hopefully the simplistic opposition between nature and nurture in the determination of intelligence has been left behind, in favour of a more complex approach which recognizes that intelligence — however that is defined, and especially if it is defined plurally as Gardner, Sternberg and others do — is a function of the interaction between the biological and the social. It seems probable that the only valid models of the lifespan are those that do not set up a dualism between the biological and the social but accept the interaction between them, and recognize that the task is to map out the patterns of interaction which exist and to discover how these patterns change over time and vary between different cultures.

One can go further by differentiating between two basic types of interaction, each dynamic in its own way. The first occurs at the level of the individual as he or she grows older. The second interaction occurs at the collective level.

Interaction at the Individual Level

The pattern of the individual's lifespan is shaped by the specific events and circumstances which are encountered over time. The rapid emergence of guidance and counselling as a crucial element in the education of adults is a case in point. Not so long ago guidance was accepted as part of the educational process, but only as a marginal part. Now, especially with the emphasis at present on modularization and credit transfer, guidance is gaining recognition as a central feature of provision. This is not just a reflection of the complexity of education, but an acknowledgement of the singularity of individual development. People's aspirations, preferences and capacities change rapidly over time, and successful education must involve the matching of provision to these dispositions. This in turn requires serious attention to be paid to their articulation, this being itself an important part of the learning process.

Such interaction is not, however, a succession of presents, since people carry their pasts with them as they go. The move towards formal recognition of prior learning is one area where the implications of this truism are beginning to be worked out. Less recognized is the importance of opportunities to unlearn, to escape from routines and habits which have become deeply embedded. Whilst the impact of early educational experiences is well documented, especially where these have been sufficiently unpleasant to deter further participation in education, the more powerful influence of daily routinization on people's propensity to learn has been largely ignored.

The influence of routines or habits on learning is by no means solely a repressive one. As Michael Young (1988) points out, habits enable us to deal economically with the predictable, and therefore free us to meet the challenge of the unpredictable:

> The relative fixity of one set of responses to expected changes in the environment allows relative flexibility in responses to the unexpected. But no sooner has the unexpected appeared than its potential for being moved into the category of the expected is assessed. If the unexpected recurs, it can be passed along for action to the general economy of habit. Once the unpredictable has been slid along into the predictable, the mental resources which have been called up can be demobilized and once again put into reserve, ready to deal with the next novelty for which there is no ready-made drill ... . Habit is not only the most precious conservative agent of society, it is also its opposite, its most precious radical agent, enabling us to pay attention to new departments. (Young, 1988, p. 124)

Despite this potential, the extent of routinization may in many cases be such as to dull the readiness to appreciate and respond to new stimuli. Providing the appropriate environments in which routine can play an enabling rather than a stultifying role is a major challenge to adult educators, as it is for schoolteachers.

Interaction at the Collective Level

The second form of interaction is at the collective or general level. However diverse individual patterns of development may be, there will be common features across members of a generation. Both the provision of public services such as education, and behaviour towards friends and strangers, are guided by certain established patterns and norms, which enable people to make assumptions about what others appear to want and to do at different moments in their lives. Yet these patterns are themselves shaped by the temporal location of the generation and the common circumstances in which it was born and raised. This form of interaction is far less acknowledged than the first, and the result has restricted our understanding of adult development. As Rossi (1980, p. 14) points out, in the United States most of what is known in social science research about middle age has come from people who were either born during the Depression or spent their early childhood in families which experienced it. "It may be the case," she goes on,

> that the timing-of-events model of adult development emerged in a period of social history — the 1950s and early 1960s — more stable and with a more "expectable life cycle" than either before or since. Many indicators in the 1970s

[and subsequently — TS] suggest a new period of increased variance in both the timing and sequence of life events. (Rossi, 1980, p. 16)

The temporal as well as the cultural specificity of much of our knowledge base needs to be borne well in mind. Such specificity has political as well as theoretical consequences. The generation of men and women now reaching the end of their working lives are precisely those who were the last not to benefit from the postwar expansion of educational expenditure. This is the issue which has prompted concern, especially in the Nordic countries, for intergenerational equality (see Thomson, 1989). Whatever the quality of the educational experience, prolonged initial schooling will embed the idea of subsequent learning in people's minds, however feebly and unevenly. Discussions of propensity to learn in later life have therefore to take account of the inhibitions laid on the current older workers by their relative lack of formal schooling, and the fact that the young are being offered opportunities which older workers collectively never received. This kind of interaction across generations has significant consequences for both learning and equity.

Time and Identity

Is lifespan development more fixed and predictable in the early than the later parts of the lifespan? Children are more closely measured, against each other and against a formal standard, by their parents and teachers. Specified age norms operate with considerable precision, most notably as children move through school grades. Adults appear to have encountered a far wider range of factors and contexts with which to interact, gaining over time a variety of experience through their work or as parents. And yet children change faster physically; and the intensity of their interaction with new experiences may outweigh the limitations. They are less the prisoners of routine, and in this sense their learning patterns may be less predictable. On the other hand, when adults do change in later life, the change may be more radical precisely because it represents a more dramatic break with an established pattern.

This realization has a number of important implications for education. It means that in at least some forms of adult education the stakes are higher than for children. Adults are more vulnerable, curiously, for the change involved in learning entails a greater potential loss of identity than it does for children for whom such changes are almost routine. For adults significant change can result in a crisis of identity, whereas for children change amounts to character development. This emerges most clearly in the types of course which cater specifically for adults returning to learn after a period away from education, for example through "access" courses which enable unqualified adults to enter upper secondary or higher education. But it may also apply to those involved in narrowly defined job-related training, in so far as this entails relinquishing previous patterns of behaviour and standards of skill and knowledge. The point at which the acquisition of a new skill shades into a change of occupational, and therefore possibly personal, identity is not easy to specify. As a corollary, the knock-on effects on the person's wider role set are often underestimated.

The contrast between adult and youth also means that the relative impact of, as it were, a given quantity of education is very different. The implication is that it needs to be established at what points in the life cycle education is most effectively offered. A key policy issue — applying to schooling as well as adult education — is to develop a realistic approach to the timing of educational opportunity.

Age, Gender, and the Reconstruction of Life Cycle

Dawning awareness of the ageing of Western societies has prompted policy makers in the United States and Europe to begin to think about education for older adults, but it may be suggested that this is because of the way old age is viewed: predominantly as a problem with stupendous implications for social expenditure. A powerful, although pragmatic, argument for more educational opportunity for older adults is the preventive one: that it is a way of staving off dependency with its horrendous personal, social and economic consequences. But the argument leads inevitably backwards into considerations of earlier phases in the life cycle, and the role education may play in personal development before the onset of old age, however that is defined.

The statistics are by now well known, at least in broad outline. The industrialized societies are witnessing an unprecedented ageing of their populations (Laslett, 1989). There is, it should be added, considerable variation between countries (see Table 2.1). Moreover, contrary to most public perceptions, the issue is not one which is confined to countries of the industrialized North, although it may have higher salience there than in the rest of the world. Third World nations are also experiencing an ageing of their populations, but the numbers of their young people are not declining as they are in the North (Tout, 1990).

Ageing and Social Structure

The political and social implications of this trend are massive; they present the need to appreciate the interaction between social structures and conceptions of the lifespan.

Table 2.1. Share of elderly (65 years and over) in population 1950-2050 (actual data and forecast)

	1950	1980	2000	2010	2020	2030	2040	2050
Canada	7.67	9.51	12.84	14.61	18.59	22.39	22.47	21.34
France	11.38	13.96	15.28	16.26	19.45	21.76	22.72	22.33
Germany	9.35	15.51	17.12	20.35	21.74	25.82	27.60	24.48
Italy	8.02	13.45	15.31	17.28	19.37	21.92	24.15	22.61
Japan	5.21	9.10	15.20	18.62	20.92	19.97	22.66	22.30
United Kingdom	10.73	14.87	14.48	14.61	16.27	19.24	20.43	18.74
United States	8.14	11.29	12.15	12.79	16.16	19.49	19.80	19.31
Unweighted average of above	8.64	12.53	14.63	16.36	18.93	21.52	22.83	21.59
Australia	8.12	9.62	11.68	12.59	15.41	18.22	19.71	19.44
Austria	10.44	15.47	14.94	17.45	19.41	22.82	23.94	21.73
Belgium	11.04	14.37	14.70	15.90	17.74	20.78	21.89	20.79
Denmark	9.13	14.41	14.87	16.67	20.11	22.56	24.70	23.17
Finland	6.66	11.98	14.43	16.76	21.73	23.78	23.14	22.70
Greece	6.76	13.14	14.97	16.76	17.80	19.49	20.99	21.06
Iceland	7.64	9.90	12.86	13.50	16.33	20.76	23.81	25.21
Ireland	10.67	10.72	11.12	11.08	12.57	14.74	16.92	18.86
Luxembourg	9.80	13.52	16.74	18.12	20.15	22.38	22.03	20.28
Netherlands	7.74	11.51	13.46	15.13	18.89	22.96	24.77	22.61
New Zealand	8.95	9.73	11.07	12.01	15.31	19.35	21.86	21.30
Norway	9.59	14.76	15.15	15.12	18.18	20.73	22.80	21.90
Portugal	6.99	10.17	13.54	14.13	15.63	18.24	20.40	20.59
Spain	7.30	10.85	14.36	15.53	17.00	19.64	22.68	22.86
Sweden	10.25	16.29	16.58	17.47	20.81	21.70	22.47	21.40
Switzerland	9.61	13.83	16.73	20.49	24.37	27.29	28.25	26.27
Turkey	3.38	4.74	5.03	5.52	6.97	8.92	10.17	11.51
OECD, unweighted average	8.52	12.20	13.94	15.36	17.96	20.62	22.09	21.36

Source: OECD, Social Data Bank, demographic section

Two implications are identified by Riley (1985). The first is the increased variety of role sequences. People change occupations more frequently; they also change partners, and consequently the family structures within which they live. These changes are only partly a function of increased longevity. It would be perfectly possible for such trends to occur within a static lifespan. But the longer people live the more options are open to them, whatever the social limitations. As a result the number of transitions which have to be negotiated have multiplied: from wife to divorcee and back again, from employee to student and back again, and so forth. Given that such transitions are widely acknowledged to be crucial learning points, the potential demand for learning opportunities is immense.

The implications for theories of the life cycle are as follows. It is not merely a question of extended duration, with more episodes having to be fitted in, but one of a different ordering, with different levels and types of experience being brought into play. A women who defers bearing children until she has established a career will have a different learning pattern, drawing on a different range of experience, to that of the early mother. She is also more likely to be distanced from the experience of her mother, so often a strong guiding model. A woman who takes up full-time work later on in life may do so with different expectations of what this work will signify, with stronger ideas of a "career" and therefore of progression because she expects to be working for an extended stretch before retiring.

The increased variety in role sequences also means that people more often than before reenter roles which they have previously occupied, albeit in a different guise. A typical example is the man who starts a second family, perhaps two decades after his first. There will be repetition as well as novelty, at the same time as the ageing process continues. Linearity is displaced, as he will revisit experiences of, for example, disturbed nights. The effect on the man's priorities and his disposition to learn may be very significant.

The point is that the replacement of linearity by *recursiveness*, however limited, is very likely to affect such educationally crucial features as motivation and creativity. It can be argued that the interplay between repetition and variation is essential not only to biological organisms but also to social beings, individual and collective (Adam, 1990). Too much repetition and the rhythm descends into montony; too much variation and the result is stress and rootlessness. Both forms inhibit creative learning.

The opportunity to revisit an experience and encounter a new variation on an old theme is potentially a significant expansion of the scope for learning. Living longer affords such an opportunity, but our educational systems are not structured to allow people to take full advantage of it.

Table 2.2. Labour force participation rates of men (60-64) and women (55-59)

	1970	1980	1984	1988
Labour force participation rates: men aged 60-64				
France	68.0	47.6	31.1	25.4
Germany	71.8	42.5	34.1	31.5
Japan	81.5	77.8	73.8	71.1
Netherlands	--	48.8	32.1	14.6
Sweden	79.5	69.0	65.8	64.1
United Kingdom	86.7	71.2	56.0	55.1
United States	71.7	59.8	55.5	53.8
Labour force participation rates: women aged 55-59				
France	46.0	47.3	42.9	45.3
Germany	36.4	37.4	36.8	38.5
Japan	48.7	50.5	50.9	50.9
Netherlands	--	18.5	18.8	16.7
Sweden	52.8	68.8	73.6	79.6
United Kingdom	50.1	53.6	50.9	54.8
United States	48.8	48.1	49.6	53.0

Source: OECD Labour Force Statistics

The second major consequence of greater longevity is increased role complexity. The two overlap to some extent. A man who starts a second family may become a father again after he has become a grandfather, and have to play the two roles simultaneously. But the major area in which such complexity is occurring is amongst older adults. In addition to the possible family roles, there is a wider range of social roles, including a mix of paid and unpaid work. This is a consequence above all of the changes which have occurred in working lives.

Changing Patterns of Employment

Far less predictable than ageing is the transformation of the labour market, especially for older men. The broad picture over the last two decades is one of a shortening of the span of working life. This can be inferred from the data in Table 2.2.

The pattern is clear. The significant group is that of men in the period before the formal pension age, whose economic activity rates have dropped very sharply. The prime force behind this has been economic; the combination of recession and restructuring leading to a mass exit from the labour force. The ways of exit have implications for how people view personal development and learning as part of their lives.

The broad trend is blurred, however, by moves in some countries to recruit older workers, as economies turn upwards and a shortage of young people is felt. This solution may prove to be short-lived, and to be merely a repetition of what is historically quite a well-established pattern of acceptance and rejection of older people, treated as a flexible workforce who are alternately encouraged to continue working and given to understand that they are better off taking it easy. In Sweden and the United Kingdom one can see a repeat by employers of the pattern of the late 1970s, as the recession takes its toll on the employment prospects of especially older workers. It is a point of political significance whether the cycle will indeed simply be repeated, or whether this particular conjuncture will see a qualitative shift in the place of older people in the labour market.

There are, of course, other labour market trends which have significance for the scope for learning and development across the lifespan. Changes in the content of work, with varying patterns of deskilling and upskilling, necessarily alter the extent to which adults are expected or required to exercise their capacity to learn as part of their everyday working lives. The growth in part-time employment is another major factor, more so in some countries than in others: for the period 1973-81, the ratio of growth in part-time jobs to total employment growth ranged from 165 in Germany through 105 in Sweden to a mere 17 in the United States (Esping-Andersen, 1990, p. 198). The extension of biological life and the shifts within this of the mix of employment and domestic patterns generate a huge number of new learning possibilities for men and women, though educational institutions do little to cater for this systematically. As Janet Giele observes:

> At the individual level, the separation of the biological and social life cycles has had consequences for sex roles ... . Delay or abstention from parenting and the long empty nest period create transitional periods that traditional age-sex roles no longer easily "handle". New forms of self-integration and new social guidelines are needed that will symbolize these transitions and help the individual to negotiate them in a way that is not just idiosyncratic but has some social shared meaning. Rather than rites of passage that move the person in lockstep fashion from one age-sex grade to the next, what is needed in modern society is a new symbolic statement of the transformations that a person will experience throughout the life course. The new image would depict movement back and forth across the different functional and hierarchical domains. (Giele 1980, p. 167)

Gender Convergence — or Crossover?

The map of life looks very different to the two sexes:

> If we try to envisage the whole course of human life, it seems that the shape of living can be very different for females and for males. Whereas time is relatively linear, relatively progressive for boys and men, this does not seems to be true for girls and women, who are likely to experience both more discontinuity and instead of a progression, a long plateau in which time may be marked rather than lived. Both boys and girls look forward to their adulthood; both, in some sense, are busily preparing for it, are climbing the slope towards being grown up. But where the path the boys are following goes steadily up, in a more or less straight line, the girls' path changes direction at certain points. Like many climbers, young men find, when they have reached what, as children, they thought was the top, that a further slope confronts them, a slope on which the path continues in much the same direction as the one they took during their childhood. For young women, things are probably seldom like this. Not only may the view from the peak look rather different from what they expected; it may also seem that there is really nowhere to go on to from there. (Salmon, 1985, p. 88)

The image seems a telling one; but it needs to be supplemented on two fronts, hailing back to the two types of interaction previously identified. The first refers to historical changes in the patterns of adolescence and early adulthood. The second is the extension to capture the second half of the life cycle, and the experiences of older men and women.

There is some evidence suggesting that the patterns of male and female behaviour and experience are converging. The data on labour market participation shown in Table 2.2 indicate that male economic activity rates decline sharply in the period immediately preceding retirement to the point where they run close to those of females, which remain relatively constant. Of course, older men still work full-time, for the most part, whereas older women mostly work part-time, so that overall preoccupation with paid employment remains quite different. Yet overall there are almost as many men as women who are not in the labour market at that stage in their lives.

An even more forceful argument can be made if one looks beyond the formal retirement age. In the United Kingdom, more women than men continue working beyond the state pension age, and more of these are working full-time. There may thus be more continuity in female lives, as indicated by economic activity.

The process of finishing paid employment has become prolonged and uncertain. The phrase "early retirement" embraces a wide range of possible transitions, from well anticipated and thoroughly welcome to abrupt and traumatic, from the purely voluntary to the overtly or covertly compulsory. In recent history, being retired has coincided with being in receipt of the state pension, but this conjunction is rapidly dissolving.

This can be highly disorienting, as the case of one man interviewed as part of a study in London illustrates:

> Mr Pollitt desperately wanted to work again but only because, the official retirement age being 65, he thought he could not count himself as retired ... . Of his job search he said: "If I don't go to the Job Centre I feel guilty. If I do, I feel depressed ... . In some respects I am lucky. We've only got to struggle through these next few years and then we shall know where we are and I could perhaps get a part-time job then. I did contemplate using some of our money to buy a new car and go cabbying but I don't think I could drive fast enough. It's mainly not knowing that causes the problem". (Young and Schuller, 1991, pp. 65-66)

For most women, on the other hand, the experience is a familiar one and, for that reason, more easily managed. Women are far more likely not only to have experienced a spell out of paid employment, but also to have found themselves in a position where they are not working but not necessarily looking for a job either. Coping with this ambiguity may well be more difficult for men, even though this may be changing as more men approach the third age with at least some experience of a situation other than straight employment or unemployment. Conversely, it may become more difficult for women, with increasingly continuous employment histories, to handle discontinuity.

Jung and other psychologists have proposed the idea that in the second half of life women give increasing emphasis to masculine components in their make-up, whilst men give more emphasis to the feminine. In his studies David Gutmann (1988) finds much support for this proposition. He concludes that, in later development,

> a significant sex-role turnover takes place, in that men begin to live out directly, to own as part of themselves, the accommodative, or Passive Mastery, qualities: sensuality, affiliation, and maternal tendencies — in effect, the "femininity" that was previously repressed in the service of productivity and lived out vicariously through the wife. By the same token, across societies, we see the opposite effect in women. As documented, they generally become more domineering, independent, unsentimental and self-centred — asserting their own desires, particularly toward social dominance, rather than serving the emotional needs and development of others. Just as men in middle life reclaim title to their denied "femininity", middle-aged women repossess the aggressive "masculinity" that they once lived out vicariously through their husbands. (Gutmann, 1988, p. 203)

Such findings set quite an agenda for learning strategies and educational policies, whether they are seen as acknowledging and encouraging these trends, or as forms of continued socialization which attempt to maintain gender differences. It is, however, highly unlikely that strategies or policies will be directly formulated in these terms.

Learning and Intergenerational Relations

The experience of different generations may be interpreted as showing that there is an imbalance in the attention being given to the various needs of the younger and older generations. This imbalance is also reflected in educational theory and practice. But for many people learning is heavily influenced by their relationships with other generations, notably within their own family. Thus it is not a question solely of how far and in what ways older people differ from or resemble younger people in their learning, but of how they affect each other's opportunities and achievements. Parental influence on children's educational attainments is a well established aspect of modern practice, at several levels. Yet the potential for mutual support seems seriously neglected. It is the quality of family relationships rather than the physical location of children and parents which counts. This raises the issue of how far the stress on individualism, evident in demographic statistics on the composition of households, affects learning and development in relation to age and gender. In this respect, Michael Young observes:

> The way things are going, if equality between the parents is attained the equality could be astride the bodies of their children. We can see now that gender equality will prove sterile unless as a follow-on to the too-long-delayed rise in the status of women there is a rise in the status of children ... . If there were gender-equality it would be no gain for children if the equality were between equal adults who kept swapping about between each other. A young child needs a person more than a role. (Young, 1990, pp. 14-15)

How does this relate to the theme at hand? Quite simply, the trends pointed to above — especially the increased longevity — multiply the potential for human beings to learn from each other: for older people to learn from younger generations, and for younger people to profit from the experience of their predecessors. But if people remain tied in to an age-stratified society, and one which in addition encourages individualism to an excessive extent, that potential will be lost. The challenge, in short, is not only to give full scope to adult development, to give it the attention which has been given over the last half-century to schooling, but to achieve an integration between the learning patterns of different generations.

A Policy Agenda

The broad policy framework for a system of lifelong learning was set out for the international community in the early 1970s, most notably by the OECD in its documents on recurrent education (CERI, 1973). The rationale still holds good, but needs to be supplemented by a more detailed appreciation of social variables, of which age and gender are two of the most significant. The following issues should be at the forefront of a policy agenda:

1. A clearer account is needed of the historical changes which have shaped the personal biographies of men and women as they move into and through adulthood. Cohort effects on learning patterns may be far stronger than is commonly appreciated.
2. These effects are particularly relevant to the differences between men and women in their motivations for learning at different moments in the lifespan. The growth of female employment and the shifts in the balance between full-time and part-time employment have fundamentally undermined the dominant model of a single continuous stretch of employment. At both ends of the working life, there are often prolonged periods of ambiguity, with young people and older adults moving uncertainly between paid work and other forms of activity, voluntarily or not. Such uncertainties have enormous implications for the provision of learning opportunities. Coping with multiple transitions requires skills which are far removed from the acquisition of defined sets of knowledge.
3. Realization of the principle of lifelong learning impacts heavily on youth education. The extension of full-time schooling runs against the grain, but there are constant pressures to allow this to happen. One may need to think more radically about bringing the initial educational system more closely into line with social and biological changes which propel young people more quickly into adulthood than before.
4. Segregation into age groups also runs counter to the philosophy of lifelong education. Increased longevity and changes in family structures put a higher premium on the need for educational opportunities which promote intergenerational understanding.
5. The notion of responsibility is intimately linked with adulthood, but also has application to youth. A key principle for the future will be the promotion of student responsibility, the organizing of learning so as to maximize the extent to which the student takes responsibility for his or her own learning. The implications of this — for educational institutions, for employer recruitment and training policies and for pedagogical practice — are substantial.

A final observation is that definitions of lifespan development are almost exclusively derived from external observation: studies of psychological growth or of sociological context. This external perspective needs to be supplemented with work which throws light on and emphasizes the adults' own understanding of the life cycle: where they stand in it, their relation to contemporaries and people of other generations, their perspectives and expectations. This would add enormously to the depth and practical utility of theories on lifespan development and adult learning.

References

Adam, B. (1990). *Time and social theory*. Cambridge: Polity Press.

Burrow, J.A. (1986). *The ages of Man*. Oxford: Clarendon Press.

CERI (1973). *Recurrent education: A strategy for lifelong learning*. Paris: OECD, Centre for Educational Research and Innovation.

Cross, K.P. (1981). *Adults as learners*. San Francisco: Jossey-Bass.

Esping-Anderson, G. (1990). *The three worlds of welfare capitalism*. Cambridge: Polity Press.

Giele, J. (1980). Adulthood as transcendence of age and sex. In N. Smelser & E. Erikson (Eds.), *Themes of love and work in adulthood* (pp. 151-173). New York: Harvard University Press.

Gilligan, C. (1982). *In a different voice: Psychological theory and women's development*. New York: Harvard University Press.

Gutmann, D. (1988). *Reclaimed powers*. London: Hutchinson.

Laslett, P. (1989). *A fresh map of life*. London: Weidenfeld and Nicholson.

Levinson, D.J. (1978). *The seasons of a man's life*. New York: Alfred A. Knopf.

McLeish, J.A. (1976). *The ulyssean adult*. New York: McGraw-Hill.

OECD (1989). *Labour force statistics*. Paris: OECD.

Riley, M.W. (1985). Women, men and lengthening life course. In A. Rossi (Ed.), *Gender and the life course*. New York: Aldine Press.

Rossi, A. (1980). Life-span theories and women's lives. *Signs 6* (1), 4-32.

Salmon, P. (1985). *Living in time*. London: Dent.

Thomson, D. (1989). The welfare state and generation conflict: Winners and losers. In P. Johnson, C. Conrad & D. Thomson (Eds.), *Workers versus pensioners* (pp. 35-56). Manchester: Manchester University Press.

Tout, K. (1990). *Ageing in developing countries*. Oxford: Oxford University Press.

Tucker, N. (1977). *What is a child?*. London: Open Books.

Turnbull, C. (1984). *The human cycle*. London: Jonathan Cape.

Young, M. (1988). *The metronomic society*. London: Thames and Hudson.

Young, M. (1990). *A harem in a heartless world — The future of the family*. London: The Royal Society of Arts.

Young, M., & Schuller, T. (1991). *Life after work: The arrival of the ageless society*. London: Harper Collins.

Chapter 3

LIFESPAN LEARNING: DEVELOPMENTAL TASKS AND THEIR MANAGEMENT

PETER G. HEYMANS
University of Utrecht, The Netherlands

All human lives come to an end. But there is no single pathway from conception to death, as research in developmental psychology has shown. Research testifies to the open nature of human development. Especially in the adult trajectory of life people actively influence their own development. Nevertheless, the diversity of human life seems somehow standardized. In the first part of this chapter, some symbolic means which serve to constrain and shape forms of human lives and occasions for learning will be presented. In the second part, attention is given to developmental tasks in the context of adult learning. The conceptualization of life as a partially ordered sequence of developmental tasks poses the question as to the availability of resources upon which the individual draws to complete particular developmental tasks. In the third part, some examples are given of the application of a technical model for the optimal management of resources for developmental tasks.

Central in this chapter is the idea of a developing individual who accomplishes a series of developmental tasks. Successful performance on these tasks depends on the adequate use of resources. Societal arrangements provide these resources to a certain degree. In controlling these resources individual development can be steered. What counts as a developmental resource for an individual depends on the type of life this individual is living. Four life styles, each of which generates a specific structure of meanings, are described.

Symbolic Aspects of Lives

The lifespan is more than the period before death. From the point of view of the individual there is a life-to-be-lived.Moreover, in our societies, the individual is acting as a person, and wants to be treated accordingly. According to Harré (1983), a person is an individual who has acquired a 'theory' about how to order his/her experiences. The term "theory" refers to a more or less coherent system of beliefs in conjunction with some rules of inference. So-called scientific theories can be subsumed under the broader term "theory," and in fact there is some trafficking between both fields, as can be seen in the phenomenon of "proto-professionalization" of lay-persons. But most of an individual's "theory" consists of images, metaphors, and narratives. Their use is in bringing order in the individual's life.

Individuals use the structure implicit in an image, metaphor, or narrative for mapping their experiences onto, so that these experiences themselves get structured. As a by-product of such a mapping the subjective feeling of "meaning" is generated. A successful mapping of experiences resulting in a "life" is beset by a number of constraints. First, the mapping must preserve some form of time-order. Time is not necessarily physical time. It can even be cyclical time, as in the image of the "seasons of human life". Time can even be running "backward," for instance for a group of people awaiting an important examination. Second, a mapping must lead to a result (i.e. a life) that can be easily shared with other people. If the mapping of experiences is based on unusual structures, it is difficult for the individual to communicate and make his or her life understood. The listeners to such a life have difficulty appreciating and remembering it, thus creating meanings different from those intended by the speaker. Third, a mapping is constrained by purpose and interest. And fourth, a mapping should be systematic.

Some examples may clarify the points made above. Figure 3.1 shows some images for describing lifespan development. Sometimes a life is compared to a ladder with rungs (Figure 3a), or with a double staircase or a journey (Figure 3b).

Metaphors can also be used; for example, the construction-metaphor implies that development should be based upon solid foundations, and that there is a plan behind it. The so-called 'Arab model of development' in Figure 3.2 depicts a young palm tree in the desert, that has been covered with a stone. It will receive water only if the sprout can lift the stone and throw it off, because in this case it is likely that the investment will eventually bear fruit. The implication for educators may be that it can be worthwhile to put young individuals under pressure, and to select at a young age.

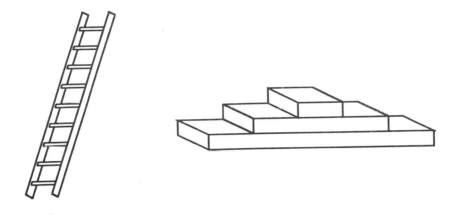

Figure 3.1. Two models of developmental change in the lifespan

Figure 3.2. The 'Arab' model of development

Consider the following story of the three little frogs, as another example of a device for structuring experience:

Three little frogs, A, B and C, lived on a farm. While playing they jumped into a bucket of fresh milk. They enjoyed drinking the milk and swimming around. However, when the fun was over they could not get out of the bucket; its walls were too high and slippery. They swam and swam, and got very tired. Frog A gave up, and drowned. Frog B and C firmly decided to continue paddling and not to give up. But suddenly frog B got cramps in his legs, and also went down. Frog C thought "I will swim as long as possible, you never know!" All of a sudden, after continued paddling, frog C felt some ground under his legs. The milk started to become butter and a little island was formed. Frog C used this island for getting some rest, and then as a basis for jumping out of the bucket.

Suppose you tell this story to people in a depressed state. When such people order their experiences by identifying with frog A or B, you understand that their outlook on the future is very gloomy. However, when people tell you, "I think I'm like frog C" then they elicit a very different expectation.

What is the lesson of these examples? Images, metaphors and stories are not just devices, providing structures for mapping a state of affairs. These devices result in mappings which have implications for action and policy. Moreover, these devices generate "meaning", and it is important to note that the meaning of an event or experience is shaped by the structures used by the individual to represent it. The meaning of an event is not necessarily stable: a change in mapping structure can generate a new meaning out of an old event. Consider the case of shoplifters. The chances are high that petty thieves refuse to acknowledge their act as theft; instead they may well use euphemisms such as "proletarian shopping". This reframing removes most of the moral implications. Finally, culture preserves a number of symbolic devices for making a life out of a set of experiences, and usually makes them available without explicit notice. Political movements may try to generate new images of human life. But these new images can only survive when they succeed in fulfilling the four contraints mentioned above.

Attention is now given to life stories and their underlying narrative structures. Stories are ubiquitous and powerful means to change or consolidate the perception of a state of affairs. The focus is on the main types of life stories which culture offers to its members as devices for bringing order into their experience.

Life Stories and Their Consequences

When are "lives" made? Children may not have a notion of life as interpreted by adults. When asked they tell a string of simply juxtaposed events ("... and then ... and then ..."). Lives in the form of structurally ordered experiences are at stake when individuals have to account for their actions in front of an audience questioning their identity. For example, suppose you see a person apparently taking your bicycle and ask "What are you doing?" This person could reply: "I am protecting your bike". This interaction centres around the possible identity of being "a thief", which is warded off by claiming that the identity "guard" should be given instead. There are many situations in which someone offers an interpretation of events in someone else's life. This occurs in speeches at weddings, farewell parties, and funerals, but also in selection committees discussing applicants, and so on.

The defence of personal identity is always based upon a previous mapping of life experience. Western culture has standard structures underlying life stories, which generate standard biographies. In the field of literary criticism an important contribution was made by Frye (1957). Frye concluded on the basis of an analysis of several hundreds of literary works that there are four basic narratives: romance, comedy, tragedy and irony. These were brought to the attention of psychologists as identity-generating devices by Gergen and Gergen (1988) and Murray (1985, 1989). A short description of each type of structure follows below.

In *romance* the narrative describes life as a medieval quest. Romantic heroes are searching for the sources of happiness, but on their journey there are regularly obstructed by representatives of evil. The hero fights these representatives. Initially there are only minor confrontations, but at some point there comes a decisive battle. Evil loses and the hero wins, although often at the price of being wounded, and receives public acclaim. Throughout this journey the hero receives help from a kind of assistant. The hero in a romantic life story is bound to solve conflict by fight, instead of consultation and negotiation. The ultimate goal in life is the preservation of honour.

In *comedy* the life of the hero is described as a sequence of periods in which a balance is wrought between forces which could impede the fulfilment of the hero's desires. Comic heroes, although not in control of the events, succeed periodically in neutralizing one negative force in their life with another. A famous theme of a comic life is the victory of youth and desire over decay and death.

In *tragedy* the individual is not so much a hero but a victim. The person sets out to do good, but cannot overcome the adversary forces which have been summoned in the effort to do good. These forces will eventually destroy the individual.

In *irony* individuals put themselves at a distance from others. They are aware of the relative value of the efforts to bring coherence in what in essence is an accidental collection of life experiences. The ironic individual tries to show others that their efforts are in vain and that their assumptions about reality are untestable and therefore untenable. So at the core of the ironic attitude is the exposure of life as an idle and random construction.

The thesis is now proposed that the above narrative structures serve as prototypic lives, and that any life or substantial life-trajectory that is communicated between people uses a form that comes close to one of these four types. The information pertinent to a life story is assimilated in moulds, in accordance with the narrative structures presented above.

Although every adult in our culture "knows" all four narratives, the use of a specific mould is functionally related to the *life context* of the individual. The four types of narrative are in fact cosmologies defining the relevant aspects of the world and the place of the individual in it. As the anthropologist Mary Douglas has shown, these cosmologies are related to two aspects of the environment: "grid", or the degree to which an environment contains prescriptions for individuals, and "group", or the degree to which an individual is embedded in social networks. Moreover, the cosmologies differ with regard to a third variable (Thompson, 1982): the degree of control that individuals have over the events shaping their life. The relationship between grid, group and control as aspects of life context and the prevailing prototypical mould is complex. A graphic representation is presented in Figure 3.3. It can be seen that a change in life context along the group axis often has no consequences for the life narrative used but there is a point where a small change in "group" is sufficient to trigger a major change in life narrative. This transition occurs at different times, depending upon the direction of the change in group. For instance, the loss of a job or the social network associated with married life following a divorce could be such a reduction in group that individuals are forced to change the structure of their life story from R- to T-type in case of a high-grid environment, and from C- to an I-type story in case of a relatively low-grid environment. This change transforms the individuals' identity at the same time as their life experiences are being reordered in a structurally different way.

An example may be needed. Take an individual who is currently under medical investigation with cancer as the possible diagnosis. Suppose this person adheres to a R(omantic)-type of life structure. Cancer will then be seen as an adversary originating in evil. The operation preceding the diagnosis is one of the minor obstacles the individual has to overcome. Suppose that cancer is indeed found. For the R-person this message signals "fight". A surgical operation is looked upon with optimism and as decisive; the surgeon and other medical personnel are assigned the role

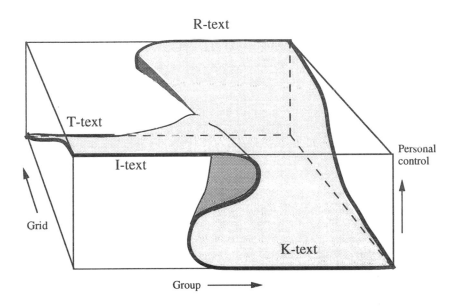

Figure 3.3. The functional relationship between three aspects of the life context of an individual (grid, group, and control) and the type of narrative structure (romance, comedy, tragedy, and irony) fitting that life context

Mutilations resulting from this surgical action are easy to endure because the scars prove that the battle was tough. That the person is still alive is evidence of success, and visiting family members are supposed to honour the person's endurance and brave performance. When, after some time, the operation turns out to be not that successful, the individual redefines the whole episode up to this operation as a minor, preparatory struggle. The thing to come is the real, decisive battle.

Folk Models are Not Neutral; They Have Consequences

The four forms of symbolic structures of the lifespan are examples of folk models: more or less interrelated systems of beliefs serving to make the world one lives in intelligible, and as guidelines for actions and feelings. There is evidence that these folk models are not just innocent ideas, awaiting study by anthropologists and psychologists. From several models it is known that they are self-fulfilling prophecies, and generate their own evidence. Three examples based on carefully conducted research are given below.

Scheper-Hughes (1985) studied mother—child interaction among the very poor in the north-east of Brazil. The people studied lived in a *favela* or slum. There was a high incidence of child mortality, mainly in the first months of life. Most mothers, who tended to be very fond of their children, held a view of life based on the idea of *luta* — "life is war". In this fight only the strong will win. When a child is *braboso* (wild, daring, energetic) it has a good chance of success, but if it is quiet and sleeps much, then the expectation is that this child is badly prepared for the struggles to come. Children in a *favela* run a high risk of catching infectious diseases. Infections weaken the child and lead to under-nourishment because mothers are hesitant to feed a child which may "waste" it. Weakened children are very quiet, doze away frequently, don't ask the attention of the mother; these children are certainly not *braboso*. So these children are gradually set onto a developmental path which through neglect causes progressive weakening and ultimately death. Scheper-Hughes' (1985) study shows how the *luta*-metaphor of life perpetuates itself by generating its own facts, visible to all people in the *favela*.

Cruts (1991) shows the influence of ideas about children's development of behavioural characteristics in parents of a newborn. For older children in classrooms, this Pygmalion-effect has been well-documented, although the nature of the processes that are involved is still debated. When an educator is made aware of the potential of a student, then the chances are high that this pupil will eventually show achievements consistent with the expectations of the teacher.

Ross (1989) studied folk models concerning menstruation. Women were ordered by the degree to which they believed that menstruation caused the swelling of the body by water retention, aches, and depressive mood changes. In the study self-reports on all these aspects were collected. Some women were asked to report in retrospect about the menstrual period, while another group of women reported on their feelings in three intermenstrual days. The data clearly show that retrospective reports were much more in line with the beliefs of the women about menstruation than the self-report data collected while the women were menstruating. Apparently, the very experiences of the women are assimilated into their "theory" about menstruation. The folk model or naive theory is thus used to restructure reality.

It is not unplausible that hidden assumptions concerning the nature of the course of life, as embodied in the narratives described above, generate their own facts in the lives of individuals. Fact and fiction thus co-constitute human lives. That is one reason why the study of important aspects of human life is difficult. It urges the investigator regularly to withdraw from the ongoing data-collection and analysis in order to search for a metaperspective from which the compass for research can be adjusted.

It may well be that some existing theories in developmental psychology tell a "scientific" story about human life structured in accordance with one of the four typical life narratives. Murray (1989) supports this hypothesis. The next section introduces the concept of developmental tasks and presents a framework for conceptualizing "meaningful" learning.

Developmental Tasks

Common to all four narratives (R-, C-, T-, and I-type) is the notion of life as a sequence of episodes in which the events derive meaning from their relation to tasks the individual undertakes. The completion of the task depends, at least in part, on the skill and ingenuity of the person. Success or failure are under the judgement of outsiders. Task success or failure has consequences for the identity status of the person. Within each prototypical life story these developmental tasks differ in both content and consequences.

The Narrative Structure Underlying Selected Developmental Theories

The narrative structure of romance underlies Erikson's theory of personal development over the lifespan (Erikson, 1950). The lifespan is seen as a succession of eight major developmental tasks, each manifesting itself in a crisis which the individual has to overcome. Successful solution of a crisis results in advanced developmental status characterized by the individual having acquired a new virtue. For example, the solution of the identity crisis in adolescence results in the trait of fidelity towards a self-chosen set of values or ideology. Unsuccessful handling of the crisis may cause stagnation. An exegesis of Erikson's theory (Capps, 1989) states that in crisis the individual is confronted with one of a set of eight "deadly sins"; in the case of the identity crisis the menace comes from the sin of "pride" — a self-centred attitude where one is continuously expecting or demanding praise and adulation (Capps, 1989). The virtue of fidelity is seen as the antidote against the sin of pride.

The narrative of tragedy is at the core of Levinson's (1986) theory on adult development. In a T-structured life the individual is — in the end — the loser who, however, can count on the sympathy of the people. The destruction of the person is the end of a series of conflicts in which the hero — who tries to be "good" — unknowingly activates a powerful adversary force, which will finally prove destructive. In the first part of adult life the developmental task is, according to Levinson, the realization of the Dream (an image of the place the individual will occupy in the world of adults). Initially it seems to individuals that they are being successful; they do not notice the threats coming up. But in midlife it becomes clear that they are arriving at a certain position in the adult world, and they are confronted by their own finiteness and mortality.

The theory of Gould (1978) on adult development from 16 to 50 years of age uses the concept of "transformational tasks". Gould's theory centres on an irony-structure to bring order in life. In the succession of transformational tasks individuals have to liberate themselves from the "false assumptions" stemming from an earlier developmental stage. For instance, according to Gould, people in their early twenties should unmask their belief that "I will always belong to my parents, and adopt their world-view" as false. In Gould's theory developmental tasks consist of searching for hidden assumptions and overcoming their influence.

Finally, C-structured life stories are present in theoretical approaches related to attachment theory. These approaches are mainly used to describe and explain social relations in the period between birth and 14 years of age (Sroufe, 1979; Van Lieshout 1987), but there are also some extensions into adult life, which mostly focus on the "romantic" life style. Developmental tasks in the C-narrative are periods in which the individual is confronted with problems that frustrate the fulfilment of wishes, and has to acquire special skills such as ego control and ego resiliency for neutralizing these adverse forces. Especially situations with a high degree of *communitas* (e.g. mother—child bond, peer friendship, love relationship) are important for learning these balancing skills, as well as for celebrating successful application.

Developmental Tasks and Meaningful Learning

The use of the concept "developmental task" for the analysis of human development was first proposed by Havighurst (1948). Recent analyses of the lifespan in terms of developmental tasks are contributed by Oerter (1986) and Baltes (1987). Unfortunately the concept lacks a precise delineation. The following definition is proposed:

A developmental task is a period or trajectory during which the individual has the opportunity to prove before a specific audience or jury that he or she is capable of performing certain actions. This capability is inferred from the controlled and goal-directed use of available personal, social and/or material resources. The individual is granted the right to act on his or her own account if an audience or jury is persuaded that the individual has achieved the new competency.

This captures the essence of the concept in relation to each of the four types of narrative. However, this is not the place to elaborate this further.

Learning can be generally defined as any change in behaviour due to certain experiences. This implies too broad a class of phenomena. Real learning, the kind of learning that education is intended for, has to do with meaningful learning: learning directed at the achievement of valued goals. The outcomes have implications for the individual's self-view (e.g., whether the individual is a competent architect or a good lover). The educational system often fails to ignite meaningful learning processes, despite the fact that meaningful learning is the only learning of significance for people, from young to old (see also Raven, 1991).

The outcome of the successful completion of a developmental task is a competency. A competency is not just a new skill. Rather it is a new skill in conjunction with a "theory of oneself" in relation to this skill. Adults, from a young age, organize their "meaningful learning" in the context of "personal projects" (Zirkel and Cantor, 1990). These projects cover similar situations as those subsumed under the term developmental task.

Managing the Lifespan

Models in behavioural research are intended to help detect how variables are related, and how "strong" a relationship may be. These models imply knowledge useful in decision making. This *praxis* asks for different tools. In this section some fictitious, but lifelike problems concerning lifespan development and education are examined with the help of linear programming and management science. It is assumed that the completion of a developmental task requires a person to integrate certain resources into a new "product". The main goal of education associated with a developmental task may well be to supply the necessary resources, as can be inferred from the examples given below:

Problem 1: Effects of delays in the completion of a developmental task on the total time needed to finish the whole developmental trajectory.

Suppose that in a certain life period people have to complete 10 developmental tasks. Completion of each task or personal project leads the individual into a certain state. Some states are only reached when two or three developmental tasks are completed. In this example there are eight such states (A-H), including a beginning- and an end-state. The states are partially ordered, that is, the completion of a certain developmental task presupposes the previous completion of other developmental tasks. Moreover, the completion of a developmental task takes a specific amount of time. The ordering of the developmental tasks and states is shown in Figure 3.4.

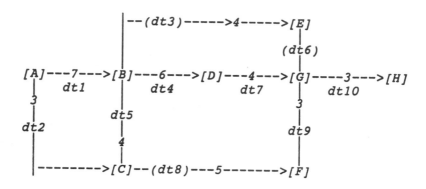

Figure 3.4. Partial ordering of 10 developmental tasks. The arrows indicate conditional relations between eight developmental states (A-H). The arrows also show the estimated completion time (in years). This corresponds to Table 1, columns 1-5 ('dt' = developmental task)

Completion of a developmental task depends upon the use of certain resources. Insufficient resources can cause a delay in the time it takes to complete a project. This could lead to the individual being 'off-time' for the next developmental phase, which lies at the basis of many problems in life. The question is whether one can predict the optimal completion time for a given sequence of developmental tasks, and predict if a delay in one project results in an overall delay?

Project evaluation and review technique (PERT) is a method that may provide answers to the above questions, provided that data are available about the *expected time* each task takes to complete. These data can be actual observations of completion time, but can also come from expert judgements about the most *probable* time ($= m$), the *optimistic* time ($= o$) or *pessimistic* time ($= p$). Measures of this kind are combined in into an estimated *expected time*.

The expected time for completing a certain developmental task is then $\{(o + 4m + p)/6\}$ and the variance around this expected time is $\{[(p -$

o)/6]^2}. Table 3.1 shows some expert judgements for the developmental tasks indicated in Figure 3.4. Table 3.1 shows the PERT answers to the two questions above in the columns 6-11. The data show that there is a *critical path*, denoted by the sequence *[1 -> 5 -> 8 -> 9 -> 10]*, which indicates that each delay in the completion of these tasks leads to a delay in overall completion time (see Table 3.1, col. 11). The slack (Table 3.1, col. 10) indicates the amount of delay allowed in working on a developmental task without running the risk of delaying overall completion. Thus the margins are zero for tasks on the critical path. Tasks 2, 3 and 6 have a large margin, while tasks 4 and 7 have narrow margins. For the tasks on the critical path (1, 5, 8, 9, 10) it is imperative that the resources are available at the right moment and in sufficient quantities. Logistics can be used to examine the relationship between the supply of resources and the time needed to complete a specific developmental task. The purpose of the examples given below is to show the kind of problems that may be addressed and the answers that might be obtained.

Table 3.1. Expert judgements about the time (in years) it takes to complete 10 developmental tasks (as in Figure 3.4). The judgements are in columns 1-3 (O=optimistic judgement; M= most probable judgement; P=pessimistic judgement. PERT-solutions are in columns 4-11)

Tasks	O 1	M 2	P 3	ET 4	VT 5	EB 6	LB 7	EE 8	LE 9	S 10	CP 11
01	5.0	6.0	13.0	7	1.33	0	0	7	7	0	*
02	2.0	2.5	6.0	3	0.66	0	8	3	11	8	-
03	3.0	4.0	5.0	4	0.33	7	12	11	16	5	-
04	4.0	5.0	12.0	6	1.33	7	9	13	15	2	-
05	3.0	4.0	5.0	4	0.33	7	7	11	11	0	*
06	2.5	3.0	3.5	3	0.17	11	16	14	19	5	-
07	2.5	4.0	5.5	4	0.50	13	15	17	19	2	-
08	3.5	4.5	8.5	5	0.83	11	11	16	16	0	*
09	2.5	3.0	3.5	3	0.17	16	16	19	19	0	*
10	2.0	3.0	4.0	3	0.33	19	19	22	22	0	*

Key to columns 4-11: ET = expected time to completion; VT = variance in ET; EB = earliest begintime; LB = latest begintime; EE = earliest endtime; LE = latest endtime; S = slack or margin; CP = on critical path?; * = yes, - = no.

Problem 2: Parsimonious allocation of scarce educational resources to three developmental tasks.

Suppose a family consists of father, mother, grandmother, and three children. Each child is working on a developmental task. Anna, who is five years old, tries to comprehend reading; Bernard (7 years) is working on the secrets of arithmetic; and Cornelia (9) years, tries to discover the rules of friendship making. Each child needs support from an adult to complete the task. Due to idiosyncracies, each child should receive help from the same adult until task completion. Moreover, each adult can handle only one child. The adults in the family are not equally good in helping in all three projects. Table 3.2 shows the amount of effort or time required from each educator.

Table 3.2. Amount of educational effort or time asked from each of three educators to help with each of three developmental tasks

Educational resource	Anna *reading*	Bernard *arithmetic*	Cornelia *friends*
Grandmother	10	15	9
Father	9	18	5
Mother	6	14	3

The problem is that the educators in this family have many obligations to handle, and that they do not want to waste their time or effort. So, the question is which educator goes best with which child?

The lifespan management approach offers the following solution: First, the *goal-function*, which represents what should be minimized, is determined. In this example it refers to the total amount of educational effort. Second, the *constraints* in the given situation are formulated. Third, the technique of linear programming is used to calculate the optimal solution for this case of minimization under constraints.

Let the dichotomous variable $X(i,j)$ indicate whether a certain educator i will help a certain child j with its current developmental task. The total amount of effort which each educator spends is estimated in Table 3.3. The constraints are given in Table 3.4. The goal-function to be minimized consists of the sum of the three rows in Table 3.3. This unweighted sum reflects our assumption that the time/effort of each educator is equally valuable.

The *optimal solution* of this family's problem is that grandmother should help Bernard with his arithmetic, father helps Cornelia with her friendship problems, and mother helps Anna with learning to read.

Table 3. Total amount of time and effort spent by each educator

Educator	Time and effort spent	
Grandmother:	$10X_{11} + 15X_{12} + 9X_{13}$	(a)
Father:	$9X_{21} + 18X_{22} + 5X_{23}$	(b)
Mother:	$6X_{31} + 14X_{32} + 3X_{33}$	(c)

Table 4. Constraints imposed upon the family

1. (grandmother can help at most 1 child):	$X_{11} + X_{12} + X_{13} \leq 1$
2. (idem for father):	$X_{21} + X_{22} + X_{23} \leq 1$
3. (idem for mother):	$X_{31} + X_{32} + X_{33} \leq 1$
4. (Anna gets only one educator):	$X_{11} + X_{21} + X_{31} \leq 1$
5. (idem for Bernard):	$X_{12} + X_{22} + X_{32} \leq 1$
6. (idem for Cornelia):	$X_{13} + X_{23} + X_{33} \leq 1$
7. (no negative assignment):	for all i,j: $X_{ij} \geq 0$

Table 6.2 shows that this takes for grandmother 15, for father 5, and for mother 6 units of effort (e.g. weeks). The optimal solution does not depend on the units, however, but on their relations as given in Table 6.2. The information should be given on a ratio scale. For this simple problem an optimal solution could have been found with trial and error. However, linear programming has the advantage that it allows for playing with variations and anticipating the consequences.

Problem 3: Choice of identity related personal projects.

Let us follow 20 year-old Maria musing about her future in the coming four years. Maria is enrolled at a university and steadily dating a boyfriend. She is in a reflective mood, as she has to make choices regarding her future life. In fact she is contemplating five "personal projects": (1) living on her own in an apartment instead of the dormitory; (2) having an income of her own that covers the minimal costs of living; (3) completing her education with a degree; (4) having a partner for life; and (5) marrying and having a baby.

Considering all projects, Maria feels interdependencies exist. Marrying implies that she has decided upon a partner for life, and also having a place to live on her own. Maria knows moreover that a reliable income is necessary to rent an apartment, and this income comes from having a job. Maria is aware that, in fact, she is contemplating quitting her study because it will take her much effort. Her parents would however be very proud of her, if she succeeded; and Maria appreciates her parents' opinions. As an alternative to the university Maria considers taking a two-year professional training course as a foreign language secretary. She speaks several languages fluently, and she is extravert; this course would not pose difficulties to her. Thus project 3 gets split up into two projects: (3a) continuing with the present study and getting a diploma, and (3b) changing to the secretarial course and obtaining a qualification.

It follows that Maria is confronted with six personal projects. The outcome of each has repercussions on the status of Maria vis-à-vis her reference persons. Each project has a different value to Maria, due to these anticipated repercussions. The diagnostic value of each project (according to Maria) is given in Table 3.5. This table also records the effort that Maria estimates each project will ask from her in the coming period. The amount of time Maria has available, given her other obligations, is also indicated. Maria's problem is one of making investment decisions: "to which personal projects should I commit myself?" A linear programming description and solution of Maria's problem is given below.

Table 3.5. The six personal projects Maria is confronted with

Project/ content	Diagnosticity		Year				Decision- variable
	Maria	advisor	1	2	3	4	
1. home	8	3	5	1	1	1	X1
2. income	7	9	8	7	7	7	X2
3a. university	6	7	12	12	12	12	X3a
3b. professional	4	4	6	6	0	0	X3b
4. partner	3	6	2	2	2	2	X4
5. family	2	4	6	8	10	10	X5
Time constraints			24	18	20	20	

Note: For each project is indicated its anticipated benefit, i.e. its diagnosticity about the self, according to Maria (column 1) and her advisor (column 2). Columns 3-6 give information about the amount of effort/energy each project takes in the coming four years. The final column contains the corresponding binary decision variable. The last row indicates the limitations that energy/effort impose upon Maria.

We start with the definition of six *decision variables*, $X(i)(i = 1,7)$, one for each personal project. This decision variable has a value of one when

Maria undertakes the project (and we assume that a project once undertaken is successfully completed), and zero otherwise. Maria's *goal function* to be maximized is the total value of all projects undertaken, that is, *{d1*X1 + d2*X2 + d3a*X3a + d3b*X3b + d4*X4 + d5*X5}*. The coefficient d(i) refers to the diagnostic value of project i. The *constraints* imposed upon Maria arise from the interdependencies among the personal projects, and from the amount of energy Maria has available each year for these projects.

Maria wants to maximize the following goal function (corresponding to her own estimates of the diagnostic benefits of each project): max [8*X1 + 7*X2 + 6*X3a + 4*X3b + 3*X4 + 2*X5] under the following 10 constraints:

1. [5*X1 + 8*X2 + 12*X3a + 6*X3b + 2*X4 + 6*X5] ≤ 24 {effort in year 1}
2. [1*X1 = 7*X2 + 12*X3a + 6*X3b + 2*X4 + 8*X5] ≤ 18 {idem, year 2}
3. [1*X1 = 7*X2 + 12*X3a + 0*X3b + 2*X4 + 10*X5] ≤ 20 {idem, year 3}
4. [1*X1 = 7*X2 + 12*X3a + 0*X3b + 2*X4 + 10*X5] ≤ 20 {idem, year 4}
5. [X3a + X3b] ≤ 1 {university and professional training exclude each other}
6. [X2] ≥ [X1] {own apartment assumes own income}
7. [X3a + X3b] ≥ [X2] {adequate income presumes diploma}
8. [X3a + X3b] ≥ [X5] {only marriage, when study is completed}
9. [X4] ≤ [X5] {marriage presumes choice of partner for life}
10. [X1 + X2 + X3a + X3b + X4 + X5] ≥ 4 {limited attention span; not more than four projects at a time}

The *optimal solution* for Maria is: (X1, X2, X3a, X3b, X4, X5) = {1, 1, 0, 1, 1, 0}. This means that she does best in undertaking project 3b (taking up a study to become a professional secretary) and project 4 (choosing a partner for life). Moreover, project 2 (acquiring own income) should be envisaged as well as project 1 (living on her own). The optimal solution also dictates what not to do: project 3a (continuing university studies) and project 5 (starting a family). The total benefit is then optimal, given the constraints, and has the value of 22 diagnostic units.

If the estimates of Maria's advisor are used then the set of projects best undertaken remains the same, despite the change in goal function, that is {1, 1, 0, 1, 1, 0}. Differences emerge when constraint 10 (number of projects maximally undertaken) is reduced from four to three. Under this scenario Maria's own estimates would give an optimal solution at {1, 1, 0, 1, 0, 0}, while the advisor's estimates would lead to {0, 1, 0, 1, 1, 0}. In the scenario of maximally only two projects, the optimal solution is again the same for both Maria's and the advisor's data on diagnosticity: {0, 1, 0, 1, 0, 0}.

Conclusions

There is no segment of the lifespan in which learning is completely absent. Learning is most intense and the need for support in learning the greatest at transitions in the lifespan. As Schuller (this volume) also concludes, these transitions or discontinuities can stem from age-graded, history-graded, or nonnormative life events. The transitions are periods or trajectories during which a specific transitional event is anticipated and preparatory learning takes place. In the aftermath of transitional events the individual accomodates the changed environment. This learning is experienced as meaningful learning because it is related to a change in the individual's identity. Adults are not passively waiting for transitional events; they often engage in personal projects to create a certain self having a specific life. Lives can be seen from four different points of view, each characterized by a specific narrative structure. Common to all these narratives is the notion that the individual has to solve a sequence of developmental tasks. In order to complete such a project the individual has to draw upon certain resources.

This conceptualization of what happens when individuals create order in their lifespan facilitates the use of methods such as operations research and linear programming. The advantage is that the choices people make in their lives can be technically described. The method assumes that individuals are active and goal directed — an aspect often neglected in psychology (cf. Heymans & Brugman, 1990).

The rational approach to managing lifespan development that is discussed in this chapter can have several benefits to practitioners and policy makers. First, they could know in advance what the optimal solution to a given problem would be, and act accordingly. Second, they would be able to manipulate certain parameters in a problem and assess the outcomes. Information concerning the likely results of implementing one policy rather than another could have critical value in decision making. On the other hand, the use of the tools described in this chapter presuppose the availability of validated scientific knowledge about developmental tasks and personal projects in adult life. Here lies a challenge for future research.

References

Baltes, P. (1987). Theoretical propositions of lifespan developmental psychology. *Developmental Psychology, 23*, 611-626.

Capps, D. (1989). The deadly sins and saving virtues: How they are viewed by laity. *Pastoral Psychology, 37*, 229-253.

Cruts, G. (1991). Folk developmental psychology. Doctoral dissertation, University of Utrecht.

Erikson, E.H. (1950). *Childhood and society*. (second enlarged edition, 1963). New York: W.W. Norton.

Frye, N. (1957). *Anatomy of criticism*. Princeton: Princeton University Press.

Gergen, K., & Gergen, M. (1988). Narrative and the self as relationship. In G. Berkowitz (Ed.), *Advances in experimental social psychology, Vol. 21* (pp. 17-56). New York: Academic Press.

Gould, R. (1978). *Transformations: Growth and change in adult life*. New York: Simon and Schuster.

Harré, R. (1983). *Personal being*. Oxford: Blackwell.

Havighurst, R. (1948). *Developmental tasks and education*. New York: McKay.

Hazan, C., & Shaver, P. (1987). Romantic love conceptualized as an attachment process. *Journal of Personality and Social Psychology, 42*, 511-524.

Heymans, P., & Brugman, G. (1990). Plasticity and ageing: At the nexus of person and context. In W. Koops et al. (Eds.), *Developmental psychology behind the dikes*. Delft: Eburon.

Levinson, D. (1986). A conception of adult development. *American Psychologist, 41*, 3-13.

Murray, K. (1985). Life as fiction. *Journal for the Theory of Social Behaviour, 15*, 173-188.

Murray, K. (1989). The construction of identity in the narratives of Romance and Comedy. In J. Shotter & K. Gergen (Eds.), *Texts of identity*. London: Sage.

Oerter, R. (1986). Developmental task through the lifespan: A new approach to an old concept. In P. Baltes (Ed.), *Lifespan development and behavior, Vol. 7* (pp. 233-269). Hillsdale: Erlbaum.

Raven, J. (1991). Developing the talents and competencies of all our children. Background paper to the Educational Research Workshop on gifted children and adolescents, Conference 'Research on Education in Europe', Nijmegen, 23-26 July 1991.

Ross, M. (1989). Relation of implicit theories to the construction of personal histories. *Psychological Review, 96*, 341-357.

Scheper-Hughes, N. (1985). Culture, scarcity and maternal thinking: Maternal detachment and infant survival in a Brazilian shantytown. *Ethos, 13*, 291-317.

Sroufe, A. (1979). The coherence of individual development. *American Psychologist, 34*, 834-841.

Thompson, M. (1982). A three-dimensional model. In M. Douglas (Ed.), *Essays in the sociology of perception*. London: Routledge and Kegan Paul.

Van Lieshout, C. (1987). De schoolloopbaan: op zoek naar de persoon van de leerling. In J. van Kuyk (Ed.). *Basisvorming in de basisschool* (pp. 103-122). Tilburg: Zwijsen.

Zirkel, S., & Cantor, N. (1990). Personal construal of life tasks: Those who struggle for independence. *Journal of Personality and Social Psychology, 58*, 172-185.

Chapter 4

AGEING AND LEARNING: AN AGENDA FOR THE FUTURE

ROGER HIEMSTRA
Syracuse University, U.S.A.

This chapter deals with "ageing and learning". The subheading "an agenda for the future" is added with the intent of providing some ideas or models that may be useful in developing policy and research.

Research has demonstrated the ability of most adults to learn throughout life. Many societies have begun to respond with an increasing array of programmes, educational resources, and learning opportunities for older adults. Three of these (Elderhostel, Seniornet, and Computers and the Elderly) are described in the chapter as examples of what is possible. Researchers also have determined that many older adults wish to assume considerable responsibility for their own learning. Professionals working with adult education and training in the future will need to transform their thinking and instructional approaches to accomodate corresponding individualized, self-directed learning needs. The chapter describes some of these needs and provides several related policy recommendations. The appendixes include concise summaries of selected literature to guide professionals and policy makers in their deliberations regarding learning across the lifespan.

Relevant Research

Although the aged are still an underserved and untapped potential, the situation is gradually improving. Growth in the number of elderly people participating in learning activities has taken and continues to take place in the United States, the Netherlands, and other OECD countries. Coinciding with this growth has been an increasing amount of research on older adults as learners. This research has focused on various areas.

Some studies have investigated the physiological problems adults may face as they age, such as various visual or hearing losses and the impact this has on learning. For example, Williams (1990) reported that recent epidemiological studies of several aging populations revealed interesting differences in the effects of visual versus hearing deficits on such functions as memory. People with declines in vision are more likely to have difficulty in remembering recently acquired information. Hearing loss appears closely associated with long-term memory and visual perception more closely associated with short-term memory.

Researchers also have studied how information is processed, short-term and long-term memory, intelligence measures, motivation, and life stages. Sternberg (1985, 1986, 1991; Sternberg and Wagner, 1986), for example, considers intelligence in terms of what he calls a "triarchic theory" and the selective combinations or comparisons that people make. He suggests that there is more to intelligence, whether it is adult intelligence or practical intelligence, than can be measured by standard IQ tests. He believes there is an external or social aspect of intelligent behaviour where people can learn to adapt or shape their world. Another aspect is what he calls "experiential intelligence". This refers to the role experience can play in developing a person's ability to cope with novelty or to automate familiar tasks. Another aspect is tied to the more common internal or mental processes of planning, encoding, and problem solving. Sternberg has created much interest in rethinking what is known about intelligence. Much research is needed to understand his work in terms of older learners, but the value of experience alone in older people makes such research vitally important.

Other research areas have included cognitive styles, learning to learn, learning needs and activities of older people, and life satisfaction. For example, Kolodny (1991) describes the importance of understanding learners' cognitive styles for teaching success. Three Syracuse university students have completed dissertations related to the life satisfaction of older adult learners finding the anticipated positive correlations between active learning and life satisfaction measures (Brockett, 1982; Estrin, 1985; Henry, 1989).

This chapter draws attention to three programmes developed for older learners in the United States that might serve as viable models for future development elsewhere. These are considered in relation to research on adult learning and instruction during the past 15 years. Some instructional implications gleaned from either research or the literature are taken up. Finally, some implications for educational policy are discussed.

Older Adults as Learners

One thing that is quite clear is that individual differences among the aged do exist. Older adults, especially if being considered as learners, cannot be treated or viewed as a single group. The elderly are heterogeneous, multidimensional in characteristics, and varied in terms of needs and abilities. For example, several researchers and programme developers have shown how successful older adults can be in educational pursuits. Fisher (1986), Galbraith and James (1984), and Peterson (1983) are among many doing such work in the United States. Hiemstra (1975, 1976) found that most adults in the 65-75 year old range spent 325 hours or more each year engaged in what Tough (1979) calls learning projects. It has been determined in a longitudinal study conducted since 1975 that many adults keep involved with learning activities well into their eighties and nineties (Hiemstra, 1982).

One viable example of such active involvement in the United States is the Elderhostel movement. Initiated in 1974 by Marty Knowlton in the New England area (Knowlton, 1977), Elderhostel is a confederation of provider institutions, mainly colleges and universities, that sponsors educational programmes for people over 60 years of age. These programmes are patterned after the youth hostels and folk high schools found in the Nordic countries and other parts of Europe. As Kinney (1989) points out, 165,000 older learners participated in programmes throughout the United States and 38 foreign countries in 1988. Those numbers continue to increase. In Syracuse, LeMoyne College, a private liberal arts college in a Jesuit tradition, hosts over 500 people each year in 30 to 40 different groups. These groups participate in about 20 week-long programmes over such topics as the Decades of the 1930s, 1940s, and 1950s, the history of New York's old canal system (the Erie Canal), and famous women throughout history.

Another example is SeniorNet, a service that comes from San Francisco, California. SeniorNet provides an electronic communication link for people 55 or older having an interest in obtaining skills on how to use a computer. SeniorNet involvement (it costs $25 per year plus phone charges) provides members with computer-related literature, a newsletter, an annual conference, and a national electronic network over the Delphi system for electronic mail, electronic conferences, and access to various data bases.

SeniorNet has several thousand members in nearly 50 cities around the United States. In a recent survey of 1400 members, it was found that they used computers for various activities ranked in the following way: word processing, personal finances management, telecommunications, business, hobbies, and miscellaneous (Why We Use Computers, 1990).

Syracuse University through the Graduate Programme of Adult Education was one of the member sites until September, 1991. It provided a campus location with several computers to older people who gathered to talk about computers, use them for various purposes, and use SeniorNet. A project in which the education of older adults is administered in direct relation to initial education was also set up. This project, entitled "Computers and the Elderly", involves training older people in various aspects of computer literacy. They in turn volunteer to introduce first and second graders in the Syracuse Public Schools to word processing and teach fifth graders language arts through computers (Hiemstra, 1987). The effort is now guided by LeMoyne College in Syracuse in cooperation with a local senior centre.

Hiemstra (1980) studied some of the practical implications related to this heavy involvement of especially older adults in learning. Much of it is related to learning how to learn, one of the scientific viewpoints considered at this symposium. Some procedures for helping practitioners teach older adults were developed (Hiemstra, 1980). Hiemstra and Sisco (1990) have worked on some new approaches for teaching adults and have developed various corresponding instructional procedures. These are based on the idea that an individualizing process of instruction has great potential for adult learners, especially because this process enables the learners to assume responsibility for their own learning.

Based on research on the self-directed learning activities of adults (Brockett and Hiemstra, 1991), and building on Sternberg and others' notions about practical intelligence and the role of experience, the six-step individualizing process includes the following:

- Step one — planning activities prior to meeting with learners;
- Step two — creating a positive learning environment;
- Step three — developing the instructional plan;
- Step four — identifying appropriate learning activities;
- Step five — monitoring the progress of learners;
- Step six — evaluating individual learner outcome.

There are various obstacles faced by older adults regardless of the instructional process being used. Although some problems specific to a location or economic group will exist, typical obstacles include inadequate transportation, time limitations, high costs, low self-esteem or self-confidence, stereotypes regarding the elderly and education, and lack of knowledge about various learning opportunities. Health-related limitations and overall health status, such as fatigue, reduced mobility, and declining hearing or visual acuity can also impact on learning ability and activity.

Here are two instructional requirements to demonstrate how such information in facilitating future programmes or research might be used:

Condition	Change Pattern	Instructional Requirement
Sclerosis or a yellowing of the lens	Causes light to become somewhat scattered; slow decline after 50	Reduce any glare; do not use colour coding; ensure proper illumination
Visual ability and distinctness; visual acuity	Sharp decline usually starts in the 50s	Be sensitive to various visual needs; help learners move closer

Such declines or losses can create various problems that may affect learning and eventually instructional success. For instance, self-concept and self-confidence may decline if a person experiences various declines in personal abilities or skills. Correspondingly, instructors should work to enhance self-concept, self-confidence, and an ability to become self-directed. An instructor using the individualizing process described above will employ various teaching approaches to accommodate losses, such as removing any competition or time barriers, limiting the possibility for learners to make errors, or reducing high risk situations.

The instructor's role also is important in terms of the speed used to present information to older learners. This means allowing for adequate response time, using recognition rather than recall techniques, providing adequate feedback on learner progress, and employing self or peer-evaluation techniques. Appendix A summarizes what the research related to several broad instructional requirements or conditions has revealed.

Another related area of study pertains to building effective learning environments (Hiemstra, 1991). A learning environment can be defined as all of the physical surroundings, psychological or emotional conditions, and social or cultural influences affecting the growth and development of an adult engaged in an educational enterprise. This entails paying attention to the physical spaces in which learning takes place. It involves understanding issues like the emotional baggage an adult learner might bring to the learning setting. It necessitates that educators and trainers be conscious of various social or cultural impediments that might affect learning activities. Appendix B summarizes what an instructor of adults might look for if analyzing the learning environment. For example, the literature related to what in the United States has become known as "women's ways of knowing" has much to say about the creation of learning environments. Appendix C presents a summary of some studies in this area. Racism, whether overt, subtle, or unconscious is another issue that needs to be confronted by those of us setting policy and developing programmes (Colin and Preciphs, 1991).

Some Policy Implications

The expectation is that some future policies associated with initial and adult education will result from the Groningen symposium's activities. The development of policy applicable for any age learner, interested educators, and educational, community, or governmental agencies is a difficult and complicated activity. It requires accumulating considerable knowledge about learners. It also necessitates recognizing the complex nature of most human or societal problems. The application of personal and institutional philosophies to building policies can also be a crucial step. Finally, incorporating policy recommendations into practice activities requires much care, dedication, and patience.

Some policy statements are presented in Appendix D. Policy is defined in this context as a recommended course of action for achieving some goal or meeting some need, such as creating new educational services for older learners. The purpose of a policy is to serve as a framework for decision making rather than as a dogmatic rule or administrative directive. Policy suggestions may help set an agenda for the future. By way of conclusion, some examples with suggestions on how they might be used to develop learning strategies for adults are given below (Brockett and Hiemstra, 1991).

Policy Area	*Policy Recommendation*	*Implementation Strategies*
Older adults as learners	Encourage older learners to examine personal strengths and weakness	Assist older adults to complete self-inventories or self-concept measures
Adult education organizations	Organizations working with older learners should provide learning environments that accommodate learning	Examine the learning environment in terms of physical, emotional, and social issues; make any needed changes

References

Brockett, R.G. (1982). Self-directed learning readiness and life satisfaction among older adults. Unpublished doctoral dissertation, Syracuse University.

Brockett, R.G., & Hiemstra, R. (1991). *Self-direction in adult learning: Perspectives on theory, research, and practice.* London: Routledge.

Colin, S.A.J. III, & Preciphs, T.K. (1991). Perceptual patterns and the learning environment: Confronting White racism. In R. Hiemstra (Ed.), *Creating environments for effective adult learning* (pp. 61-70). San Francisco: Jossey-Bass.

Estrin, H.R. (1985). Life satisfaction and participation in learning activities among widows. Unpublished doctoral dissertation. Syracuse University.

Fisher, J.C. (1986). Participation in educational activities by active older adults. *Adult Education Quarterly, 36*, 202-210.

Galbraith, M.W., & James, W.B. (1984). Assessment of dominant perceptual learning styles of older adults. *Educational Gerontology, 10*, 449-458.

Henry, N.J. (1989). *A* qualitative study about perceptions of lifestyle and life satisfaction among older adults. Unpublished doctoral dissertation. Syracuse University.

Hiemstra, R. (1975). *The older adult and learning* (ERIC Document Reproduction Service No. ED 117 371).

Hiemstra, R. (1976). The older adult's learning projects. *Educational Gerontology, 1*, 331-341.

Hiemstra, R. (1980). *Preparing human service practitioners to teach older adults* (Information Series No. 209). Columbus, Ohio: Ohio State University (ERIC Document Reproduction Service No. ED 193 529).

Hiemstra, R. (1982). The elderly learner: A naturalistic inquiry. *Proceedings of the 23rd Annual Adult Education Research Conference* (pp. 103-107). Lincoln, Nebraska: Adult and Continuing Education Department, University of Nebraska.

Hiemstra, R. (1987). Older people master personal computer use. *Perspectives on Aging, 16* (1), 19.

Hiemstra, R. (Ed.). (1991). *Creating environments for effective adult learning* (New Directions for Adult and Continuing Education, Number 50). San Francisco: Jossey-Bass.

Hiemstra, R., & Sisco, B. (1990). *Individualizing instruction: Making learning personal, empowering, and successful.* San Francisco: Jossey-Bass.

Kinney, M.B. (1989). Elderhostel: Can it work at your institution? *Adult Learning, 1* (3), 21-24.

Knowlton, M.P. (1977). Liberal arts: The elderhostel plan for survival. *Educational Gerontology, 2*, 87-94.

Kolodny, A. (1991, February 6). Colleges must recognize students' cognitive styles and cultural backgrounds. *Chronicle of Higher Education,* A44.

Peterson, D.A. (1983). *Facilitating education for older learners.* San Francisco: Jossey-Bass.

Sternberg, R.J. (1985). *Beyond IQ: A triarchic theory of human intelligence.* New York: Cambridge University Press.

Sternberg, R.J. (1986). *Intelligence applied: Understanding and increasing your intellectual skills.* Orlando, Florida: Harcourt Brace Jovanovich.

Sternberg, R.J. (1991). Understanding adult intelligence. *Adult Learning, 2* (6), 8-10.

Sternberg, R.J., & Wagner, R.K. (Eds.). (1986). *Practical intelligence: Nature and origin of competence.* New York: Cambridge University Press.

Tough, A.M. (1979). *The adult's learning projects 2nd edition.* Austin, Texas: Learning Concepts.

Why We Use Computers. (1990). *Seniornet Newsline,* Fall, p. 4.

Williams, T.F. (1990, June). Research needs in aging and vision. *NCVA Aging and Vision News, 3* (1), 1-2.

Appendix A
Age-related Changes: Instructional Implications

The following are adapted and updated from Hiemstra and Sisco (1990) and Hiemstra (1991).

Learners' Needs and Experiences
1. Learning activities and instructional approaches should be based on learners' needs and interests;
2. Differing needs, interests, and abilities will exist and change over time among older learners, so instructors must be flexible;
3. Life stages and changes in life will impact on learning needs;
4. Social interactions among learners may have value as a learning motivator;
5. Small group discussion can be used for analyzing individual and group needs;
6. Learners should be helped to relate new knowledge to past experiences;
7. Learners should be helped to understand the advantages and disadvantages of being an older person in terms of educational needs;
8. Help learners tie any necessary text material to their own current knowledge base;
9. Instructional approaches should be tailored for different cognitive styles.

Involving Learners in Instruction
1. Learners should become active in all aspects of efforts to individualize the instructional process;
2. Learners should be encouraged to be self-directed in determining personal goals, learning approaches, and learning resource needs;
3. The development of confidence and a positive self-concept can be enhanced when learners engage in completing learning contracts;
4. Increasing opportunities for personal responsibility reduces learner dependency on the instructor;
5. Learners should be encouraged to become more efficient and self-motivated in the educational planning efforts;
6. Discovery teaching techniques can be used to involve and motivate learners;
7. Use a process orientation to increase perceptions of control and lead to improved self-confidence.

Personalizing the Instructor's Approach
1. Be helpful, positive, and supportive;
2. Assist older learners to compensate for intellectual or noncognitive changes;
3. Promote learning confidence, self-discipline, and self-respect;
4. Provide a learning environment of informality and levity;
5. Help learners feel welcome in any new learning setting;
6. Help learners feel at ease.

The Learning Pace
1. Provide long periods of time between stimuli for discussion or answering questions;
2. Provide adequate time for all aspects of the learning experience;
3. Eliminate sudden surprises or changes;
4. Be aware of learner perceptions about life satisfaction and locus of control;
5. Provide information in short sessions (50-60 minutes);
6. Minimize time pressures;
7. Provide for self-pacing by learners;
8. Move from easy to difficult material to promote success.

Assessment and Evaluation
1. Use outside validators if they are the most knowledgeable;
2. Reduce any chances for drastic failure or making grave errors;
3. Utilize peer review or feedback, positive feedback on progress, and various review strategies;
4. Reduce or eliminate homework and testing procedures;
5. Help learners talk about their learning, problems, and aspirations;
6. When testing is required use multiple-choice questions;
7. Utilize recognition techniques rather than more traditional recall methods.

Learning Activity: Organization and Meaningfulness
1. Become highly organized as an instructor;
2. Provide instructional goal suggestions and help learners develop personal objectives;
3. Provide outlines, study guides, and various advanced organizing techniques;
4. Encourage a belief in personal learning ability;
5. Assist learners in processing received information;

6. Facilitate and increase their ability and self-perception in terms of reading proficiency;
7. Assist learners in organizing planned learning activities;
8. Encourage learners to use learning contracts;
9. Facilitate the practising of techniques;
10. Show learners how to take notes and make outlines;
11. Let organizing material be part of the learning process;
12. Encourage the learner to connect concepts or information with a personal experience base;
13. Use materials with real meaning to learners;
14. Appeal to several senses;
15. Have concrete examples that tie to a learner's past experiences;
16. Be aware of differences in cognitive or learning styles;
17. Use various cuing devices;
18. Urge learners to use mnemonic devices;
19. Utilize headings, summaries, and review aids;
20. Facilitate a recognition of personal meaning;
21. Provide clear instructions in an attention-getting manner.

Recognize Barriers, Obstacles, and Physiological Needs
1. Be sensitive to diminishing hearing and associated problems for some older adults;
2. Assist learners to move closer to sound sources if needed;
3. Utilize voice and media amplification whenever appropriate;
4. Be sensitive to diminishing vision and associated problems for some older learners;
5. Provide time for adjustments when an older learner moves from light to dark areas;
6. Provide adequate light for classroom and visual aids;
7. Ensure that glare or direct sunlight is not a problem;
8. Utilize adequate contrast on visuals and reading material;
9. Emphasize visual as well as interactive approaches;
10. Be sensitive to short-term memory problems;
11. Read material aloud when feasible;
12. Utilize both auditory and visual presentation modes;
13. Diagnose learners' needs, abilities, and limitations;
14. Minimize learning distractions;
15. Be sensitive to various obstacles that can interfere with learning;
16. Be sensitive to physical environment problems;
17. Check for comfortable heating and proper ventilation;
18. Have periodic bathroom or refreshment breaks;
19. Help any learners with limited mobility or declining energy;
20. Reduce the use of colour coding as a category discriminator;

21. Accommodate those learners who need or desire to sit near the front;
22. Determine if all learners can focus on and see all visual aids;
23. Be alert to differences in ways of learning by gender categories;
24. Help responsible administrators become aware of troublesome barriers.

***

Appendix B
A Checklist for Analyzing the Learning Environment

The following checklist, adapted from Hiemstra and Sisco (1990) and Hiemstra (1991) can be used for analyzing various aspects of the learning environment. Analyze the agency in terms of whether or not these concerns seem to exist. This can be done by means of interviews, observations, or reading of available documents.

Sensory Concerns
• adequate lighting
• absence of glare
• lighting adequate for A/V devices
• attractive/appropriate colours and decorations
• adequate acoustics
• adequate sound amplification
• any noise to be reduced or eliminated
• temperature adequate for season of the year
• adequate ventilation or air conditioning
• "warm" or "caring" setting

Seating Concerns
• adjustable seats or alternative choices
• adequate cushioning if used for long periods
• person's legs can be crossed comfortably
• straight back and flat seat for people with back problems
• adequate sturdiness/size
• easily moved around
• seat height from floor adequate
• left-handed learners provided for

Social-Cultural Concerns
• no overt or subtle gender discrimination operating
• no overt or subtle age discrimination operating

Furnishing Concerns
• adequate table or writing space
• furnishing can be rearranged for small group work or to facilitate social interaction

- no overt or subtle racial discrimination operating
- facilitators trained for age, race, and gender sensitivity
- discussion/seating arranged so as to facilitate social interaction
- knowledge of various cultures as associated histories incorporated into learning
- women learners not disempowered or devalued in any way

- table space available for refreshments or resources
- if sitting at tables learners can cross their legs
- if learners sit at tables they can be arranged in a square, circle, or U-shape
- absence of ragged or sharp edges on all furnishings
- adequate sturdiness for all furnishings
- learners can see each other adequately when seated
- learners can see facilitator adequately when seated

General Concerns
- adequate access to site for learners
- adequate signs to direct learners to appropriate sites
- lavatory/cafeteria/refreshment machines nearby
- adequate parking nearby
- adequate lighting in parking area and building hallways
- adequate space shape and size in learning site
- breakout rooms/areas available if needed
- learning site provides for learner movement if needed
- learners facilitated in using computer technology

Psychological Concerns
- learners helped to become acquainted with each other
- learners helped to feel at ease and relaxed
- special attention given to the very first encounter with learners
- barriers learners may face when addressed by facilitators considered
- barriers learners may face when addressed by administrators considered
- learners helped to take more control of own learning
- facilitators trained in adult learning literature and theory
- facilitators trained in adult teaching techniques and theory

Appendix C
Some Sources on Women's Ways of Knowing:
Brief Annotated Bibliography

- Belenkey, M.F., Clinchy, N., Goldberger, L. and Tarule, J.M. (1986). *Women's ways of self, voice and mind.* New York: Basic Books. This book has perhaps done more than any other to popularize and help promote the new understanding that many women learn in ways different from those of men. Based on interviews with both students and women in professional roles, five distinct categories for "knowing" emerged: (a) a position of silence, subject to the whim of authority; (b) received knowledge from others; (c) subjective knowledge often associated with an inner voice; (d) procedural knowledge involving learning how to apply objective means for acquiring and communicating information; (e) constructed knowledge where women view themselves as knowledge creators. Several ideas for fostering women's development in learning situations are presented.

- Collard, S. and Stalker, J. (1991). Women's trouble: Women, gender, and the learning environment. In R. Hiemstra (Ed.), *Creating environments for effective adult learning* (New Directions for Adult and Continuing Education, Number 50). San Francisco: Jossey-Bass. Institutional settings both create and mirror a learning environment that devalues and disempowers women learners.

- Gilligan, C. (1982). *In a different voice: Psychological theory and women's development.* Cambridge, Massachusetts: Harvard University Press. Gilligan was one of the first American authors to discuss distinctive developmental characteristics of women. Although focusing primarily on moral development issues, there is much in this book about adult development in general that the interested adult education practitioner may want to consider.

- Hayes, E.R. (1989). Insights from women's experiences for teaching and learning. In E.R. Hayes (Ed), *Effective teaching styles* (New Directions for Adult and Continuing Education, Number 43). San Francisco: Jossey-Bass. Hayes presents a rationale for a feminist pedagogy and describes what the corresponding process should entail: collaboration in teaching and learning activities, cooperative communication styles, holistic approaches to learning, strategies for theory building, and action projects. She urges consideration of these strategies in the light of women's needs as learners, and appreciation of women's strengths and experiences.

- Kolodny, A. (1991, February 6). Colleges must recognize students' cognitive styles and cultural backgrounds. *Chronicle of Higher Education*, A44. Kolodny explains why educators must think about not only what they are teaching but also who and how. Although directed primarily at undergraduate teaching, she offers several ideas appropriate for adult education as well. She describes how high attrition rates for women in engineering courses in the United States were traced to teaching approaches that failed to account for the way women prefer to learn and discuss subject matter.

- Luttrel, W. (1989). Working-class women's ways of knowing: Effects of gender, race and class. *Sociology of Education, 62*, 33-46. This article describes and analyzes how black and white working-class women use knowledge. These women's perspectives challenge feminist views of a universal mode of knowing for women. Instead, the author suggests that complex power relations of gender, race, and class exist that shape how women think and learn. For adult educators concerned with creating equitable learning environments, the authors suggests that ethnic, class, and race issues specific to women's experiences must be carefully examined.

- Tannen, D. (1990). *You just don't understand: Women and men in conversation.* New York: William Morrow. This book helps us to better understand some of the sociolinguistic differences between men and women that can affect learning environments. Recent research from linguistic and social sciences that indicates how women and men use language differently is included. Men see themselves as autonomous individuals, where conversations are attempts to achieve and maintain an upper hand. Women see themselves as enmeshed in a web of relationships that they want to maintain, and conversations are negotiations for closeness, confirmation, and support.

Appendix D
Policy Recommendations

These recommendations and implementation strategies are adapted and updated from Brockett and Hiemstra (1991).

I Older Adults as Learners

Recommendation 1: Older adult learners should be acknowledged as having unlimited learning potential and given respect as self-directed learners.
Implementation strategies:
1. Use small groups discussion or create learning networks, including electronic networks, for assisting older learners to discover personal talents.
2. Provide opportunities for older learners to discover their own individual strengths.
3. Make educational resources available that teach about learning skills and how to use learning materials.
4. Assist teachers and trainers to understand their role in promoting individualized, self-directed learning.

Recommendation 2: Encourage older learners to examine personal strengths and weaknesses.
Implementation strategies:
1. Assist the older adult to complete self inventories or self-concept measures.
2. Ensure that teachers and counsellors have skill in discussing self-inventory information with older learners.

Recommendation 3: Help older learners develop or strengthen internal reinforcement mechanisms.
Implementation strategies:
1. Promote skill in using various reinforcement resources (meditation techniques, diary writing processes, and critical thinking techniques).
2. Train teachers to assist older learners in strengthening personal growth skills.
3. Secure learning resources that assist older learners with internal reinforcement.

Recommendation 4: Help older learners to understand their personal learning or cognitive style and to use such information in their educational efforts.

Implementation strategies:
1. Help learners to complete learning and cognitive style measures.
2. Train teachers and counsellors to interpret and use learning style information in helping learners with their planning.

Recommendation 5: Encourage older learners to form autonomous learning and support groups.
Implementation strategies:
1. Create learner information sources in libraries, universities, and senior centres.
2. Develop learning exchange or support networks in various settings.
3. Develop study circles or study groups similar to the Nordic model.
4. Develop support groups related to various content areas.

Recommendation 6: Provide older learners with opportunities for taking individual responsibility for their own learning.
Implementation strategies:
1. Create the necessary administrative support in order to facilitate individual adult initiative (convenient scheduling, adequate resources, transport support, adult counselling, etc.).
2. Provide workshops or learning materials to develop learning skills in time management and planning.

Recommendation 7: Continue the research necessary to understand the various aspects of individualized, self-directed learning.
Implementation strategies:
1. Determine learning techniques and skills necessary for learners and teachers.
2. Determine means for enhancing learner's problem-solving skills.
3. Study reasons why some people are reluctant to utilize self-directed approaches.
4. Examine the relationship between life stages and individualized, self-direction learning approaches.

Recommendation 8: Provide educators of adults with training in utilizing theories and practices related to adult learning.
Implementation strategies:
1. Students in formal adult education training programmes need an understanding of adult learning concepts and approaches.
2. Develop in-service training programmes on adult learning for the many educators who have not received any related formal training.

II Adult Education Organizations

Recommendation 9: Help organizations serving older adults to incorporate the concepts of individualized, self-directed learning into normal operating procedures.
Implementation strategies:
1. Develop individualized resources, create self-study materials, and establish appropriate learning settings.
2. Carry out learner needs assessments to determine possibilities for individualized, self-directed learning and provide the information to administrators.
3. Help organizations in co-ordinating the delivery of necessary resources and services related to individualized, self-directed learning.

Recommendation 10: Organizations working with older adult learners need to provide opportunities for administrators, faculty, and staff to become knowledgeable about adult learning.
Implementation strategies:
1. Promote an awareness of research and literature pertaining to adult learning.
2. Carry out workshops for employees, in-service training, and resource material dissemination related to adult learning.

Recommendation 11: Organizations working with older adult learners should develop and maintain various measures or criteria for accountability and evaluation.
Implementation strategies:
1. Create reporting systems that accommodate nontraditional data collection and reporting mechanisms (learning contracts, internship reports, credit for experience of work, etc.).
2. Try "innovative" evaluation methods (interviewing, networking assessments, validation via outside experts, etc.).

Recommendation 12: Organizations working with older adult learners should seek national legislation and funding to promote and facilitate adult learning at all levels.
Implementation strategies:
1. Provide learning resources and study opportunity information to a multitude of community agencies.
2. Attempt to influence legislation through professional associations.

Recommendation 13: Organizations working with older adult learners should provide support services that help those desiring to be self-directed in their learning efforts.
Implementation strategies:
1. Create centres or special locations within agency settings where learners can gather, obtain learning resources, and support each other.
2. Ensure personnel have the expertise to counsel and help older adults make effective use of self-directed learning skills.

Recommendation 14: Organizations working with older adult learners should provide learning environments that accommodate learning.
Implementation strategies:
1. Examine the learning environment in terms of physical, emotional, and social issues and make any necessary changes.
2. Maintain on-site specialists on learning environments who can work with educators and learners to design appropriate learning conditions.

Part 2

Capacity to Learn in the Lifespan

Chapter 5

FLUID ABILITIES AND EPISTEMIC THINKING: SOME PRESCRIPTIONS FOR ADULT EDUCATION

DAVID F. LOHMAN
The University of Iowa, U.S.A.

GEOFFREY SCHEURMAN
The University of Iowa, U.S.A.

There is a new interest in human intelligence. The rooms that were once occupied by the stodgy old men of psychometrics have been renovated by a new generation of upstarts. Some of the new tenants have remodelled their rooms into quarters that their predecessors would not recognize. But others, after much ado, merely succeeded in rearranging the furniture a bit and hanging new curtains on the windows. Indeed, one does not have to know too much about the history of research on human intelligence to see much that is old in the new house of intellect.

One of these older theories has had a surprisingly large impact on both contemporary theories of intelligence and on the tests constructed to estimate it. The theory has received considerable attention in factor analytic theories of intelligence (e.g., Horn, 1985; Gustafsson, 1984), information processing theories of intelligence (e.g., Sternberg, 1985; Snow, 1981), and has served as the theoretical model for at least two major intelligence tests — the Woodcock-Johnson (1989) and the Stanford–Binet Fourth Edition (Thorndike et al., 1986). The theory is Cattell's (1943, 1963) theory of fluid and crystallized intelligence.

In this chapter, it is argued that this theory holds great promise for the improvement of education at all levels, but that the opportunity has been missed because of some mistaken beliefs about the nature of fluid abilities. It supports those who see fluid abilities not as a measure of innate capacity or physiological integrity of the organism, but as one of the more important products of education and experience.

The view that ability constructs at all levels in the hierarchy fo human abilities can be decomposed in this same way is upheld. Thus, as Snow (1981) suggests, one might better speak of the processes of fluidization and crystallization than of one fluid and one crystallized ability. Implications of this view for adult education and development are then briefly noted, and explanations for the decline in general fluid abilities across the lifespan proposed.

Recent theories of adult intellectual development, which identify a stage or level of adult cognitive development characterized as epistemic knowing, are reviewed subsequently. The theories suggest that current tests of fluid abilities seem to provide good estimates of the ability to solve well-structured novel problems of the sort school children must face, but do not provide estimates of the ability to solve the sort of ill-structured novel problems that characterize the most advanced levels of adult thinking. It is concluded that a new understanding of fluid abilities would have important implications both for the assessment of adult competence and for education at all levels. But the story must be told from somewhere near the beginning, and so the evolution of the theory of fluid and crystallized abilities is briefly examined first.

Historical Overview

Cattell first proposed the concept of two intelligences at the 1941 meeting of the American Psychological Association. Coincidentally, Hebb (1949) also outlined his theory of Intelligence A and Intelligence B at the same meeting. Intelligence A referred to the innate, genotypic potential of the individual whereas Intelligence B referred to the phenotypic expression of this intelligence. The earliest published account of Cattell's theory appeared two years later. At that time, he argued that fluid ability (Gf) was "a purely general ability to discriminate and perceive relations between any fundaments, new or old" (Cattell, 1943, p. 178). Fluid intelligence was also hypothesized to be the cause of the general factor found among ability tests administered to children and among "speeded or adaptation-requiring" (p. 178) tests administered to adults. Crystallized intelligence (Gc), on the other hand, was thought to consist of "discriminatory habits long established in a particular field" that were originally acquired through the operation of fluid ability. Thus, in this earliest version of the theory, the two intelligences were given equal status.

The theory lay dormant for 20 years while Cattell returned to an earlier research interest of applying factor analysis to the study of personality. In the 1963 formulation of the theory, however, fluid ability was given a more important role. Gf was now hypothesized to reflect the physiological integrity of the organism useful for adapting to novel situations that, when invested in particular learning experiences, produced Gc. The new Gf was thus much closer to Hebb's (1949) Intelligence A. Although Cattell (1963) tried to distinguish his theory from Hebb's, others, including Horn (1985), equate Cattell's interpretation of the Gf-Gc dichotomy with Hebb's (1949) distinction between Intelligence A and B.

The hypothesis that Gf reflects physiological influences and is thus a better measure of the true intelligence of the individual conforms with our intuitive or naive theories of intelligence. But there is considerable evidence that these theories are only partially correct and that the investment theory of aptitude — at least as formulated by Cattell — may be more misleading than helpful. Indeed, several prominent theorists accept the fluid - crystallized distinction, and some also subscribe to the investment theory of aptitude. But they do so without assuming that fluid ability is somehow more innate than crystallized ability. For example, Cattell's student and collaborator Horn (1976) interpreted Gf simply as "facility in reasoning, particularly in figural or non-word symbolic materials" (p. 445). Cronbach (1977) went even further when he argued that "fluid ability is itself an achievement" that reflects the "residue of indirect learning from varied experience" (p. 287). More recently, Horn (1985) has echoed the same theme: "There are good reasons to believe that Gf is learned as much as Gc, and that Gc is inherited as much as Gf" (p. 289). Gc, said Horn, reflects individual differences in "acculturation learning" whereas Gf reflects individual differences in "casual learning" and "independent thinking" (Horn, 1985, pp. 289-290). Horn and others point out that, if tests of fluid abilities were better indicators of the psychological integrity of the organism and if crystallized abilities were more the product of experience, then scores on tests of fluid abilities should show relatively higher heritabilities, which they do not (Horn, 1985; Humphreys, 1981; Scarr and Carter-Saltman, 1982). For example, Humphreys' analyses of the Project Talent data showed that heritabilities were higher for a Bible knowledge test than for nonverbal reasoning tests.

The Psychology of the Fluid—Crystallized Distinction

If the fluid-crystallized distinction does not correspond to the difference between innate and acquired abilities, then what does it represent? Snow (1981) gives one answer:

> Gc may represent prior assemblies of performance processes retrieved as a system and applied anew in instructional or other performance situations not

unlike those experienced in the past, while Gf may represent new assemblies of performance processes needed for more extreme adaptations to novel situations. The distinction is between long-term assembly for transfer to familiar situations and short-term assembly for transfer to unfamiliar situations. Both functions develop through exercise, and perhaps both can be understood as variations on a central production system development. (Snow, 1981, p. 360)

There are two key assertions here: first at a process level, fluid and crystallized abilities may be not all that dissimilar since both can be modelled as variations on a common production system. The primary difference is between successfully executing certain processes in the present (Gf) and having successfully executed those processes in the past and stored the products as knowledge (Gc), or between process and product, to use Cattell's (1963) terms. Second, fluid abilities are understood to be as much learned as crystallized abilities. Indeed, elsewhere Snow claims that fluid abilities are among the most important products of education and experience (Snow and Yalow, 1982).

Explaining the Decline in Gf

If this is the case, then why do we observe a decline in general fluid abilities over the lifespan? There are several possibilities, including brain damage, changes in memory, and lack of practice in confronting novelty (see also Horn, 1985).

Cumulative Damage to the Brain

The assumption here is that fluid abilities reflect the physiological integrity of the organism. The decline in Gf with age reflects the cumulative impact of ageing on the efficiency of the brain.

Changes in Working Memory and Attention

Kyllonen and Christal (1990) report strikingly high correlations between performance on tests that require subjects to manipulate information in working memory and the sort of reasoning tests that often define Gf. One interpretation of these correlations is that Gf in large measure reflects the ability to manipulate symbolic information in working memory. However, working memory is not a seven-slotted box. Anderson (1983) models working memory as simply knowledge that is in an active state. This knowledge consists of both temporary knowledge structures and the active parts of long-term memory. However, activation spreads automatically in long-term memory to nodes that are related to the source node. Thus, the more knowledge one has associated with a particular source node, the lower the activation of each ancillary node.

This is sometimes called the fan effect. By this explanation, then, increases in knowledge lead to a gradual diffusion of attentional resources among larger segments of memory. One is slower searching this knowledge base, both because there are more paths to traverse and activation of each node in the network is lower. One older man explained it this way: "When I was young," he said, "my mind was like a bright light that I could focus on a problem and keep it there until the solution appeared. Sometimes I almost felt it was like a laser beam. But now it is much harder to focus the beam". Another older genius reported that the only real change he had noticed in his thinking over the years was that with age, the internal noise had increased. Both of these accounts are consistent with an explanation of decline in Gf as reflecting a shift in attentional resources. Note, however, that the chief culprit here is the breadth and depth of knowledge, not age *per se* or brain damage correlated with age.

Lack of Practice in Confronting Novelty

The third possibility is the most intriguing, yet certainly the most speculative of all. The hypothesis can be stated in many ways. One version is what can be called the empty-head theory. When an adult is confronted with a problem, the first tendency is to search memory for analogues somewhere in the (often distant) past. "It seems that I remember something like this back in 1964", or 1945, or whatever. Further, experience teaches most of us that it is wise to use one's experience. A little searching through memory can often pay handsome dividends. But when one is 16 years of age, the search through memory for relevant prior experiences proceeds rather quickly. There is at most one decade of accumulated memory to search rather than four or five. Thus, the search is often aborted quickly and the process of assembling a solution from scratch begun at once. Experience thus rather naturally leads one to rely more on Gc-type knowledge and skills and less on Gf-type knowledge and skills. The assumption then, is that fluidization of abilities occurs through repeated attempts to cope with novelty, whereas crystallization occurs through repeated applications of old knowledge to new situations. The hypothesis is that both general fluid ability or fluid applications of more specific abilities develop through exercise and decline through lack of exercise, as E.L. Thorndike (1920) and Snow (1981) suggest. This is easy to see for more specific skills like speaking a foreign language. But it probably also applies at the level of general academic ability. For the child in school, each day brings new problems, each semester brings new courses and new instructors. One is constantly confronted with novelty. Indeed, fluid-ability tests show their highest correlations with school performance at those points where the transition is greatest, such as from elementary school to high school, or from high school to the university, especially when the university experience differs markedly from high school experience. Thus, the decline in general fluid ability over the adult years may occur in large measure because these abilities are not much exercised. Once again, this may be easier to see at the level of more specific abilities in the hierarchy. In other words, is the decline in general fluid abilities mirrored at the level of more specific abilities? If so, is this because knowledge and skills become increasingly crystallized through the repeated application in familiar situations? Can it be counteracted by occasionally changing the context or nature of the problems faced? There is much anecdotal evidence that this is the case. Large corporations routinely move employees into different positions. Is the individual who has had a varied employment history better at solving unfamiliar problems than the employee who has stayed in the same position for as many years? Probably. The point is simply that if we stop thinking of the decline in fluid abilities as the inevitable product of cumulative brain damage then many other possibilities open up.

The Development of Fluid Abilities

The assertion that fluid abilities develop through exercise and decline with disuse has important implications for educators. Unfortunately, examination of existing tests of fluid ability give no clear guidance for how one might teach fluid abilities or assess them in instructionally useful ways. The key to making this transition lies in the realization that the processes of crystallization and fluidization of knowledge occur at all levels in the hierarchy of human abilities. Cattell, Horn, and others have studied this continuum at the highest level, that of general mental ability. Cattell took Spearman's g and decomposed it into two constructs. Actually, fluid and crystallized general abilities can be placed along a continuum, as several theorists have suggested (Lohman, 1989). This is indicated in Figure 5.1. But this same continuum can be applied to ability constructs at any level in the ability hierarchy. We can speak of the process of fluidization or crystallization of knowledge and skills in any domain, whether it be learning to speak a foreign language, to play a musical instrument, to write short stories, or to sail on the IJselmeer. Crystallization occurs through chunking and automatization of knowledge for repeated applications to familiar situations; fluidization occurs through the elaboration and application of old knowledge to unfamiliar situations.

Education at all levels must be increasingly concerned with the fluidization of abilities. The ability to apply one's learning to unfamiliar situations has always been an important outcome of education.

Tests of immediate learning	Final course exams	General academic achievement (Gc)	General fluid ability (Gf)	Insightful and creative problem solving

Familiar problems and contexts	Novel problems and contexts
Near transfer	Far transfer

Figure 5.1. A continuum of transfer for describing the fluid-crystallized ability distinction.

In a world in which the half-life of ideas declines yearly, perhaps solving new problems (or old problems in new ways) is the most important task for students of all ages. Unfortunately, both instruction and educational assessment tend to focus on the familiar rather than on the novel. There are many reasons for this. One of the more important is that like beauty, novelty is in large measure in the eyes of the beholder. What is novel for one person at one point in time may not be novel for another person or even for the same person at another time. Thus, measurement of the ability to cope with novelty, to borrow Sternberg's (1985) phrase, becomes increasing problematic as the average novelty of tasks for the group tested increases. Stern's (1914) solution to this problem — which was the solution accepted by most subsequent investigators — was to use puzzle-like tasks that were moderately novel for most test takers. But such tasks have little if any instructional utility. What is needed, then, are instructionally useful measures of the ability to solve novel problems in a domain, and instructional methods that encourage the development of these abilities.

Lohman (1991) has argued that instructionally useful tests of fluid abilities can be devised by requiring students (a) to solve increasingly unfamiliar problems in a domain, and (b) to impose one or more organizational schemes on their learning. The first avenue emphasizes the skill or procedural aspect of knowledge, whereas the second focuses on the factual or declarative aspect of knowledge. Both require a shift in perspective from that of the test administrator to that of the test taker. In other words, the goal of measurement is to gain a glimpse of the learner's perception of a problem and of the richness (or poverty) of the knowledge the learner brings to bear on the problem. Marton (1983) has developed a procedure for doing this that he calls phenomenography. His approach has much in common with Langer's (1989) theory of mindfulness.

In our work, we have used a simpler procedure of asking the test-taker to rate or sort problems according to their novelty. All of these approaches challenge the assumption of psychometrics that all subjects must run the same race or be rank ordered on the same scale before meaningful measurement is possible. Rank ordering subjects by their performance on a common set of tasks is generally most useful somewhere near the beginning of the learning cycle; carrying it beyond that can artificially constrict one's understanding of what students have learned and, when this information is used to guide instruction, the subsequent learning of students. For example, consider the task of measuring artistic ability. We could ask all students to draw the same scene from the same perspective and then get judges to rank order their drawings. Indeed, this is how art instructors often proceed at the elementary levels. But we would lose much if we insisted on this same procedure as students develop. Some rough ordering of students is still possible even if each attempts a unique drawing. But the goal of rank ordering everyone along a single scale must decline in importance as we move to higher levels of competence. At the highest levels there are probably as many different rank orders as there are judges.

This same principle applies to all areas of development. A common set of tasks is useful only when the experiences of the group are constrained to be more or less equal. Diversity of experience increases as competence increases, often abruptly so, such as when the period of common schooling ends and adults enter the workforce or pursue diverse forms of higher education. Calls for better estimates of the life competencies of adults must recognize that such assessments will rarely apply to more than a small segment of the population.

Thus, although there seems to be consensus that the school-type tasks used to estimate Gc skills in children and adolescents are inappropriate for adults, and that a wider net must be cast to capture the important life competencies of adults, a single, wide-ranging test may still be inappropriate. Although some of these competencies are shared by many in the society (e.g., filing taxes, borrowing money, voting), most are even more domain specific than the academic accomplishments of the student. Thus, Wagner and Sternberg (1986) investigated the practical knowledge of academic psychologists and business managers using separate scales. Such tests need not be administered to everyone to be useful. Putting everyone on a common scale is less useful than understanding the variations in competence within the group who claim training or expertise in a domain.

In summary, the distinction between fluid and crystallized general ability is but one example of the fluidization or crystallization process that occurs with all abilities, broad and narrow. The knowledge and skills represented in any ability construct can be made more fluid through practice that encourages the flexible organization and elaboration of declarative knowledge and the application of procedural knowledge to diverse and unfamiliar problems. The great challenge for education, then, is to encourage fluidization, not merely crystallization of knowledge and skills. Doing this will require a commitment to instructional methods and assessment techniques that go beyond the conventional (see Lohman, 1991, for more discussion). It also requires a commitment to long-term rather than immediate educational outcomes. Too much educational research has looked at immediate outcomes. But the long-term effects of instruction can be quite different from the short-term effects, especially when the goal is transfer of knowledge to new learning or applying it to the solution of unfamiliar problems. Taking the long view is facilitated by a theory of adult intellectual development.

Models of Adult Intellectual Development

In order to contrast the intellectual abilities of adults with children, theorists have devised a language for describing types of problems and the different systems of inquiry required to think about them intelligently (Churchman, 1971; Wood, 1983; Kitchener, 1983). For well-structured problems, including puzzles used on most current tests of fluid ability, all the parameters necessary for a complete solution are present. What distinguishes a puzzle is that the proper application of previously agreed upon rules, evidence, and procedures leads to a single, absolutely correct solution. By contrast, postadolescent functioning often requires the solution of ill-structured problems, where the problem solver is faced with multiple solutions that are contextually relative or even antithetical. Higher-order intelligence is operationalized as the ability to decide which set of competing or conflicting assumptions and procedures best fit the evidence at hand and the ability to integrate them into a single solution. For example, making judgements about arguments often requires synthesizing several perspectives into a more general model of the problem. Rather than absolute truths, solutions to ill-structured problems are more likely to be reasoned, tentative judgements (Wood, 1983).

Whereas the solution of well-structured problems is likely to involve cognitive and metacognitive resources in the application of logical thought, it has been argued that ill-structured problems are likely to require "epistemic" cognitive processes that influence how individuals understand problems and decide which strategies are appropriate in dealing with them.

Alternative Frameworks

In response to the call for better ways to measure intellectual growth (Sternberg, 1982), a number of models have been proposed to explain the structure and processes best suited to deal with ill-structured situations. In each of these formulations, the assumption is that formal operations — the kind of hypothetical-deductive reasoning described by Piaget — are inadequate to describe differences in adult intelligence. An example of this kind of modelling is the attempt to distinguish problem-solving from problem-finding abilities (Arlin, 1986, 1990). This work represents an attempt to identify a unified picture of mental functioning which describes more advanced adult developmental characteristics associated with the discovery of problems.

A second model describes the development of dialectical thinking (Baseeches, 1986, 1989), where intelligence is described by an age-related increase in cognitive schemata which permit relationships among informational input to be integrated and transformed into larger units. Like problem finding, dialectical processes are beyond the formal analyses required to succeed on traditional measures of intelligence or formal reasoning.

A third effort seeks to explain the unique features of adult intelligence in terms of life planning, or what has been called the fundamental "pragmatics of life" (Baltes and Smith, 1990; Smith and Baltes, 1990; Smith et al., 1989). These authors argue that age-related increases in crystallized intelligence can be explained by certain skills which become good enough to compensate for others such as fluid abilities, which are declining. Solving ill-structured problems, however, requires more than internal and external information search strategies; integration skills and practice at making evaluative judgements are necessary as well. Using an expertise analogue, their work has begun to show that current formulations of declarative and procedural knowledge are not sufficient to identify the more complex processes needed to deal with open-ended, multi-dimensional and dialogical problems.

Though these and other adult models possess unique features, they are conceptually similar. Intelligent behaviour depends on cognitive structures which continue to evolve into adulthood. Successful solution of ill-structured problems may require a recognition of the relativistic nature of knowledge, the limits imposed by context, as well as increased differentiation between subject and object in an increasingly complex social environment (Cavanaugh et al., 1985). Other characteristics of adult cognitive development are clearly articulated in the work of Perry (1970) and Kitchener (1983, 1986).

The Perry Scheme

Perry (1970) described a fixed sequence of nine cognitive stages of growth representing transitions in the processes young adults use to understand intellectual and ethical discourse. The college student is seen as a naive epistemologist who often enters school with a dualistic conception of knowledge. One's view of reality is polarized (right-wrong, we-they, good-bad) while knowledge is an unorganized set of absolute and discrete truths. One evolves from total dependence on authority through a stage of uncertainty where multiple perspectives are accepted as having equal claims on truth. A more mature conception of knowledge is eventually accepted where certainty is once again found in the integration and interpretation of context-dependent propositions (Ryan, 1984a, 1984b). The fundamental transition, then, is from a position of egocentric certainty to one of contextual relativism where judgements can be made on the basis of evidence and argument. The development of epistemological maturity as described by the Perry Scheme assumes that growth occurs when one comes to see knowledge as ultimately constructed rather than given, contextual rather than absolute, and mutable rather than fixed (Moore, 1991).

The Reflective Judgement Model

The Reflective Judgement Model is a purely cognitive theory of post-adolescent thinking which defines seven stages corresponding roughly to the first five stages of the Perry Scheme (Kitchener and King, 1981). The stages are predicated on a three-level model of cognitive processing (Kitchener, 1983). While cognition refers to familiar information-processing activities such as storing and transforming knowledge, metacognition includes knowledge about one's own processing strategies as well as the distinctive features of a given cognitive task. It is argued that while metacognitive abilities may be sufficient to solve many well-structured activities, ill-structured problems require an additional level of epistemic cognition. The focus of this third type of intellectual processing is on an individual's assumptions about the manner in which knowledge is acquired, the criteria and certainty of what counts as knowledge, as well as the methods and limitations of justifying truth claims.

Subjects at the earliest stages of reflective judgement are also characterized by the view that reality can be known with absolute certainty. Knowledge is based either on direct experience or transmitted by an authority, who either knows truth or will someday discover it. Like the dualist perspective in the Perry Scheme, the person at these stages assumes all problems are well-structured (Kitchener, 1986). As subjects evolve through the sequence of stages, they become increasingly aware that the answer to some problems cannot be known with certainty. Eventually, the subject begins to recognize the relativistic context in which ill-structured problems thrive, and that knowledge is therefore constructed out of a higher order synthesis of multiple perspectives. Intelligence is again seen as progression from dogmatic certainty through various stages of relativistic uncertainty in which judgements must be made in the face of subjective evaluation. Those at higher stages of reflective judgement assume that interpretations themselves are subject to empirical and conceptual scrutiny, and regard criteria such as soundness, validity, relevance, and parsimony as increasingly important (King et al., 1990).

In summary, subjects tend to approach intellectual problems from a particular conceptual orientation. These orientations can be described by stage models described in research on adult intellectual development. The major positions of the Perry Scheme — dualism, multiplism, contextual relativism and commitment — as well as the primary stages of the Reflective Judgement Model — dogmatism, scepticism, rationality — share a common view of adult naive certainty about knowledge. It is possible for adults to evolve through stages of relative uncertainty, and culminate with a tentative certainty about the validity of claims to truth which is complex, mature, and rational.

Beyond Existing Measures of Fluid Ability

Theories of adult cognitive development all point to a stage of development evolving during young adulthood which is characterized by an ability to know about knowledge — its certainty, its limits, and most importantly, the criteria by which we determine what counts as knowledge at all. Metacognition is thinking about thinking and an awareness of the products of one's thinking. Epistemic cognition or knowledge is a kind of reasoning about reasoning (it's been called meta-metacognition). It includes the ability to form a representation of representational systems, or to execute a network of meta-assumptions and metaprocedures that have to deal with deciding which set of assumptions and procedures should be implemented in the context of a particular problem. Indeed, Kuhn (1983) has concluded that the discussion on metacognition has blurred the distinction between Executive 1 strategies (knowledge about the task or problem itself) and Executive 2 strategies (knowledge of whether a particular strategy is appropriate to apply in a problem-solving situation). Executive 2 strategies differ from Executive 1 strategies in that they deal with knowing about knowledge itself — such as whether a truth claim is valid or that, for some problems, no solution is ever absolutely true (Kitchener, 1983). This is more than metacognition.

This transition from metacognitive to epistemic knowing has an important implication for the way we should understand and assess fluid abilities in adulthood. The key is to be found in differences between the way mature adults and children confront novel, ill structured problems. Fluid abilities are estimated through performance on novel problems. For children, these are invariably well-structured puzzle problems that admit a single correct answer. Several theorists (Brown and Campione, 1986; Sternberg, 1985) have argued that performance on such tasks depends heavily on metacognitive processes, that is, on how efficiently and effectively the child can monitor the task of assembling a strategy to solve the task, monitoring its effectiveness, and adapting it in the face of changing task demands. While the ability to engage in metacognitive processing clearly differentiates between retarded and normal performance during childhood, it is not the source of the more sophisticated forms of adult thinking, especially on the sort of ill-structured problems which adults confront.

Here what we have termed epistemic thought is more important. Epistemic thought may be described by the manner in which one either ignores the novel dimensions of a problem (such as turning an uncertain, dialogical problem into a dualistic one by refusing to admit into the problem space those assumptions that conflict with one's egocentric view) or takes the conflicting assumptions and synthesizes them into a reformulated model of the problem. According to this view, then, epistemological assumptions held by an individual actually impose a level of novelty on a task.

The claim, then, is that while general fluid abilities of children may well be estimated by their performance on well-structured puzzle-like tasks, fluid abilities of adults may require the presentation of ill-structured problems and a scoring system that goes beyond judgements of right/wrong in order to estimate the epistemological sophistication of the perspectives offered. Such assessments would probably benefit more form Kitchener and King's (1990) Reflective Judgement Interview, Marton's (1983) phenomenography, or Langer's (1989) concepts of mindfulness than from existing puzzle-like tasks.

Finally, it should be noted that although we may indeed estimate a general fluid ability for children who are all participants in a common march through the educational system of a nation, we may not be able to estimate a general fluid ability in adults that has anything like the generality of the corresponding ability estimated for children. The specialization for adult knowledge may require that we estimate fluid abilities with problems that allow adults to use their uniquely adult forms of knowledge.

Conclusions

1. Intelligence at all ages is in significant measure the product of education and experience. Naive beliefs of ability as innate have misled theorists and practitioners. These beliefs are reinforced by a misinterpretation of research on the heritability of ability. Genetic factors are important. However, the limits placed on development by genetics are soft, vary over the lifespan, and are unknowable in advance. Those who find this hard to understand should try reading "achievement" for "intelligence" in discussions of heritability, since heritability coefficients are usually higher for measures of school achievement than for IQ scores. Yet no one would suggest that school achievement is not in significant measure the product of experience.

2. Those who view intelligence as a reflection of the biological integrity of the organism naturally look for biological causes for the observed decline in general fluid abilities over the lifespan. However, other explanations are equally plausible, including (a) the dispersion in attentional resources brought about by an increase in knowledge, and (b) the relative decline of such abilities through disuse.

3. It was claimed that, at all developmental levels and in all domains, it is useful to distinguish between the ability to solve relatively familiar problems and the ability to solve relatively novel problems. Cattell (1963) refers to these as crystallized and fluid abilities. However, Snow (1981) argues that it is better to think of ability development as a process of fluidization and/or crystallization.

4. It was argued that fluidization is encouraged when learners are asked to stretch their knowledge to solve increasingly unfamiliar problems or to organize concepts in new ways. Unfortunately, existing tests of fluid ability do not provide instructionally useful information about the extent to which learners have developed these abilities in different domains. New measures are thus sorely needed.

5. Theories of adult development describe one or more additional stages of development that go beyond the level of formal operations described in Piaget's theory. These stages are characterized by an understanding of knowledge as constructed rather than as given, as contextual rather than as absolute, and as mutable rather than as fixed. Such epistemic awareness is particularly important in attempts to solve the sorts of ill-structured problems adults confront after they leave school. Measures of adult intelligence need to be developed which estimate both the crystallized and fluid aspects of such problem solving.

6. Education has traditionally sought only to develop crystallized abilities and has presumed that fluid abilities were unalterable. We now know better. Further, we know that fluid abilities are at once

both the most important products of education as well as the most important aptitudes for learning in that medium (Snow and Yalow, 1982). Therefore, both initial and adult education must take seriously the charge to develop fluid as well as crystallized abilities, especially in a world in which the economic and political stability of countries depend on the abilities of their citizenry to adapt to change.

7. Adults continue to develop those abilities that they use; abilities that show decline in the later adult years either emphasize speed or require the solution of novel problems. In both cases, disuse may be a significant factor in explaining the decline, although other factors are also involved. Thus, recent research on the development of adult intelligence shows the value of adult education in maintaining old abilities and in developing new, uniquely adult forms of thinking.

References

Anderson, J.R. (1983). *The architecture of cognition*. Cambridge, Massachusetts: Harvard University Press.

Arlin, P.K. (1986). Problem finding and young adult cognition. In R.A. Mines and K.S. Kitchener (Eds.), *Adult cognitive development: Models and methods* (pp. 22-32). New York: Praeger.

Arlin, P.K. (1990). Wisdom: The art of problem finding. In R.J. Sternberg (Ed.), *Handbook of human intelligence* (pp. 230-243). New York: Cambridge University Press.

Baltes, P.B., & Smith, J. (1990). Toward a psychology of wisdom and its ontogenesis. In R.J. Sternberg (Ed.), *Wisdom: Its nature, origins, and development* (pp. 87-120). London: Cambridge University Press.

Baseeches, M. (1986). Dialectical thinking and young adult cognitive development. In R.A. Mines and K.S. Kitchener (Eds.), *Adult cognitive development: Models and methods* (pp. 33-56). New York: Praeger.

Baseeches, M. (1989). Intellectual development: The development of dialectical thinking. In E.P. Maimon, B.F. Nodine and F.W. O'Connor (Eds.), *Thinking, reasoning, and writing* (pp. 23-45). New York: Longman.

Brown, A.L., & Campione, J.C. (1986). Psychological theory and the study of learning disabilities. *American Psychologist, 41*, 1059-1068.

Cattell, R.B. (1943). The measurement of adult intelligence. *Psychological Bulletin, 40*, 153-193.

Cattell, R.B. (1963). Theory of fluid and crystallized intelligence: A critical experiment. *Journal of Educational Psychology, 54*, 1-22.

Cavanaugh, J.C., Kramer, D.A., Sinnott, J.D., Camp, C.J., & Markley, R.P. (1985). On missing links and such: Interfaces between cognitive research and everyday problem solving. *Human Development, 28*, 146-168.

Churchman, C.W. (1971). *The design of inquiring systems: Basic concepts of systems and organization*. New York: Basic Books.

Cronbach, L.J. (1977). *Educational psychology* 3rd edition. New York: Harcourt, Brace, Jovanovich.

Gustafsson, J.E. (1984). A unifying model for the structure of intellectual abilities. *Intelligence, 8*, 179-203.

Hebb, D.O. (1949). *The organization of behavior*. New York: Wiley.

Horn, J.L. (1976). Human abilities: A review of research theory in the early 1970s. *Annual Review of Psychology, 27*, 437-485.
Horn, J.L. (1985). Remodeling old models of intelligence. In B.B. Wolman (Ed.), *Handbook of intelligence* (pp. 267-300). New York: Wiley.
Humphreys, L.G. (1981). The primary mental ability. In M. P. Friedman, J.P. Das and N. O'Connor (Eds.), *Intelligence and learning* (pp. 87-102). New York: Plenum.
King, P.M., Wood, P.K., & Mines, R.A. (1990). Critical thinking among college and graduate students. *The Review of Higher Education, 13* (2), 167-186.
Kitchener, K.S. (1983). Cognition, metacognition, and epistemic cognition. *Human Development, 26*, 222-232.
Kitchener, K.S. (1986). The reflective judgement model: Characteristics evidence, and measurement. In R.A. Mines & K.S. Kitchener (Eds.), *Adult cognitive development: Methods and models* (pp. 76-91). New York: Praeger.
Kitchener, K.S., & King, P.M. (1981). Reflective judgement: Concepts of justification and their relationship to age and education. *Journal of Applied Developmental Psychology, 2*, 89-116.
Kitchener, K.S., & King, P.M. (1990). The reflective judgement model: Ten years of research. In M.L. Commons, C. Armon, L. Kohlberg, F.A. Richards, T.A. Grotser and J.D. Sinnott (Eds.), *Adult development: Models and methods in the study of adolescent and adult thought* (pp. 63-78). New York: Praeger.
Kramer, D.A. (1983). Post-formal operations? A need for further conceptualization. *Human Development, 26*, 91-105.
Kuhn, D. (1983). On the dual executive and its significance in the development of developmental psychology. In D. Kuhn & J. Meacham (Eds.), *On the development of developmental psychology* (pp. 81-111). Karger: Basel.
Kyllonen, P.C., & Christal, R.E. (1990). Reasoning ability is (little more than) working memory capacity?! *Intelligence, 14*, 389-434.
Langer, E.J. (1989). *Mindfulness*. Reading, Massachusetts: Addison-Wesley.
Lohman, D.F. (1989). Human intelligence: An introduction to advances in theory and research. *Review of Educational Research, 59* (4), 333-373.
Lohman, D.F. (1991). Encouraging the development of fluid abilities in gifted students. Paper presented at the Henry B. and Jocelyn Wallace National Research Symposium on Talent Development, Iowa City.
Marton, F. (1983). Beyond individual differences. *Educational Psychology, 3*, 291-305.
Moore, W.S. (1991, March). The Perry Scheme of intellectual and ethical development: An introduction to the model and major assessment approaches. Paper presented at the annual meeting of the American Educational Research Association, Chicago.
Perry, W.G. (1970). *Forms of intellectual and ethical development in the college years: A scheme*. New York: Holt, Rinehart and Winston.
Ryan, M.P. (1984a). Monitoring text comprehension: Individual differences in epistemological standards. *Journal of Educational Psychology, 76*, 248-258.
Ryan, M.P. (1984b). Conceptions of prose coherence: Individual differences in epistemelogical standards. *Journal of Educational Psychology, 76*, 1226-1238.
Scarr, S., & Carter-Saltman, L. (1982). Genetics and intelligence. In R.J. Sternberg (Ed.), *Handbook of human intelligence* (pp. 792-896). New York: Cambridge University Press.
Smith, J., & Baltes, P.B. (1990). Wisdom-related knowledge: Age/cohort differences in response to life-planning problems. *Developmental Psychology, 26*, 494-505.
Smith, J., Dixon, R.A., & Baltes, P.B. (1989). Expertise in life planning: A new research approach to investigating aspects of wisdom. In M.L. Commons, J.D. Sinnot, F.A. Richards and C. Armon (Eds.), *Adult development: Comparisons and applications of developmental models*, Vol. 1. New York: Praeger.
Snow, R.E. (1981). Toward a theory of aptitude for learning: Fluid and crystallized abilities and their correlates. In M.P. Friedman, J.P. Das and N. O'Connor (Eds.), *Intelligence and learning* (pp. 345-362). New York: Plenum Press.

Snow, R.E., & Yalow, E. (1982). Education and intelligence. In R.J. Sternberg (Ed.), *Handbook of human intelligence* (pp. 493-585). New York: Cambridge University Press.

Stern, W. (1914). *The psychological method of testing intelligence* (G.M. Whipple, Trans.). Baltimore: Warwick and York.

Sternberg, R.J. (1982). Reasoning, problem-solving and intelligence. In R.J. Sternberg (Ed.), *Handbook of human intelligence* (pp. 225-307). New York: Cambridge University Press.

Sternberg, R.J. (1985). *Beyond IQ: A triarchic theory of human intelligence.* Cambridge, Massachusetts: Cambridge University Press.

Thorndike, E.L. (1920). Intelligence and its uses. *Harper's Magazine, 140,* 227-235.

Thorndike, R.L., Hagen, E.P., & Sattler, J.M. (1986). *The Stanford-Binet intelligence scale: Fourth edition technical manual.* Chicago: The Riverside Publishing Company.

Thorndike, R.M., & Lohman, D.F. (1989). *A century of ability testing.* Chicago: The Riverside Publishing Company.

Wagner, R.K., & Sternberg, R.J. (1986). Tacit knowledge and intelligence in the everyday world. In R.J. Sternberg and R.K. Wagner (Eds.), *Practical intelligence: Nature and origins of competence in the everyday world* (pp. 51-83). Cambridge, Massachusetts: Cambridge University Press.

Wood, P.K. (1983). Inquiring systems and problem structure: Implications for cognitive development. *Human Development, 26,* 249-265.

Woodcock, R.W., & Johnson, M.B. (1989). *The Woodcock-Johnson tests of cognitive ability: Standard and supplemental batteries.* Allen, Texas: DLM/Teaching Resources.

Chapter 6

FOSTERING THE ACQUISITION AND TRANSFER OF INTELLECTUAL SKILLS

ERIK DE CORTE,
University of Leuven, Belgium

Thinking and problem solving are nowadays generally considered as a major component of intelligence. For example, Sternberg (1981) has defined intelligence as: "a set of developed thinking and learning skills used in academic and everyday problem solving" (p. 18).

Therefore, the acquisition and varied application of those skills constitutes a major objective of instruction in schools as well as in post-school educational settings such as industrial training and permanent education. In Resnick's (1987a) terms one could say that while in a preceding era mass education focussed on "low literacy", that is, the acquisition of the basic skills of reading, computation, health, and citizenship training, it has now become an educational challenge to aim at "high literacy" for all.

Responding appropriately to this challenge requires an answer to the following three questions:

1. What, precisely, does skilled thinking, learning, and problem solving, involve?
2. How can the acquisition of those skills be fostered through systematic instruction?
3. What are the conditions for obtaining transfer of cognitive skills to problem and learning situations that differ from the original learning context?

Skills Involved in Competent Learning and Problem Solving

Over the past 20 years a substantial amount of research has been carried out aiming at the identification of knowledge and skills involved in competent learning and problem solving. In the early days of the cognitive psychological approach, the skill in approaching and solving new cognitive tasks was studied in laboratory settings using mainly "knowledge-lean" tasks. This research has convincingly shown the heuristic nature of human problem solving (Newell and Simon, 1972). But in the mid-1970s the question has been raised whether the principles underlying the solution of this kind of tasks can be generalized to more complex and less well-defined problems in semantically rich domains. Consequently, a large number of investigations were carried out in a variety of fields such as physics, mathematics, computer programming, medical diagnosis, economics, and ecology. This research has led to the identification of the following four categories of skills that a problem solver or learner should master with a view to approaching a problem or learning task with a good chance of being successful (De Corte, 1990b):

1. Flexible application of a well-organized domain-specific knowledge base, involving concepts, rules, principles, formulas, and algorithms.
2. Heuristic methods, that is, systematic search strategies for problem analysis and transformation, such as carefully analyzing a problem specifying the knowns and the unknowns; decomposing the problem into subgoals; visualizing the problem using a diagram or drawing.
3. Metacognitive skills, involving knowledge concerning one's own cognitive functioning, and activities that relate to the self-monitoring and regulation of one's cognitive processes, such as planning a solution process, and reflecting on one's learning and thinking activities.
4. Learning strategies, that is, activities that learners engage in during learning in order to acquire any of the three preceding types of skills (see e.g., Levin and Pressley, 1986 for this category).

There is substantial evidence that many students in the formal school system do not sufficiently master those categories of knowledge and skills that are required to approach new tasks and problems in an efficient and successful way. The following examples can illustrate this statement.

Instead of the classic parallelogram example from Wertheimer's (1959) work is used as a first illustration. The example is about solving numerical problems such as:

$$\frac{274 + 274 + 274}{3} \qquad \text{or} \qquad \frac{812 + 812 + 812 + 812 + 812}{5}$$

Wertheimer found that many learners proceeded as follows: they added the terms in the numerator, and then divided the sum by the denominator. Their correct response shows that they master the arithmetic procedures, but at the same time that they lack understanding of the relationships between the different elementary operations.

In one of our own studies (De Corte et al., 1988) 116 sixth graders (12-year olds) were administered a series of multiplication word problems in which we varied in a systematic way the nature of the multiplicand and the multiplier: integer, decimal larger than 1, or decimal smaller than 1. The task consisted of choosing the correct operation between the following alternatives: a + b; a - b; b - a; a x b; a : b; b : a. Table 6.1 shows the percentage of correct answers for the three problems.

Table 6.1. Percentage of correct answers on three different multiplication word problems in a group of 116 sixth graders

Multiplicand	Multiplier	Problem	% correct
Integer	Integer	Spinach is priced at 65 Bfr a kilogram Ann buys 3 kilogram How much does she have to pay?	98
Decimal < 1	Integer	One piece of sugar costs 0.4 Bfr. How much would it cost for 60 pieces?	99
Integer	Decimal < 1	Milk is priced at 20 Bfr a litre. Ann buys 0.8 litre. How much does she have to pay?	32

Source: De Corte, Verschaffel and Van Coillie (1988)

The major finding from this study, and one that was replicated in other studies, is the negative effect on the proportion of correct responses of a decimal multiplier smaller than 1. Almost all errors consisted of choosing division instead of multiplication. This error can be explained in terms of a frequently occurring misconception, namely that the result of a multiplication is always bigger than the multiplicand ("multiplication makes bigger").

In a study with 11-year-old children in Canada and Poland, Rabijewska and Szetela (1988) administered the following problem:

A school received 18 cartons of mathematics books with 21 mathematics book each. Later 16 cartons with 32 books each were received. How many mathematics books were received?

Only one third of the Canadian pupils and less than a half of the Polish children gave the correct solution. Two fifths of the Canadian learners simply added the four given numbers, a clear proof of their orientation toward blind ciphering without any trace of heuristic or metacognitive activity with a view to constructing an appropriate representation of the problem.

A last example derives from the results of the Third National Assessment of Educational Progress (Carpenter et al., 1983) in the United States, involving a national sample of 45,000 pupils. The 13-year-olds were given the following problem:

An army bus holds 36 soldiers. If 1,128 soldiers are being bused to their training site, how many buses are needed?

Seventy per cent of the pupils performed the division algorithm correctly, but only 23 per cent gave the exact answer. Twenty nine per cent of the other children wrote that the number of buses needed is "31 remainder 12", while 18 per cent answered "31". In other words, less than one third of the children who performed the calculation correctly, gave the right answer; the others neglected to make an otherwise simple analysis of the meaning of the problem situation.

Those examples, that are fairly representative in research in the domain of mathematics, point to a number of important shortcomings and deficiencies in many learners, that can to an extent be attributed to current teaching practices. Pupils often acquire only deficient, superficial, and rote knowledge of basic concepts; in many domains they are even afflicted with misconception (e.g., "multiplication makes bigger") and defective skills (e.g., buggy algorithms); they do not master a variety of usable heuristic and metacognitive strategies; finally, they often develop incorrect beliefs about cognitive activities (e.g., being able to solve a problem is a mere question of luck) and about subject-matter fields (e.g., the view that mathematics consists of a set of rules and procedures that one has to use in a mechanical way, and among which they do not see any connections nor relations with reality).

The illustrations discussed are all taken from the domain of mathematics. But there is no doubt that the series could easily be expanded with instances from other fields that are symptomatic for similar shortcomings in pupils. For example, one often has the impression that language teaching, no less than mathematics instruction, focuses on imparting a set of rules from spelling and grammar, and that the essential aspects of reading and writing, namely comprehension and communication fall into the background.

A plausible explanation for this lack of mastery of basic knowledge and cognitive skills is that current teaching-learning situations are not designed in accordance with a number of crucial features of appropriate and effective processes of knowledge and skill acquisition. A few of these basic features will be reviewed in the next section.

Basic Characteristics of Effective Acquisition Processes

Research on learning and instruction has led to the identification of a number of characteristics of acquisition processes that provide a sound basis for instructional design. Without attempting to be exhaustive the following series represents some of the major aspects: the constructive nature of learning; the importance of the integrated acquisition of domain-specific knowledge and more general cognitive skills; the necessity to take into account individual differences in prior knowledge, abilities, approaches to learning, needs, and motivation between learners; the necessity to embed learning activities in realistic contexts involving social interaction. Each of these aspects can only briefly be discussed here (see De Corte, 1990a for a more detailed review).

Although one should not judge the entire school system in one sweeping statement, it is nevertheless the case that nowadays the prevailing view of learning in educational practice is still the information-transmission model. Yet this view, which usually results in the design of weak learning environments, is strongly contradicted by the conception supported by a substantial body of recent research, namely that learning is an active and constructive process. Learners are not passive recipients of information, but they actively construct their knowledge and skills on the basis of their prior — informal as well as formal — knowledge, and through interaction with their environments.

In the preceding section it has been argued that there is now robust evidence showing the crucial and complementary role in skilled learning and problem solving of domain-specific knowledge on the one hand, and heuristic and metacognitive activities on the other. Therefore, it is important to teach more general cognitive skills embedded in the different semantically rich domains.

The important role of prior knowledge in learning is implied in the constructivist view of learning processes: it is indeed on the basis of what they already know and can do that learners actively process the information they encounter and, thus, construct new knowledge and skills. One aspect of prior knowledge that has been well-documented in recent research in a diversity of content domains is learners' informal knowledge and problem-solving strategies, including their misconceptions and deficient procedures.

Another area of individual differences in which the constructive nature of acquisition processes becomes obvious, relates to distinct qualitative approaches to learning as identified by Marton and Säljö (1984), namely a "deep" versus a "surface" approach. Students adopting a deep approach try to understand the intention and meaning of a given material, and search for relations within it; in contrast surface learners focus on memorizing the information.

While in current education knowledge is often acquired independently of the social and physical context from which it derives its meaning and usefulness, recent research points to the need to anchor learning in more realistic and authentic situations. Typical examples are the investigations comparing so-called "street arithmetics" with formal word problem solving in the classroom (Carraher et al., 1985), and anthropological studies of learning and cognitive activities in informal, real-life situations. This work has led to the identification of a number of interesting and relevant differences between learning in formal and informal settings, summarized as follows by Resnick (1987b):

1. The dominant form of learning and performance in formal education is individual, whereas outside school far more activities are undertaken in a group.
2. In formal education "pure thought" activities without the use of tools prevail. In contrast, the use of aids and tools such as books and calculators is common in real-life cognitive activities.
3. Formal education stresses symbol-based learning and thinking independent of concrete objects and events, while outside school activities are intimately related with objects and events.
4. Schooling focusses on the teaching of general, widely applicable knowledge and skills. In real life, however, situation-specific skills are emphasized.

Summarizing one can say that typical learning in school settings is often decontextualized, whereas real cognitive activities and learning occur in context. The recently introduced situated cognition paradigm stresses precisely the importance of contextualized learning, and puts forward the "cognitive apprenticeship" view of learning and instruction as an approach embracing the basic characteristics of situated acquisition of knowledge and skills. Brown et al. (1989) define this approach as follows: Cognitive apprenticeship methods try to enculturate students into authentic practices through activity and social interaction in a way similar to that evident — and evidently successful — in craft apprenticeship (p. 37). In other words, constructive learning processes should be embedded in contexts that are rich in resources and learning materials, that offer opportunities for social interaction, and that are representative of the kinds of tasks and problems to which the learners will have to apply their knowledge and skill in future.

A Framework for Designing Powerful Learning Environments

Cognitive learning across the lifespan should focus on the progressive mastery and further improvement of the four categories of skill described above, namely a well-organized and flexibly accessible domain-specific knowledge base, heuristic methods, metacognitive skills, and efficient learning strategies. Pursuing those skills in children, students, and adult learners requires the design and implementation of powerful teaching-learning environments, that is, situations that elicit in learners the appropriate learning activities for achieving the intended outcomes.

This instructional design activity should be guided as much as possible by the basic characteristics of effective learning processes described in the previous section. This implies especially that learning environments should stimulate and support the constructive acquisition processes in learners and, moreover, must try to develop and enhance more active and deep learning strategies in passive and surface learners. However, it is important to stress that conceiving learning as an active process does not exclude that the construction of knowledge and skills can be mediated through appropriate interventions and guidance of teachers, peers, and educational media. In other words, a powerful learning environment is characterized by a good balance between discovery learning and personal exploration on the one hand, and systematic instruction and guidance on the other, taking into account the individual differences in prior knowledge, abilities, approaches to learning, learner needs, and motivational orientations.

Recently at least two models for the design of learning environments have been proposed that are largely in line with the preceding ideas, namely the cognitive apprenticeship model of Collins et al. (1989), and Van Parreren's (1988) developmental instruction model. These frameworks derive from different, but nevertheless related, theoretical perspectives, namely the situated cognition and learning paradigm, and the activity theory approach. However, they both aim at eliciting goal-oriented learning activity in appropriate social contexts. Consequently, they share a number of basic ideas relating to learning and instruction, such as a moderate constructivist conception of learning; the importance of dialogue and social interaction for learning; the effectiveness of teaching methods such as coaching, scaffolding, and reflection, the need for a well-organized sequence of learning tasks; and the importance of motivation. I will restrict myself here to a brief outline of the model by Collins et al. (1989).

Collins and his colleagues have thoroughly analyzed three successful American teaching experiments involving major characteristics of cognitive apprenticeship, namely Palincsar and Brown's (1984) reciprocal teaching of reading comprehension, Scardamalia and Bereiter's (1985) procedural facilitation of writing, and Schoenfeld's (1985) heuristic teaching of mathematics. Their analysis resulted in a general framework for designing ideal learning environments involving four dimensions: content, teaching method, sequence of learning tasks, and social context for learning.

Content

With respect to content an ideal learning environment should focus on the acquisition of all categories of knowledge that experts master and apply. More specifically the four categories mentioned in the first section of this chapter should be taught, namely domain-specific knowledge, heuristic methods, metacognitive strategies and learning strategies.

Teaching Methods

With a view to helping students to acquire and integrate those different categories of knowledge and skills the teacher can apply six different methods falling roughly into three categories.
1.   Three techniques constituting the heart of cognitive apprenticeship, are based on observation, guided and supported practice and feedback; they aim at the acquisition of an integrated set of cognitive and metacognitive skills.
(a) *Modelling* involves the observation by the student of an expert who is performing a certain task; this allows the student to construct an appropriate mental model of the activities that are required for skilled performance.
(b) *Coaching* refers to the observation of the student by the teacher during task execution as a basis for giving hints and feedback with a view to improving performance.
(c) *Scaffolding* encompasses the provision of direct support to the student while they are carrying out the task; this method derives from the Vygotskyan concept of proximal development (Vygotsky, 1978).
2.   Two other methods aim at making students explicitly aware of their own cognitive and metacognitive activities.
(a) *Articulation* refers to any technique that helps students to spell out and make explicit their knowledge and problem-solving procedures.

(b) *Reflection* leads students to compare their own cognitive strategies and solution processes with those of experts, of other learners and ultimately with a mental model of expert performance.
3. *Exploration*, finally, intends to increase the learner's autonomy in skilled problem solving as well as in discovering, identifying and defining new problems.

Sequence of Learning Tasks

Collins et al. (1989) present two principles relating to the sequence of learning tasks.
1. Progressive complexity and diversity, such that competent performance requires more and more of the domain-specific knowledge as well as a larger variety of cognitive and metacognitive skills.
2. Global before local skills, meaning that the orientation towards the complex task as a whole should precede the practising of partial, lower-level skills.

Social Context for Learning

Finally, Collins et al. (1989) describe a series of guidelines that are important with a view to realizing a favourable social context for learning.
1. Situated learning involving students being given tasks and problems representing the diversity of situations to which they will have to apply their knowledge and skills afterwards.
2. Organizing opportunities for contact with and observation of experts.
3. Enhancing intrinsic motivation for learning.
4. Fostering cooperative learning through small-group problemsolving.
5. Organizing classroom dialogues aiming at the identification, analysis, and discussion of students' problem-solving strategies and processes.

The situated learning and cognition paradigm and the cognitive apprenticeship model for knowledge and skill acquisition imply that learning and instruction take place in authentic, real-life contexts that have personal meaning and value for the learner. There is no doubt that this is a worthwhile idea that should be taken into account in instructional design. In fact, there are a number of examples of instructional programmes or approaches that are very much in line with major aspects of cognitive apprenticeship, even without being directly derived from it.

One example is the so-called realistic approach to elementary mathematics teaching developed in the Wiskobas-project at the University of

Utrecht, The Netherlands (Treffers, 1987). Two major principles underlying this project represent basic features of effective acquisition
processes discussed before, namely taking children's informal prior
knowledge and strategies as the starting point for engaging them in
mathematical activity, and embedding mathematics learning in real situations and contexts.

A second example is the approach to foreign language acquisition and
communication training with individual adult learners developed by
Leuven Language Learning, a section of the Institute for Language
Teaching at the University of Leuven, Belgium. The following two principles underly the approach to language and communication training.
1. The learner should become more and more aware of, and should
   acquire cognitive and metacognitive strategies; as a consequence, he
   or she should progressively become a more skilled and autonomous
   learner.
2. Language is considered not as a goal in itself, but as a tool to communicate or convey a message in realistic and authentic situations.
   This implies that communicative efficiency is more important than
   linguistic accuracy.

This raises the question whether the cognitive apprenticeship model is
as generally applicable as its advocates assume. In this respect, some
doubts have been put forward especially concerning the feasibility of
transforming school instruction into apprenticeship (Palincsar, 1989;
Wineburg, 1989). Some interesting developmental work aiming at this
transformation is currently being undertaken, for example at the Vanderbilt Learning Technology Centre where the notion of anchored
instruction is elaborated using the situated cognition perspective as a
framework for deriving instructional principles (Cognition and
Technology Group at Vanderbilt, 1990). In this technology-oriented
instructional design project instruction is anchored in videodisc-based
complex problem spaces, called macrocontexts because they enable
learners to explore a problem space for extended periods of time from a
diversity of perspectives. But still some questions remain.

First, there are important differences between formal educational
settings and apprenticeship. Schools for general education especially
have been deliberately created as self-contained and — by their nature —
somewhat artificial settings which are not directly product-oriented nor
serve immediate utilitarian purposes.

Second, schools as well as other formal training settings aim at the
teaching and learning of knowledge and skills that are often not easily
encountered in everyday life. This holds, for example, for domains like
history, geography and chemistry. In a domain like physics everyday
experience and intuition even leads to deep-rooted and resistent miscon-

ceptions. In other words, certain subject-matter domains may not lend themselves easily to the apprenticeship approach (Palincsar, 1989).

Third, research shows that substantial learning and even transfer effects can be obtained in contexts in which learning and instruction is not at all situated or bound to real-life experience (Wineburg, 1989).

In other words, although educational settings can benefit from the basic ideas and the specific methods of apprenticeship, it is doubtful whether this model represents the only approach to learning and teaching that embodies appropriately the basic features of effective acquisition processes described above. In fact, certain activities that seem to be highly motivating children and youngsters are not at all apprenticeship-like, such as programming in Logo (De Corte et al., 1990).

Transfer: Highly Desired, But Difficult to Achieve

The importance of being able to transfer acquired knowledge and cognitive skills to new learning tasks and problem situations is recognized with respect to schooling, but also in nonschool educational and instructional settings. This issue is obviously not only of theoretical significance, but is also of utmost practical importance, as has been clearly voiced by McKeachie:

> Nonetheless, many researchers and educators, as well as hordes of businessmen, government officials, and others, hope to find ways of teaching and learning general problem solving skills. If we grant that prior knowledge is necessary for effective problem solving in most areas, the question becomes one of *whether or not problem-solving skills developed in one field can be taught in ways that enable the skills to be transferred to other fields in which the individual has some prior knowledge* (McKeachie, 1987, p. 445).

Taking this into account it is not surprising that considerable attention has been paid to the topic in the recent literature (see e.g., Clark, in press; Cormier and Hagman, 1987; De Corte, 1987; Mayer, 1988; Prawat, 1989; Salomon and Perkins, 1989; Singley and Anderson, 1989).

However, the available research shows that transfer is a very complex phenomenon, that transfer effects do not occur spontaneously, and are even difficult to obtain deliberately (see e.g., Butterfield and Nelson, 1989; Clark, in press; Perkins and Salomon, 1989). The latter findings have been accounted for in the recent literature by a robust result of the analysis of expertise in a variety of domains, namely that competence in a certain field depends to a large extent on the availability of a well-organized domain-specific knowledge base (see e.g., Glaser, 1987). However, another explanation does not deny the importance of domain-specific knowledge for skilled performance, but stresses that the lack of positive transfer is mainly due to the absence of appropriate conditions needed for transfer (De Corte and Verschaffel, 1986; Perkins and Salomon, 1989). Those conditions relate to characteristics of the learners (subject variables), to features of the tasks (task variables), and to the nature of the instruction (instructional variables).

Concerning the subject variables the extensive research programme of Brown, Campione, and their colleagues (see e.g., Brown, 1989; Campione and Brown, 1990) has shown that skilled learners and transferrers distinguish themselves from their less skilled fellows with respect to one of the four categories of skills involved in competent learning and problem solving mentioned before, namely metacognitive skills. Recently Campione and Brown have summarized their findings as follows:

> More efficient learners and more flexible transferrers spend more time planning, and analyzing and classifying the problems before they attempt to offer an answer. They are more likely to take advantage of opportunities to check their reasoning during the course of working on a problem. They are better able to engage in a number of efficient fix-up strategies when they seem to be getting off track. Poorer performers, in contrast, begin generating solutions much more quickly. They try out alternative rules in a fairly random order, trying to see if it works, and when informed that they are wrong, moving on to another one, etc. When beginning to work on a new problem, they are less likely to refer back to prior problems. Overall, the global learning and transfer indices do appear to reflect the operation of an array of monitoring and self-regulatory skills, or weak but general methods. (Campione and brown, 1990, p. 168)

In terms of Kuhl's (1985) theory of self-regulation one could say that skilled learners and transferrers are characterized by a high level of action control, that is, a systematic and persistent orientation toward a preconceived objective. This implies that such learners are constantly monitoring their activity, and, whenever necessary, make the required corrections. These findings are the more interesting because they question the currently prevailing standpoint that individual differences in competency as well as differences between developmental levels are mainly determined by domain-specific knowledge.

As far as the task variables are concerned it is quite generally accepted that far transfer is more difficult to obtain than near transfer. This notion of transfer distance relates to the degree to which the transfer task is remote or novel in comparison with the original learning task.

However, recent work suggests that reality is more complex. Indeed, Bassok and Holyoak (1989) have reported asymmetric results: while they found substantial transfer effects from algebra to physics, the opposite outcomes hardly occurred. These findings were interpreted in terms of the degree of content-specific embedding of the original learning outcomes, in the sense that physics is a semantically more rich domain than algebra. But a more recent study by Bassok (1990) showed that this does not provide a sufficient explanation for the lack of transfer from physics to algebra; indeed, she observed transfer from economics — which is also a content-rich domain — to algebra. All these results lead to the conclusion that as far as the task aspects are concerned, the probability of transfer cannot be reduced to the distance variable, but that more qualitative task features and their mutual relations influence the occurrence of transfer.

A major aspect that has to be taken into account when explaining the disappointing findings in many transfer studies, is their lack of an intentional and systematic orientation toward instruction for transfer. In these investigations, it was often more or less implicitly assumed that learning would produce transfer in a direct and automatic way. However, on the basis of the acquired research experience on the one hand, and the transfer literature in general on the other, this assumption is now disposed as "wishful thinking". Indeed, it has been shown over and over that concepts and skills learned in one domain are not spontaneously generalized to other content domains (Gick and Holyoak, 1983; Pressley et al., 1987).

Most investigators nowadays share the standpoint that in order to achieve cognitive transfer in learners, it is necessary to teach explicitly and intentionally for transfer. This implies that the teacher has to show children how the skills learned in one context can be usefully applied in other problem situations, to teach them how to do so, and to give them experiences in applying their skills in different contexts. Recent research, especially a series of studies relating to transfer from learning to programme (De Corte et al., 1990; Mayer, 1988), in which more attention has been paid to the design of transfer-oriented learning environments, have indeed shown transfer effects, albeit that in most cases only near transfer has been achieved, that is, transfer to tasks that are closely related to the original learning task.

This raises the question as to which are the instructional variables that have facilitated the occurrence of transfer in successful studies? Taking into account the preceding results on the subject variables, transfer-oriented instruction should aim at fostering the metacognitive skills and the action control of the learners. Simultaneously the initial learning of the knowledge and skills the transfer of which is aimed at, has to result in thorough mastery (Gick and Holyoak, 1987; Salomon and Perkins, 1989; Simons, 1990).

To pursue more directly and intentionally the transfer of certain knowledge and skills, the "high road to transfer" as described by Salomon and Perkins (1989) has to some degree been adopted in the successful studies referred to above. This involves mainly the following two aspects: *Mindful abstraction* of the skills one wants to transfer, and *decontextualization* of these skills by demonstrating their usefulness in other situations (Salomon and Perkins, 1987). This distinction is echoed in the discrimination of two instruction components proposed by Littlefield et al. (1988), namely: *Framing*, involving "the act of relating a specific set of behaviours to a broader framework of problem solving"; and *bridging*, involving "the act of relating processes that occur within one context to similar processes occurring elsewhere" (p. 356).

Conclusions

Although continued research is certainly necessary, hopefully the preceding sections have shown that research on learning and instruction over the past 10 to 15 years has produced a substantial and empirically underpinned knowledge base that can guide and orient the design of powerful learning environments in initial as well as adult education.

First of all, the acquisition of the four basic categories of aptitudes, namely domain-specific knowledge, heuristic methods, metacognitive skills, and efficient learning strategies, has to be pursued throughout the lifespan. Taking into account the available evidence that competent learning, thinking, and problem solving requires the integrated acquisition and application of domain-specific knowledge on the one hand, and (meta-)cognitive skills on the other, learning and teaching of the latter general skills and strategies should be embedded in multiple and many-sided contexts. As argued by Perkins and Salomon (1989) such an approach will induce and elicit domain-specific adjustments of the general skills, while at the same time showing their general power and applicability.

The preceding conclusion involves a plea for a better continuity between initial schooling on the one hand, and continuing education and industrial training on the other, but it does not exclude a differential accentuation of the distinct categories of knowledge and skills depending on the level of expertise that the learners have already acquired. In this respect the distinction made by Spiro et al. (1988) between introductory learning, advanced knowledge acquisition, and the achievement of practised expertise is relevant. For example, they have found that medical students easily develop biomedical misconceptions due to oversimplification of the subject-matter content during introductory learning. Therefore, the stage of advanced knowledge acquisition should focus on the mastery of conceptual complexity, the multiple interconnectedness of concepts, and the selective and appropriate application of domain-specific knowledge.

The ultimate goal of all pedagogic endeavours in initial as well as in adult education, should be that the learners become progressively more autonomous and take responsibility for their own learning. In designing powerful learning environments for achieving this goal the following basic principles can be used as guidelines: (a) those environments should elicit and support active and constructive acquisition processes in the learners; (b) these processes can be mediated through appropriate guidance and interventions of teachers, peers, and educational media; (c) learning should as much as possible be situated, that is, contextually and socially embedded in situations and tasks that are representative for those in which they will have to use their knowledge and skills afterwards. In this respect, the apprenticeship model of learning and instruction which is in line with those principles, can certainly be used as an orienting framework. However, taking into account its limitations, this model will have to be complemented with other approaches. One alternative that deserves further exploration in this regard is the hobbyist model.

Becoming an autonomous learner involves the ability to transfer one's knowledge and skills to new learning tasks and problem situations. This requires that powerful learning environments include a systematic and intentional orientation toward transfer. In other words, transfer has to be taught explicitly. A promising approach in this respect seems to be Salomon and Perkins' (1989) high road to transfer involving mindful abstraction and decontextualization of the knowledge and skills to be transferred. Recent research suggests that the development of the learners' metacognitive skills and increasing their level of action control can have a beneficial influence on their transfer ability.

References

Bassok, M. (1990). Transfer of domain-specific problem-solving procedures. *Journal of Experimental Psychology: Learning, Memory and Cognition, 16*, 522-533.

Bassok, M., & Holyoak, K.J. (1989) Interdomain transfer between isomorphic topics in algebra and physics. *Journal of Experimental Psychology: Learning, Memory and Cognition, 15*, 153-166.

Brown, A.L. (1989). Analogical learning and transfer: What develops? In S. Vosniadou & A. Orotny (Eds.), *Similarity and analogical reasoning* (pp. 369-412). Cambridge: Cambridge University Press.

Brown, J.S., Collins, A., & Duguid, P. (1989). Situated cognition and the culture of learning. *Educational Researcher. 18* (1), 32-42.

Butterfield, E.C., & Nelson, G.D. (1989). Theory and practice of teaching for transfer (ERIC Annual Review Paper). *Educational Technology Research and Development, 37* (3), 5-38.

Campione, J.C., & Brown, A.L. (1990). Guided learning and transfer: Implications for approaches to assessment. In N. Frederiksen, R. Glaser, A. Lesgold, & M.G. Shafto (Eds.), *Diagnostic monitoring of skill and knowledge acquisition* (pp. 141-172). Hillsdale, New Jersey: Lawrence Erlbaum.

Carpenter, T.P., Lindquist, M.M., Mathews, W., & Silver, E.A. (1983). Results of the third NAEP mathematics assessment: Secondary school. *Mathematics Teacher, 76* (9), 652-659.

Carraher, T.N., Carraher, D.W., & Schliemann, A.D. (1985). Jathematics in the streets and in schools. *British Journal of Developmental Psychology, 3,* 21-29.

Clark, R.E. (in press). Facilitating domain-general problem-solving: Computers, cognitive processes and instruction. In E. De Corte, M. Linn, H. Mandl, & L. Verschaffel (Eds.), *Computer-based learning environments and problem solving.* Berlin: Springer-Verlag.

Cognition and Technology Group at Vanderbilt (1990). Anchored instruction and its relationship to situated cognition. *Educational Researcher, 19* (6), 2-10.

Collins, A., Brown, J.S., & Newman, S.E. (1989). Cognitive apprenticeship: Teaching the craft of reading, writing and mathematics. In L.B. Resnick (Ed.), *Knowing, learning, and instruction. Essays in honor of Robert Glaser* (pp. 453-494). Hillsdale, New Jersey: Lawrence Erlbaum.

Cormier, S.M., & Hagman, J.D. (Eds.) (1987). *Transfer of learning. Contemporary research and applications.* San Diego, California: Academic Press.

De Corte, E. (Ed.) (1987). Acquisition and transfer of knowledge and cognitive skills. *International Journal of Educational Research, 11,* 601-712.

De Corte, E. (1990a). Acquiring and teaching cognitive skills: A state-of-the-art of theory and research. In P.J.D. Drenth, J.A. Sergeant, & R.J. Takens (Eds.), *European perspectives in psychology. Volume 1* (pp. 237-263). London: Wiley.

De Corte, E. (1990b). Towards powerful learning environments for the acquisition of problem-solving skills. *European Journal of Psychology of Education, 5,* 5-19.

De Corte, E., Verschaffel, L. (1986). Effects of computer experience on children's thinking skills. *Journal of Structural Learning, 9,* 161-174.

De Corte, E., Verschaffel, L. & Schrooten, H. (1990, March). Cognitive effects of computer-oriented learning. Paper presented at the Seventh International Conference on Technology and Education, Brussels, Belgium.

De Corte, E., Verschaffel, L., & Van Coillie, V. (1988). Influence of number size, problem structure, and response mode on children's solutions of multiplication problems. *Journal of Mathematical Behavior, 7,* 197-216.

Gick, M.L., & Holyoak, K.J. (1983). Schema induction and analogical transfer. *Cognitive Psychology, 15,* 1-38.

Gick, M.L., & Holyoak, K.J. (1987). The cognitive basis of transfer. In S.M. Cormier & J.D. Hagman (Eds.), *Transfer of learning. Contemporary research and applications* (pp. 9-46). San Diego, California: Academic Press.

Glaser, R. (1987). Learning theory and theories of knowledge. In E. De Corte, H. Lodewijks, R. Parmentier, & P. Span (Eds.), *Learning and instruction. European research in an international context. Volume 1* (pp. 397-414). Oxford/Leuven: Pergamon Press/Leuven University Press.

Kuhl, L. (1985). Volitional mediators of cognition-behavior consistency: Self-regulatory processes and action versus state orientation. In J. Kuhl & J. Beckman (Eds.), *Action-control: From cognition to behavior* (pp. 101-128). Berlin: Springer-Verlag.

Levin, J.R., & Pressley, M. (Eds.) (1986). Special issue: Learning strategies. *Educational Psychologist, 21,* 1-161.

Littlefield, J., Delclos, V.R., Lever, S., Clayton, K.N., Bransford, J.D., & Franks, J.J. (1988). Learning LOGO: Method of teaching, transfer of general skills, and attitudes toward school and computers. In R.E. Mayer (Ed.), *Teaching and learning computer programming. Multiple research perspectives* (pp. 111-135). Hillsdale, New Jersey: Lawrence Erlbaum.

Marton, F., & Säljö, R. (1984). Approaches to learning. In F. Marton, D.J. Hounsell, & N.J. Entwistle (Eds.), *The experience of learning* (pp. 36-55). Edinburgh: Scottish Academic Press.

Mayer, R.E. (Ed.) (1988). *Teaching and learning computer programming. Multiple research perspectives.* Hillsdale, New Jersey: Lawrence Erlbaum.

McKeachie, W.J. (1987). The new look in instructional psychology: Teaching strategies for learning and thinking. In E. De Corte, H. Lodewijks, R. Parmentier & P. Span

(Eds.), *Learning and instruction. European research in an international context. Volume 1* (pp. 443-456). Oxford/Leuven: Pergamon Press/Leuven University Press.

Newell, A., & Simon, H.A. (1972). *Human problem solving.* Englewood Cliffs, New Jersey: Prentice Hall.

Palincsar, A.S. (1989). Less charted waters. *Educational Researcher, 18* (4), 5-7.

Palincsar, A.S. & Brown, A.L. (1984). Reciprocal teaching of comprehension-fostering and comprehension-monitoring activities. *Cognition and Instruction, 1,* 117-175.

Perkins, D.N., & Salomon, G. (1989). Are cognitive skills context-bound? *Educational Researcher, 18* (1), 16-25.

Prawat, R.S. (1989). Promoting access to knowledge, strategy, and disposition in students: A research synthesis. *Review of Educational Research, 59,* 1-41.

Pressley, M., Snyder, B.L., & Cariglia-Bull, T. (1987). How can good strategy use be taught to children? Evaluation of six alternative approaches. In Cormier, S.M. & Hagman, J.D. (Eds.), *Transfer of learning. Contemporary research and applications* (pp. 81-120). (Educational Technology Series). San Diego: Academis Press.

Rabijewska, B., & Szetela, W. (1988). A study of problem solving in Poland and Canada. In *Proceedings of 1987 Meeting of the International Commission for Study and Improvement of Mathematics Teaching (CIEAEM): The role errors play in the learning and teaching of mathematics.* Sherbrooke, Quebec, Canada: University of Sherbrooke.

Resnick, L.B. (1987a). Instruction and the cultivation of thinking. In E. De Corte, H. Lodewijks, R. Parmentier, & P. Span (Eds.), *Learning and instruction. European research in an international context. Volume 1* (pp. 415-442). Oxford/Leuven: Pergamon Press/Leuven University Press.

Resnick, L.B. (1987b). Learning in school and out. *Educational Researcher, 16* (9), 13-20.

Salomon, G., & Perkins, D.N. (1987). Transfer of cognitive skills from programming: When and how? *Journal of Educational Computing Research, 3,* 149-169.

Salomon. G., & Perkins, D.N. (1989). Rocky roads to transfer: Rethinking mechanisms of a neglected phenomenon. *Educational Psychologist, 24,* 113-142.

Scardamalia, M., & Bereiter, C. (1985). Fostering the development of self-regulation in children's knowledge processing. In S.F. Chipman, J.W. Segal, & R. Glaser (Eds.), *Thinking and learning skills. Volume 2. Research and open questions* (pp. 563-577). Hillsdale, New Jersey: Lawrence Erlbaum.

Schoenfeld, A.H. (1985). *Mathematical problem solving.* New York: Academic Press.

Simons, P.R.J. (1990). Transfervermogen. (Transfer ability). Nijmegen, the Netherlands: K.U. Nijmegen.

Singley, M.K., & Anderson, J.R. (1989). *The transfer of cognitive skill.* Cambridge, Massachusetts: Harvard University Press.

Spiro, R.J., Coulson, R.L., Feltovich, P.J., & Anderson, D.K. (1988). Cognitive flexibility theory: Advanced knowledge acquisition in ill-structured domains. In *Tenth Annual Conference of the Cognitive Science Society* (pp. 375-383). Hillsdale, New Jersey: Lawrence Erlbaum.

Sternberg, R.J. (1981). Intelligence as thinking and learning skills. *Educational Leadership, 39,* 18-21.

Treffers, A. (1987). *Three dimensions. A model of goal and theory description in mathematics instruction. The Wiskobas Project.* Dordrecht: D. Reidel.

Van Parreren, C.F. (1988). *Ontwikkelend onderwijs. (Developmental instruction).* Leuven: Acco.

Vygotsky, L.S. (1978). *Mind in society. The development of higher psychological processes.* Cambridge, Massachusetts: Harvard University Press.

Wertheimer, M. (1959). *Productive thinking.* New York: Harper & Row.

Wineburg, S.S. (1989). Remembrance of theories past. *Educational Researcher, 18* (4), 7-10.

Chapter 7

PRACTICAL INTELLIGENCE

Florida State University, U.S.A.

The present chapter is concerned with the measurement of practical intelligence and tacit knowledge as additional indicators of competence at work. The sections that follow will describe what practical intelligence and tacit knowledge are about, and indicate how changes in managerial training and practice provide a naturally occurring demonstration of the importance of tacit knowledge. A carefully controlled study of managerial problem solving that compares the value of tacit knowledge to other constructs such as IQ and aspects of personality will also be presented. Furthermore, the question of how the acquisition of tacit knowledge might be enhanced through adult education and training will be considered.

Background of the Problem

With surprising frequency, individuals with superior academic records in primary and secondary school have only modest success in their careers thereafter. Conversely, individuals who become superstars in their chosen careers often have unremarkable academic records.

The experience of Florida State University's psychology department is similar. Students who have had the most success in their subsequent careers have not necessarily had either the best academic records upon admission to graduate school nor the best academic records while enrolled in our programme, even though the career pursuit we are preparing the students for — to be psychology professors — is decidedly "academic".

Some years ago the author undertook a study based on interviews with highly successful individuals from several career pursuits. The results show that much was different across the various career pursuits, and even across individuals in the same career pursuit, but one common observation stood out. By and large, these individuals believed that much

109

of the learning that mattered most to their success happened *after* completion of their formal schooling (Wagner, 1987).

Some support for the idea that school learning is a necessary but not sufficient preparation for successful performance in later life comes from the fact that IQ tests and related aptitude and achievement tests are better predictors of performance in the classroom than out of the classroom. The typical correlations between measures of classroom achievement and common IQ, aptitude, and general achievement tests fall in the range of 0.40 to 0.70. However, the typical correlations between these same measures including employment tests and various indices of job performance fall at the 0.2 level (Ghiselli, 1966; Wigdor and Garner, 1982).

Careful research into the nature of school and work environments documents what most of us have learned from our first day at work — there are important differences between the kind of problems besetting everyday life, including the world of work, and the kind of problems found in the school and on traditional tests.

Practical Intelligence and Tacit Knowledge

The kind of problems found in school, which are here referred to as *academic problems*, have a number of familiar characteristics (Neisser, 1976; Wagner and Sternberg, 1985). Some of these characteristics are shown in Table 7.1.

Table 7.1. Characteristics of academic problems

---

1. Well-defined.
2. Formulated by others.
3. Complete information provided.
4. Single correct solution.
5. One or at most several methods for obtaining solution.
6. Disembedded from ordinary experience.

Consider the academic problem: What are the factors of the algebraic equation $a^2 - b^2$? Even if one were not sure how to obtain the answer, there is little question about the definition of the problem. The problem is formulated by someone else, usually the author of a text or teacher. Assuming that one had learned to factorize algebraic equations, all information required to solve the problem is contained in the problem description. There is a single correct solution (a + b, a - b), and only a couple of ways of obtaining the solution. Finally, the problem is not amenable to the application of knowledge acquired through everyday life experience.

The kind of problem found in the everyday world, including work, which are referred to as *practical problems*, have different characteristics. These are presented in Table 7.2.

Table 7.2. Characteristics of practical problems

1. Ill-defined.
2. Unformulated.
3. Incomplete information provided.
4. No one correct solution.
5. Multiple methods for obtaining a solution.
6. Grounded in ordinary experience.

Consider the practical problem of improving the morale of workers in a unit of a given organization. Although this problem appears to be as well-defined as the prior algebraic problem, what really is the problem here? Do the workers have unrealistic expectations of the level of performance? Does the organization expect too much for too little? Is the problem a reaction to poor supervision? The true definition of the problem is unclear, and may in fact never be known. It will be up to the problem solver to provide a satisfactory formulation of the problem. One formulation can render a particular problem insoluble, whereas another may provide a partial solution. Clearly if progress is to be made, additional information must be sought to help in problem formulation, solution search, and solution implementation. Knowing how much information to obtain can be crucial to avoid both a premature ineffective solution and inordinate delay. Rarely is there one perfect solution to this kind of problem. More likely, there will be several solutions, each of which is associated with both liabilities as well as assets. Often there are a number of methods available for coming up with a solution, ranging from getting the workers to provide their own solution to asking a trusted superior to provide one.

Of course nothing is as black and white as the distinction between academic and practical problems made above. Academic problems can be found in the workplace, especially for technical positions (e.g., what is the load capacity of a proposed bridge built to the following specifications?) and practical problems can be found in schools (e.g., what can I do to improve my grade in my French language class?). Many problems are furthermore best described as a mixture of academic and practical characteristics. Nevertheless, the characteristics described so far are useful for distinguishing among problems, and the proportion of academic problems to total problems declines precipitously upon leaving school.

Until the last decade or so, most of what was known about intelligence concerned the intellectual competencies required for success in classroom environments. In keeping with the terminology so far used, this kind of intelligence is referred to as *academic intelligence*. This concept refers to the intellectual competencies that are required for effective solution of academic problems. The hallmark of academic intelligence is facile acquisition of academic knowledge in school environments.

For the majority of normal children and adults, it is this kind of intelligence that is assessed, albeit indirectly, by the ubiquitous IQ and aptitude tests. IQ tests are not very direct measures of the construct of intelligence. Rather, they are general achievement tests for material that has been learned over the past few years. This explaines the fact that the subtest that correlates most highly with full-scale IQ is not one of the reasoning subtests or a subtest that measures learning such as a concept identification task, but rather simple vocabulary. By making assumptions about (a) equal opportunity and motivation to learn, (b) equal familiarity with the testing materials, and (c) equal motivation to perform well, the inference is made that the individual who has learned the most is the one with the most learning ability or intelligence.

But there appears to be a second kind of intelligence, namely *practical intelligence*. This concept refers to the kinds of intellectual competencies that are required for effective solution of practical problems. A hallmark of practical intelligence is facile acquisition of *tacit knowledge*: practical know-how that is rarely formally taught or even talked about. Tacit knowledge typically is acquired informally as a consequence of one's experience, although in some cases it may be provided by others such as mentors. A number of expressions in everyday language refer to the acquisition of tacit knowledge, including "learning the ropes", "getting your feet wet", and "finding out what goes without saying around here".

A Naturally Occurring Demonstration of the Importance of Tacit Knowledge in Managerial Problem Solving

The evolution of the training and practice of managers reveals a fascinating interplay with implications for the present discussion. (A more complete presentation of these arguments and a broader analysis of managerial problem solving is available in Wagner, 1991). The field of management is split in two. Simply put, the split, which affects managerial theory, training, practice, hiring and promotion, is between those who view managers as rational technicians and those who view them as craftspersons.

Management as Practised by Rational Technicians

Taylor (1947) is credited with promoting the view that management can be explained by a set of scientific principles, just as one might attempt to explain the orbit of the moon around the earth. This view became institutionalized as management science, and the various approaches that emerged collectively are referred to as *rational* approaches to problem solving (Isenberg, 1984). What is common to rational approaches to managerial problem solving is a set of problem-solving principles of nearly universal applicability. Belief in the value and generality of such principles supported development of general managers — individuals whose training in management science enabled them to move from location to location in order to solve problems regardless of the specific context in which they appear.

An example of a rational approach to managerial problem solving is provided by Kepner and Tregoe (1965; see Plunkett and Hale, 1982, for a similar but more recent approach). The approach consists of five principles, which are presented in Table 7.3.

Table 7.3. Principles of problem solving

---

1. Problems are identified by comparing actual performance to an expected standard of performance.
2. Problems are defined as deviations from expected standards of performance.
3. Prerequisite to identifying the cause of a problem is generating a precise and complete description of the problem.
4. The cause of the problem will be found by comparing situations in which the problem is found to similar situations in which the problem is not found.
5. Problems are the result of some change that has caused an unwanted deviation from expectations.

Source: Kepner and Tregoe (1965)

Consider the application of this approach to a problem involving rancid butterfat that was described by Kepner and Tregoe (1965). After several years of smooth functioning, a customer calls the midwestern plant of a butterfat producer to inform them that the butterfat was turning rancid during the manufacture of various food products. The problem was referred to the main office in another state. The general manager who was assigned the problem defined it in terms of deviation from expected standards of performance as follows: "Some bags of butterfat produced by the midwestern plant turn rancid prematurely". By making a number of phone calls, the manager constructed the following description of the problem: "The problem began a week ago; it is confined to a single customer; it affects only about 20 per cent of this customer's butterfat". By comparing situations in which the problem occurred to those in which it did not, the manager pieced together the following scenario: "A new freezer was installed a week ago. The affected customer is the only one whose bags of butterfat are built into a square on a pallet before freezing. The reason the problem is confined to part of the shipment to the single customer whose bags are built into a square on a pallet is that the outer bags act to insulate the inner bags from the cold of the freezer". The manager instructed the plant to insert temperature probes to various depths in a pallet. The results confirmed that the inner bags were not freezing. The problem was solved by instructing the plant to leave an inch of space between bags on the pallet.

Note that in this example, adapted from Kepner and Tregoe (1965), the problem is solved without the general manager even having to visit the plant at which the problem was occurring, thus reinforcing the view that the principles of problem solving have great generality.

Several strengths of rational approaches to managerial problem solving are obvious. First, the approach is explicit and thus easily taught to others. Second, the approach is general with respect to both the problem and the problem solver. There is no need to adapt it on account of differences across problems or managers who attempt to use the approach. Third, the approach is based on sound principles of logic and scientific reasoning. It encourages managers to avoid premature conclusions and to minimize bias.

Given these obvious strengths, one might expect that proponents of managerial science would have wiped out the opposition that view management as a craft that cannot be reduced into a simple set of principles. However, the view of the manager as craftsperson, which historically has been the longer-standing one of the two, not only has not been wiped out but is showing signs of resurgence. For one example, recent handbooks of managerial problem solving give little coverage to rational approaches (e.g., Albert, 1980; Virga, 1987). Three problems appear to be at work.

First, influential studies (beginning with Mintzberg, 1973, and continuing with Isenberg, 1984, and McCall and Kaplan, 1985) of what managers actually do — as opposed to what they say they do — revealed little evidence of rational management. For examples, managers did not follow a step-by-step sequence but rather groped along with only a vague impression about the nature of the problem solving process as opposed to waiting until the end to make a move.

Second, much of what we have learned about problem solving in the last decades casts doubt on the true effectiveness of general principles of problem solving when there is an absence of content knowledge of the specific problem-solving domain.

Third, managers — like everyone else — are subject to bias that reduces the effectiveness of their rational intellect. A list of common biases is presented in Table 7.4.

Table 7.4. Common biases in managerial problem solving that limit the effectiveness of rational approaches

---

1. Managers overestimate the prevalance of highly salient or publicized events, and underestimate the prevalance of less salient or publicized events.
2. Information acquired early in problem solving is given too much weight; information acquired late in problem solving is given too little weight.
3. Managers discover what they expect to discover.
4. Once an option has been formed, it is unlikely to be changed even in the face of conflicting information.
5. Managers overestimate the stability of data based upon small samples.

Source: Hogarth (1987)

Management as Practised by Craftspersons

With a growing realization of the limitations of managerial science, there is a renewed interest in understanding aspects of managerial problem solving, as practised by craftspersons, that are not reducible to a handful of basic principles. Consider four examples of results from the study of managers as craftspersons.

The first result comes from an approach to studying the craft of managerial problem solving that was taken by Isenberg (1986), who compared thinking-aloud protocols of managers and college students as they solved a brief business case. Note that the case approach, which is a mainstay of the curriculum of the Harvard Business School, is designed to convey the craft of management through discussion of and participation in elaborately described managerial situations. The most interesting difference that Isenberg found between the performance of managers and students was that the managers took action sooner. In fact, whereas students read the complete problem before proceeding to solution, the managers began trying out solutions before they had read a complete description of the problem. Of course, this kind of behaviour flies in the face of managerial science.

A second example is provided by the work of Mintzberg (Mintzberg et al., 1976), who observed another way in which the behaviour of managers differs from that predicted by managerial science. Managers do not solve problems in the linear fashion that is characteristic of rational approaches. Rather than beginning with definition and working through to solution implementation, managerial problem solving is better described by *recursive and interrupted cycles* of problem reformulation and solution seeking.

For a third example, McCall and Kaplan (1985) identified two common kinds of managerial problem solving that differ from rational approaches. The first, called *convoluted action*, is characterized by sporadic work on the problem by different groups of individuals over a period of time that typically is measured in months if not years. The second, called *quick action*, is just the opposite. Here, the nature of the problem calls for nearly immediate implementation of a solution. The solution is formulated by a single individual after only a cursory search for information and alternative solutions, because there simply is not time enough for a more complete analysis.

The final example is provided by Schon (1983), whose work suggests that rational approaches do not suffice because managers are not confronted with simple, isolated problems, but rather with complex, turbulent, and interwoven ones. What is required is a manager who can imagine a more desirable future, and invent the means of achieving it.

Managerial competence, which consists of as much intuition as reasoning, is reflected in action that is sponaneous for the most part. If asked to explain their behaviour, managers may either be at a loss for words or may provide a fictitious account in the spirit of trying to provide an answer. According to Schon, much of what managers know is tacit, and only available implicitly through action. On occasion, managers attempt to reflect on their actions as they perform them, as a way of testing their intuitive understanding of the problem. These conversations managers have with themselves are called *reflections-in-action*. An example is when managers ask themselves why they feel uneasy about an action they are contemplating.

A final approach that fits here expands upon the idea that tacit knowledge plays an important role in problem solving by managers and others in their career pursuits and in their daily lives. The particular example that will be discussed is a more controlled study of managerial problem solving.

A Relatively Controlled Study of Tacit Knowlegde in Managerial Problem Solving

The study to be described (Wagner and Sternberg, 1990) was carried out to compare the roles of tacit knowledge, IQ, and various personality indices in managerial problem solving. The study was carried out with the cooperation of the Centre for Creative Leadership in Greensboro, North Carolina. The Centre has a variety of programmes designed to enhance the leadership, problem-solving skills, and creativity of managers. Their flagship programme, which is known as the Leadership Development Programme (LDP), was the site of the present study.

The subjects were 45 LDP participants. The sample was mostly male, with an average age of 44 years and an age range from 32 to 58.

To measure managerial tacit knowledge, the participants were given the Tacit Knowledge Inventory for Managers (TKIM) (Wagner and Sternberg, 1991). This measure samples managerial tacit knowledge by asking individuals to rate the quality of various response alternatives in the context of a problem solving scenario. An example is presented in Table 7.5.

Table 7.5. Sample scenario and response alternatives from the knowledge inventory for managers

---

Problem: an employee who reports to one of your subordinates has asked to talk with you about waste, poor management practices, and possible violations of both company policy and the law on the part of your most trusted and valued subordinate. You have had no previous reason to doubt your subordinate. The employee has not discussed the matter with the subordinate because of its delicate nature and to avoid negative repercussions.

Rate the quality of the following response alternatives:

a. Refuse to meet with the employee until the individual discusses the matter with your subordinate.
b. Meet with the employee, but only with your subordinate present.
c. Meet with the employee privately.
d. Turn the matter over to your administrative assistant.

In addition to completing the TKIM, the participants completed the normal battery of measures that is given to participants in the Leadership Development Programme (LDP). This battery included an IQ test and several common self-report measures of personality characteristics, including the California Psychological Inventory (CPI), the Myers-Briggs Type Indicator, the Fundamental Interpersonal Relations Orienta-

tion-Behaviour (FIRO-B), and the Hidden Figures Test (a measure of
field independence).

The criterion to be predicted was Behavioural Assessment Data
(BAD) ratings of performance in two small-group managerial
simulations called Earth II and Energy International. The following
categories of performance were rated: activity level, led the discussion,
influenced others, problem analysis, task orientation, motivated others,
verbal effectiveness, and interpersonal skills. To obtain a summary
variable with satisfactory reliability, the ratings were averaged across
categories and the average ratings summarized across problems. The
resultant variable had a corrected split-half reliability of 0.59.

The following results were obtained. The best predictor of managerial
performance in the simulation was the measure of tacit knowledge ($r =$
.61, $p < .001$). The second best predictor was IQ ($r = .39$, $p < .001$). The
correlation between tacit knowledge and IQ was not reliably different
from zero ($r = .14$). To determine whether the relation between tacit
knowledge and managerial performance was independent of other
measures, a series of hierarchical regressions was carried out. For each
regression analysis, one or more variables were first used to predict
performance in the behaviour simulation. Then the tacit knowledge
variable was added to the prediction equation. If adding tacit knowledge
to the prediction equation resulted in a significant increase in variance
accounted for, then the tacit knowledge variable was measuring something other than what was being measured by the variables already in the
prediction equation. These results are presented in Table 7.6.

Table 7.6. Hierarchical regressions to determine independence of relation
between tacit knowledge and problem solving performance

Other Measures	R^2	Delta R^2 for Tacit Knowledge
1. IQ	.46***	.32***
2. CPI, IQ	.66***	.22***
3. FIRO-B, IQ	.65***	.32***
4. Hidden Figures, IQ	.47***	.28***
5. Myers-Briggs, IQ	.56***	.35***
6. All predictors significantly correlated with criterion	.54***	.17***

The results were clear cut. No matter which variables were included in
the prediction equation, adding tacit knowledge resulted in a large and
significant increase in variance accounted for. Thus, these results suggest
that the construct of tacit knowledge is not subsumed by the personality

sand ability constructs measured by the other variables. In fact, the combination of tacit knowledge, IQ, and selected personality measures predicted nearly all of the reliable variance in the measure of managerial problem solving.

Enhancing the Acquisition of Tacit Knowledge

Having argued the importance of tacit knowledge to managerial performance, we turn to the issue of whether the rate of acquisition of tacit knowledge can be enhanced through adult education and industrial training. We are only beginning to explore this issue, and our initial efforts are focussed on two fronts.

The first front is to identify situation and person variables that are associated with increasing tacit knowledge. Working with Robert Sternberg, Carol Rashotte, and Wendy Williams, the author has begun a study of Cooperative Education. Cooperative education involves combining traditional teaching in college classes with work experience. We are assessing a wide variety of characteristics associated with the cooperative learning experience such as amount of contact with experienced individuals, the presence of a mentor, and the degree of responsibility given the student, as well as characteristics of the students, to determine which are related to growth in tacit knowledge in a longitudinal study.

We have completed a pilot study for the purpose of trying out our measures, using a group of cooperative education students with less than four months of work experience, and a control group. We were surprised to discover a few differences in practical know-how between the groups with such little work experience.

The second front is to explore the possibility of directly teaching at least some tacit knowledge that appears to be useful to a wide variety of circumstances. Just because tacit knowledge typically is not taught directly does not mean that it cannot be. However, the problem is figuring out what to convey and how to convey it. In this effort we have adopted the idea of a rule of thumb: a useful principle with wide application, not intended to be strictly accurate. Examples of such rules of thumb include, "Think in terms of tasks accomplished rather than hours spent working", and "Favour action over reflection".

The challenge is in discovering the rules of thumb to solve problems. Because such knowledge is presumably tacit, little is to be gained by asking experts directly to provide them. A less direct approach that we have begun to employ with some success is to represent a given rule of thumb in a pair of response alternatives that are embedded in scenarios of the sort found on the Tacit Knowledge Inventory for Managers. For example, the rule of thumb about the value of thinking in terms of tasks accomplished would be presented by the following two response items in a scenario: "Treat yourself to dinner out after an unusually long day at work", and "Treat yourself to dinner out after completing a major task". Support for the rule of thumb is provided by a significantly larger difference in ratings given the two items (in favour of the second item) for top performers in a domain than for average performers.

Conclusions

Three conclusions can be drawn from the research that has been described. The first conclusion is that what utility there is to the construct and measures of academic intelligence (e.g., IQ tests) is confined to initial education. What is necessary to understand the capabilities of adult learners and how those capabilities may be enhanced through adult education is the construct of practical intelligence.

The second conclusion is that one conceptualization of practical intelligence that may be useful in the context of adult education is that of facile acquisition of tacit knowledge. Much of the competence that adults have and continue to develop derives from their practical know-how as opposed to their "book knowledge".

The third conclusion is that a high priority for research is to understand whether and how the rate of acquisition of tacit knowledge can be enhanced through adult education. Education always involves relating new knowledge to old knowledge, but what differentiates adult education from initial education is the degree of practical knowledge that adults bring to bear on a situation. Although the technology now exists for measuring tacit knowledge and its development, as yet there have been few studies of the effectiveness of various strategies for enhancing the rate of acquisition of tacit knowledge that might be implemented in adult education programmes.

References

Albert, K.J. (Ed.) (1980). *Handbook of business problem solving*. New York: McGraw-Hill.

Ghiselli, E.E. (1966). *The validity of occupational aptitude tests*. New York: Wiley.

Hogarth, R.M. (1987). *Judgment and choice*. New York: Wiley.

Isenberg, D.J. (1984). How senior managers think. *Harvard Business Review 62*, 81-90.

Isenberg, D.J. (1986). Thinking and managing: a verbal protocol analysis of managerial problem solving. *Academy of Management Journal 4*, 775-788.

Kepner, C.H., & Tregoe, B.B. (1965). *The rationale manager: a systematic approach to problem solving and decision making*. New York: McGraw-Hill.

McCall, M.W., & Kaplan, R.E. (1985). *Whatever it takes: Decision makers at work.* Englewood Cliffs, New Jersey: Prentice-Hall.

Mintzberg, H. (1973). *The nature of managerial work.* New York: Harper & Row.

Mintzberg, H., Raisinghani, D., & Theoret, A. (1976). The structure of "unstructured" decision processes. *Administrative Science Quarterly 21,* 246-275.

Neisser, U. (1976). General, academic, and artificial intelligence. In L. Resnick (Ed.), *The nature of intelligence* (pp. 135-144). Hillsdale, New Jersey: Erlbaum.

Plunkett, L.C., & Hale, G.A. (1982). *The proactive manager.* New York: Wiley.

Schon, D.A. (1983). *The reflective practitioner.* New York: Basic Books.

Taylor, F.W. (1947). *Scientific management.* New York: Harper and Brothers.

Virga, P.H. (Ed.) (1987). *The national management association handbook for managers.* Englewood Cliffs, New Jersey: Prentice-Hall.

Wagner, R.K. (1987) Tacit knowledge in everyday intelligent behavior. *Journal of Personality and Social Psychology 52,* 1236-1247.

Wagner, R.K. (1991). Managerial problem solving. In P. Frensch and R. Sternberg (Eds.), *Problem solving.* Hillsdale, New Jersey: Erlbaum.

Wagner, R.K., & Sternberg, R.J. (1985). Practical intelligence in real-world pursuits: The role of tacit knowledge. *Journal of Personality and Social Psychology 48,* 436-458.

Wagner, R.K., & Sternberg, R.J. (1990). Street smarts. In K. Clark and M. Clark (Eds.), *Measures of leadership.* Greensboro, North Carolina: Center for Creative Leadership.

Wagner, R.K., & Sternberg, R.J. (1991). *The Tacit Knowledge Inventory for Managers (TKIM).* San Antonio, Texas: The Psychological Corporation.

Wigdor, A.K. & Garner, W.R. (Eds.) (1982). *Ability testing: Uses, consequences, and controversies.* Washington, D.C.: National Academy Press.

Part 3
Skills Formation in the Work Place

Chapter 8

INFORMAL LEARNING ON THE JOB

BEN VAN ONNA
University of Nijmegen, The Netherlands

This chapter is concerned with informal learning in the workplace. The focus is on questions such as: why should learning on the job be considered as an essential part of a future-oriented policy for skill formation in work organizations, and what are the means by which this can be encouraged?

Some of the factors that may explain the recent interest in informal learning in the workplace, and the various contexts in which it occurs, are examined in the first part of this chapter. New developments in industry that make learning on the job an imperative for acquiring and maintaining professional competence are also described.

The second part deals with the significance of informal learning on the job as a vehicle for improving the skills of the labour force. It is claimed that, for qualified professionals in industry and services, learning on the job cannot and should not be viewed as being independent from formally provided continuing education and training. In contrast, independent learning on the job can be relevant in the training of comparatively low-skilled workers. Hence the role of informal learning on the job varies according to the specific needs of different categories of workers.

The place of informal learning on the job in a dual learning strategy that also involves formal education and training is discussed in the concluding part of this chapter. It is argued that the integration of working and learning, which is at the heart of current developments, has major consequences for the relationship between initial and postinitial education. Some of these consequences, as well as the effects of informal learning in the workplace on, for example, personality development and the alleviation of social deprivation, are examined. It is concluded that, because of the paucity of empirical information on the subject, more extensive research, for example regarding the consequences for the provision of guidance and counselling, should be initiated.

Topical Interest

Informal learning on the job or at the workplace has become a popular topic for research. It implies the rediscovery of the importance of work-oriented learning on the job, as distinguished from "artificial" situations created to achieve particular educational goals. In a broader sense it has been a relevant issue of topical interest for quite some time now for policy making as well (Kraayvanger and Van Onna, 1985, p. 9 ff.). During the 1970s, when reforms in initial education were put into effect in different Western European countries, one of the questions for close reflection concerned the possibilities and limits of the employment system in continuing the learning process and advancing it into adult life.

A reformist policy for initial education was assumed to yield positive results in case the employment system would provide opportunities for and encourage further learning. The idea was that opportunities for learning on the job would be created if workers were allowed to "sidestep" the regular production process, which would give them an opportunity to participate in planning, regulating, and controlling functions. Another view was that workplace reform, particularly the "humanization" of work would increase, although not automatically, the workers' opportunity to learn. According to some, the best way to ensure that some of the benefits of reform would accrue to workers would be to assist them in implementing innovations, applying their innovative qualifications, and shaping their work situation starting from their own interests as employees. Concern with the sex-based division of labour is also relevant in the context of developing informal learning on the job. Because women are overrepresented in certain labour markets, for example services, and underrepresented in others, and since they traditionally occupy lower positions than men, their opportunity to learn at the workplace may also differ. Hence a redistribution of labour in favour of women would involve not only a quantitative shift but also a qualitative one, since the prospects of both men and women for learning and personal development on the job would be affected.

Despite initial optimism, the research evidence suggests that informal learning on the job is necessary, but not exclusively so. The relationship with formal training is also important. The latter can be successful if the work situation invites the application of new skills, whereas the success of informal learning depends on the adequacy of the workplace as an environment for learning. The importance of this relationship is generally being recognized at present. Compared with the previous positions, a substantial shift in emphasis has taken place. It seems that, today, informal learning is appreciated less for its potential labour-external effects on society than for its possible effects on productivity. The productivity-relevant benefits of informal learning on the job are considered to be high, even in comparison with the value added due to formal training.

The relevance of informal learning on the job is discussed below. But the various contexts in which informal learning occurs need to be taken into account first.

Contexts of Learning on the Job

The first question is: how should this learning be interpreted? When projects and measures are designed to improve learning within organizations, it is often unclear whether informal learning on the job is seen as an end in itself, as a means to other goals, as a side-effect or as an explicit topic of organizational, educational, and training management resulting in certain qualifications (Onstenk, 1991). In addition, the type of industry and the social and national contexts can make a great difference. The significance of informal learning on the job may also differ according to distinct combinations of working and learning, for example in relation to practical or dual training, and firm-based or inservice training. Informal learning may also serve different functions depending, for example, on whether it occurs within the context of a training course for qualified professional work at a CNC machine with workshop programming as opposed to when workers are required to get familiar with operating a CNC machine with a semi-academic control concept at short notice. This example shows that informal learning on the job may serve different purposes when work organizations try to match available and required qualifications through specific strategies. In Mintzberg's (1983) terminology: in a machine-bureaucracy, where adjustment of qualifications to the tasks to be performed takes a prominent position, informal learning will take on the character of an optimalization of work activities, component actions and, particularly, motor skills. In an adhocracy, which specifically involves the mutual adjustment of high-grade qualifications and high-quality work, informal learning includes the creative exchange and evaluation of internal and external work experiences. By contrast, in a professional bureaucracy, this type of learning may look somewhat different again and has a different function (Van Der Krogt, 1992).

Many researchers associate almost exclusively positive connotations with learning on the job in that they see advantages to both the work organization and the individual workers (or students), although it is equally true that skills are also lost on the job, and probably on a large scale. There is moreover great variation in the interests of the different stakeholders and in social appreciation of informal learning on the job. If learning on the job is not primarily to be considered an attractive normative idea in training and educational discourse, let alone a fashionable trend, then our analyses should take these differences into account and present arguments as to the reasons and contexts in which this type of learning can be important.

This diversity of contexts and objectives makes it evident that "informal learning" is an ambiguous concept. Even if it were possible to give it a clear definition, which many doubt, some modifications would be needed depending on the actual situation. With such a flexible approach rough distinctions can be made between the types of work places where learning actually takes place, without these work places having explicitly been selected or shaped for their learning relevance. It may emerge, then, that learning is by-product of working under general and specific economic and social conditions. Naturally, these conditions, considered as learning conditions, will show qualitative variation. Another case in which these conditions are present involves the learning processes that are both internal and external to the work organization, and in which productive work will be functional to this learning. A further important distinction can be made between independent learning at the workplace and learning under guidance, through instruction or at a distance, of which also various levels and forms exist. It can be assumed that the learning processes themselves will also differ, accordingly.

Thus we may think of several ways in which workers may learn new things on their jobs, but empirical research has not yet given us much understanding of the importance of these types of learning within the context of a firm or branch of industry.

Informal Learning and Training Policy

There is a vast literature to explain the divergence between working and learning, which have become relatively separate, independent institutions in the course of time. Recent studies also discuss the reasons why working and learning may grow less far apart, in fact are converging (cf. De Vries, 1988, for a summary review). We are now in a stage in which attention is focused more on convergence, judging also by the popularity of learning on the job (Kraayvanger and Van Onna, 1985). Support for the "convergence hypothesis" can also be found in the literature on training and education, where the advantages and limitations of job training are the subject of much discussion (Kessels and Smit, 1991). The striking thing about this discussion is that some authors apparently consider it impractical or even impossible to provide systematic and high-quality training on the job. The conditions of work in modern industry are seen as a limiting factor, despite the fact that many workers spend some time on the job while being trained. The following arguments are used to question the practicality of training on the job: the complexity of machinery and equipment is too great, the pace of work is too high, the risk of accidents will increase, the opacity of the work process does not encourage learning, and the risk of damaging expensive machinery is too great. Another argument is that training courses that squarely fall within the specific area of competence of a given enterprise entail a risk of conferring firm-specific qualifications that limit the flexibility and career opportunities of employees. These arguments, which seem valid to an extent, can be interpreted as implying that informal learning on the job, whether or not as part of a formal training course, does not yield much productive learning. These arguments may not be as valid as they seem, however, and informal learning on the job cannot easily be brushed aside as being irrelevant.

After all, trade and industry also show developments that may give rise to the question whether the alternative to informal learning, that is a systematization of qualifying processes under simulated conditions, will actually enable prospective workers to learn and update the professional skill and competence they need at work. This includes the capacity to plan, execute, and control: in other words, the ability of being able to shape qualified professional work independently. The acquisition of professional competence is the central criterion in the design of educational programmes and training courses. Hence there is every reason to discuss the significance of learning on the job in further detail.

New Developments

What, then, are the developments that make informal learning on the job an imperative for acquiring professional skills and competence, and why do they necessitate a review of this type of learning and its specific objectives? Three developments seem especially important (cf. Herz et al., 1990).

First, the demand on professional competence has changed in connection with the implementation of computer technology in the workplace. The requirement is for "fluid" and "tacit" competence, which is less formalized than that conferred by traditional qualifications and yet forms an essential part of the ability to function in modern work processes. This competence can be given various labels: basic skills, key qualifications, tacit knowledge, and so on. The research shows that some of these competences, however general they may be, can only to a limited extent be taught in an explicitly didactic manner and in simulated learning environments (see Wagner in this volume). For example, the ability to think in terms of complex interrelationships is not fully acquired until practised in real-life situations (De Jong et al., 1990; Nijhof and Remmers, 1989).

Second, the rapid development of integrated technological systems in medium- and large-size companies has given rise to the belief that it is no longer feasible to simulate this technology realistically in learning situations. They have become too complex for that. Specific qualifications, for example those needed in order to maintain integrated systems and repair technical failures, can increasingly be obtained in real-life situations only. Hence the workplace may be the most appropriate place for acquiring this specific competence. The acquisition of certain key qualifications for working life thus depends on situations that bear the hallmark of authenticity.

There is yet a third perspective from which pressure is brought to bear on the argument that working and learning ought to be separated. Since much modern technology involves standard equipment technical adjustments, if any are required, can often be made after the installation. However, in the case of sophisticated technologies, the products are usually not fully developed, tested, and adapted to the wishes of the users upon delivery. Adaptation may be needed in applied situations, since the full range of applications may well become sufficiently clear only when the work process has resumed. This situation is associated with a bottom-up strategy for implementing new technology. At the core of this strategy is the idea of learning in and from practice on the job: the workers who will have to operate the new technology should change with it, so that they learn to discover new possibilities for applying and shaping that technology. This type of informal learning may be part of a training course for workers, but also of a learning programme directed towards young students. Thus the work situation of both adults and young people may objectively turn into a learning situation. Hence future-oriented work processes may make the reintegration of working and learning unavoidable (Feijen, 1989). Pedagogues and other educationalists play a small role in this merger; technologists, engineers, and organizational experts have an important contribution to make.

However, the reintegration of working and learning will certainly not occur automatically, if only because the mechanisms that have resulted in their separation are still effective. The obstacles cannot be overcome by lengthening the period of time spent by prospective workers on the job. The challenge is rather to create an environment in the work organization that is open to learning processes without explicitly setting up a pedagogic or educational framework. When informal learning is involved, the technological and organizational conditions of the work place need not become an explicit part of the learning perspective, which implies that the original flow of production can be maintained.

The Perspective of Vocational Education Theory

It follows from the above that the reintegration of working and learning is motivated by a desire to increase the professional competence of future workers by incorporating a greater part of their formal education and training into work-based activities. This can only be achieved if several conditions are met. Theories on human resource development and writings on the ideal characteristics of the "learning organization" have made a contribution to our understanding of these conditions. Research studies on training placements (De Vries, 1988; Onstenk et al., 1990; Kloas and Puhlmann, 1991; Nieuwenhuis, 1991) and on the factors that determine the provision of learning opportunities at the workplace (Frei et al., 1984; Van Onna, 1981; Herzer et al., 1991). These factors may become the object of the training policies of work organizations. Similarly, the learning-intensive design of technology is no longer a completely unventured territory (Heidegger and Rauner, 1990).

From an educational perspective there are at least two issues that warrant special interest (Herz et al., 1990). These concern the definition of informal learning on the job and its relation to initial and post-initial education and training; and the provision of guidance and counselling to both trainers and trainees.

Educators can help in designing ways of improving current approaches to the guidance and counselling of students and workers. Guidance is needed especially with respect to the acquisition of professional competence and the design of personal strategies for informal learning on the job (Marsick and Watkins, 1990). If informal learning is to be upgraded and made a structural element of formal training courses, then close attention must be given to guidance and counselling. Without personal guidance informal learning as part of a regular training course is not likely to be a success. This draws the role of the tutor into focus. It cannot be taken for granted that instructors — often experienced professionals who provide support for training in addition to performing their regular job tasks — will be sufficiently able to meet the challenges implied, that is, to understand work situations as learning situations and to make them accessible to the individual so that he or she may profit from it (Bauer and Herz, 1991). A supplementary course in vocational teacher training could enable these tutors to analyze the job tasks of professional workers and to make use of the learning potential carried by given work situations in the enterprise. In order to encourage the use of the workplace and the job itself as a place for learning, tutors should also be capable of linking the training with the educational level and the performance and expectations of individuals. Some Dutch enterprises occasionally offer training courses for professional tutors and supervisors. It is not clear at present whether these courses are successful in satisfying the demands, however.

Secondly, a detailed definition is required of the link and the division of responsibility between the training offered initially in educational institutions and the formal training courses sponsored by employers, on the one hand, and informal learning on the job on the other. Of course, this is also an organizational problem. Given that the new developments discussed in a previous section have stupendous implications for training policy, it seems clear that this definition ought to take the new dimensions of learning on the job into account. This implies that training objectives should be adjusted and that the distribution of working and learning be reconsidered.

The learning objectives behind the provision of formal training, which often confer recognized qualifications, can be tested; one can find out whether the students are able to meet certain standards of performance. But this does not necessarily mean that their competence is sufficient or that they can adequately perform qualified professional tasks. For this, informal learning under guidance and as part of the formal training course may be needed. Informal learning is at a relative disadvantage because it usually does not lead to a certification of competence. Yet this is also an advantage, as flexibility is enhanced.

The question of the redistribution and integration of work and learning over the lifespan has been the subject of extensive debate for several decades. The learning and training strategies that are being followed at present by a number of "enlightened" companies should be viewed in this context. Training and learning in work organizations has gained in relevance and has now even become an explicit part of government policy, for example where the dual nature of vocational education in schools and apprenticeship training is concerned. Since dualism adds an element of flexibility to the relationship between education and work, it presents an instrument by which the correspondence between working and learning can be strengthened and, thus, discrepancies between the skills needed on the job and the key qualifications of the workforce reduced.

The arguments so far advanced in this chapter support the view that it would be a grave mistake to believe that informal learning in the work place plays only a marginal role in the effort to improve the efficiency of the job matching process. Current business practice appears to favour formal training over informal learning in the work place. However, when the new developments previously discussed are beginning to take a hold on companies, then a rigidly formulated policy of further education and training, in which informal learning processes are hardly accomodated, may prove counter-productive.

Support for the view that informal learning should be seen as an integral part of education and training policy can also be derived from the economics of educational choice. Recruitment to vocational schools will remain imbalanced, and perhaps become even more so in future, as long as vocational education is considered by both students and parents as a second-best choice. If governments are to succeed in pursuing policy to encourage students to opt for vocational education, which hitherto has had a markedly lower status compared with general secondary education, then vocational education will have to undergo a structural adjustment that enhances its attractiveness. This may not be enough, however. The quality of the education offered, and in particular the quality of work and the career opportunities which students can look forward to, must also be considerably improved and broadened. Informal learning in the work place can contribute to this. Informal learning should therefore be seen not only as a strategy for invigorating training policy in industry, but also as a means of upgrading and modernizing vocational education.

Effects of Informal Learning

There is a dearth of empirical research on the possible external effects of learning on the job. Any discussion of such external effects is highly speculative because many claims about the expected benefits of informal learning on the job have not yet been substantiated. One reason for this paucity of empirical information is that aspects of the learning process must be measured before any systematic assessment of the outcomes of learning can be made. In the absence of hard data, a first priority is to review some of the common hypotheses concerning the externalities of learning on the job, and to put these into a broad social frame of reference.

The first hypothesis concerns the effects of informal learning on social inequality. There are good reasons to assume that differences in work situations and particularly in opportunity to learn at the work place are implicated in the reinforcement of social differences between individuals and groups (Netherlands Scientific Council for Government Policy, 1977). It is possible that training and learning on the job may not only reinforce social inequality caused by initial education but even create new aspects of inequality. If there is a strong relationship between the level of initial education and the quality of the work place, then inequality may be perpetuated because the initially poorly educated people may end up in work situations which offer few opportunities for personal development, whereas those with a high level of initial education may be employed in work place environments that provide ample opportunity for learning and personal enrichment. Hence it may be practically impossible for initially poorly educated workers to compensate later in life for the discrepancies created by means of unequal initial schooling. The significance of this discriminatory effect has to be understood in the context of the process whereby social inequality is reproduced across the generations. The central hypothesis advanced here is that one of the means to break through this chain of social deprivation and the perpetuation of inequality is to reorganize unskilled and semiskilled jobs so that these may offer sufficient opportunities for learning and personal advancement.

A second important hypothesis concerns the matter of personality development in working life: How might work support both the intellectual-cognitive development and the social and emotional development of an individual person? There is an inclination to define education in relation to the school, the family, and the peer group. Yet sufficient empirical evidence (see Kohn and Schooler, 1983) shows that there is a connection between job level (including learning opportunities) and the possibilities of individual personal development. The findings of present research on changes in work situations also indicate that students are being socialized differently through and for their work: they need to have a broad professional orientation, they must learn to think both methodically and in terms of technical and social relationships, and they should be able to apply acquired knowledge and skills in new situations.

One aspect of the transition from school to work concerns the transmission of cultural values. As this transition has become increasingly problematic, training courses are now often given objectives in addition to those concerning professional development: they should improve the work motivation of students and their identification with the firm and job task. This, too, has now led to other learning arrangements (learning by discovery, individualized learning, creative assignments, working in projects, etc.). These new methods might be used to help students overcome social or personal problems, for example a negative self-image, lack of perseverance or fear of failure. The second crucial hypothesis advanced in this chapter is therefore that informal learning on the job can play an important role in the transition from school to work, by creating a close relationship between working and learning, and by offering a means for personality development at the work place.

Conclusions

Informal learning processes at the work place have not yet been the subject of extensive research. It is only known how things develop when particular conditions are present or when motor, technological or cognitive operations and skills are involved that can be defined unequivocally.

If professional qualifications, key qualifications and design qualifications of higher levels are involved, their small measure of formalizability seems to be an important obstacle to the acquisition of knowledge and therefore to a definition of the learning objectives of informal learning. This does not mean that progress cannot be made. The Netherlands is one of the countries where exploratory research into this matter has been initiated (Onstenk, 1991). The Dutch Ministry of Social Affairs has recently commissioned a research project on schooling activities in work organizations. Interesting empirical data on the role and function of informal learning on the job in everyday work situations can be expected to result from this project, which is being conducted by J. Van Den Berg and J. Warmerdam of the Institute for Applied Social Sciences at the University of Nijmegen.

It is important to be modest about what the research has achieved so far, however. Job training is often discussed without making reference to informal learning processes and the accompanying problems as presented in this contribution. This approach may yield misleading results, since it is not clear how formal training and informal learning on the job relate to one another and to work place conditions. Further research, for example in the form of evaluations of practical experiments, will therefore have to be undertaken. Such studies may eventually explain the nature and significance of informal learning on the job. With this knowledge it may be possible to decide whether present training technologies and methodologies, which seem to focus on the acquisition of qualifications that can be formalized and tested, offer an adequate means of facilitating informal learning.

References

Bauer, H.G., & Herz, G. (1991). The "complete process of work" (CPW). An instrument for the analysis of work situations and future-oriented ways of vocational qualification. In Institut für Technik und Bildung (Ed.), *Qualifikation: Schlüssel für eine soziale Innovation, Vol. 3* (pp. 47-58). Bremen: ITB.

De Vries, B. (1988). *Het leven en de leer. Een studie naar de verbinding van leren en werken in de stage.* Nijmegen: ITS, University of Nijmegen.

Feijen, T. (1989). Nieuwe technologieën, medezeggingschap en vormingswerk. *Vorming 5*, 35-55 & 107-119.

Frei, F., Duell, W., & Baitsch, C. (1984). *Arbeit und Kompetenzentwicklung. Theoretische Konzepte zur Psychologie arbeitsimmanenter Qualifizierung.* Bern: Huber.

Heidegger, G., & Rauner, F. (1990). *Berufe 2000. Berufliche Bildung für die industrielle Produktion der Zukunft.* Düsseldorf: Ministerium für Arbeit, Gesundheit und Soziales des Landes Nordrhein-Westfalen.

Herz, G., Bauer, H., Brater, M., & Vossen, K. (1990). Der Arbeitsplatz als Lernfeld. Ein innovatives Weiterbildungskonzept. *Berufsbildung in Wissenschaft und Praxis 19*, 10-14.

Herzer, H., Dybowski, G., & Bauer, H. (1991). *Methoden betrieblicher Weiterbildung.* Eschborn: RKW.

Jong, M. de, Moerkamp, T., Onstenk, J., & Babeliowsky, M. (1990). *Breed toepasbare beroepskwalificaties in leerplan en beroepspraktijk.* Amsterdam: SCO, University of Amsterdam.

Kessels, J., & Smit, C. (1991). Opleiden op de werkplek. In *Handboek Opleiden in Organisaties.* Capita Selecta, No. 6.

Kloas, P. W., & Puhlmann, A. (1991). *Arbeit qualifiziert — aber nicht jede.* Berlin: Bundesinstitut für Berufsbildung.

Kohn, M., & Schooler, C. (1983). *Work and personality: An inquiry to the impact of social stratification.* Norwood, Massachusetts: Ablex.

Kraayvanger, G., & Van Onna, B. (1985). *Arbeid en leren. Bijdragen tot de volwasseneneducatie.* Baarn, The Netherlands: Nelissen.

Marsick, V., & Watkins, K. (1990). *Informal and incidental learning on the workplace.* London: Routledge.

Mintzberg, N. (1983). *Structure in fives. Designing effective organizations.* Englewood Cliffs, New Jersey: Prentice Hall.

Netherlands Scientific Council for Government Policy (1977). *Over sociale ongelijkheid.* The Hague: Staatsuitgeverij.

Nieuwenhuis, A. (1991). *Complexe leerplaatsen in school en bedrijf.* Groningen: RION, University of Groningen.

Nijhof, W., & Remmers, L. (1989). *Basisvaardigheden nader bekeken.* Enschede: OCTO, University of Twente.

Onstenk, J. (1991). Immanent leren in het arbeidsproces (Interim report). Amsterdam: SCO, University of Amsterdam.

Onstenk, J., Moerkamp, T., Voncken, E., & Van Den Dool, P. (1990). *Leerprocessen in stages.* Amsterdam: SCO, University of Amsterdam.

Van Der Krogt, F. (1992). Aansluitingsstrategieën en opleidingsactiviteiten in verschillende organisatietypen. *Tijdschrift voor Arbeidsvraagstukken 8* (4), 3-15.

Van Onna, B. (1981). Arbeid — leren — educatie. *Tijdschrift voor Agologie 10,* 396-42.

Chapter 9

SKILLS NEEDED IN THE WORK PLACE

JEROEN ONSTENK
SCO, Centre for Educational Research,
University of Amsterdam, The Netherlands

This chapter deals with skills needed in the modern work place. It is concluded that learning skills, practical competence, situational skills and transferable skills are becoming more important. Some of the implications for employees, especially "rank-and-file" and low-educated production workers, are described.

Changing Models for the Organization of Work

Changes in skills needed in the work place must be analyzed in relation to changes in the work organization. According to the classic Taylorist model companies are expected to think for their workers to ensure optimal production. Today one can witness the emergence of a new model (Kochan and Osterman, 1991). Optimization of production in terms of efficiency, flexibility, product quality and orientation to changing consumer demands is called for, and this results in new demands on the organization of work and higher standards for skills compared with the classic model.

As can be seen from Table 9.1, the new work place is characterized by job rotation and teamwork. Supervision is done by team leaders, whereas quality control becomes a team responsibility. Staffing policies are committed to ensuring employment continuity. Careers are determined by competency rather than seniority — although Japanese companies seem to be an exception in this respect. Pay criteria are based on performance. Training and human resource development are considered a major commitment of the company, and worker training is directed at the development of broad skills. Contrary to the old model, the company expects workers to learn and "think for the company", to be flexible, quality conscious, oriented to continuous improvement and being able to work in teams. As a result a growing number of employees is expected to need increasingly complex intellectual, methodical, strategic and social skills on the job. Lifelong learning is thus becoming a decisive factor for both the career development of individuals and the profitability of firms.

Table 9.1. Alternative human resource management systems

	Traditional	Transformed
Work place Level		
Job design	Narrow	Broad
Job assignment	Single job	Job rotation
Work organization	Individual jobs	Teamwork
Training	Job specific	Broad skills
Career progression	Seniority based	Competency based
Supervision	First line management	Team leader
Quality control	Specialized function	Team function
Participation	Grievance procedure	Employee involvement
Personnel policy level		
Pay criteria	External comparisons	Firm, group, individual performance
Staffing	Layoff policy	Commitment to employment continuity
Training and development	Limited commitment	Major commitment

Source: Kochan and Osterman (1991)

The new model is widely discussed in writings on work organization and management (see Carnevale et al., 1990b). Many managers and research workers, however, have doubts about the possibilities of implementation on a broad scale (Van Hoof, 1991). For example, it can be argued that when information technology is introduced organizational change often lags behind as a result of "structural conservatism". Thus, rather than one new model it seems that several models coexist, sometimes even within a company. Three possible organizational models can be distinguished (Laur-Ernst, 1990): (a) computerized neo-Taylorism; (b) polarized production labour; and (c) qualified, cooperative production labour. The first model is still predominant in many companies, whereas the third model is only realized in a very limited way. The most realistic option for the near future seems to be the polarization and internal differentiation of jobs (Spenner, 1988).

When, in this chapter, learning is stressed as a basic skill and the development of methodical, strategic and social competences is recommended, then the focus is not on uncontested "necessary" skills, but on the challenge to relate skill formation to modern technology and work place renewal involving the promotion of the new organizational paradigm and human-centred labour relations.

Three Approaches to the Analysis of Skills

Three possible ways of identifying changes in skills requirements can be distinguished: the "objective", which is concerned with job content; the "subjective", which primarily involves the worker, and the "activity" approach, which concentrates on the relationship between the worker and the job.

Task-centred Skills Analysis

In this approach, needed skills are determined by an "objective" analysis of job tasks. In Germany psychological models of establishing levels of "psychic" action regulation have become influential (Mickler et al., 1976). The degree of worker autonomy is the central variable in the analysis. It has a counterpart in organization theory, as it is largely compatible with the sociotechnical approach (Christis, 1989), which analyzes jobs in terms of adequate levels of "regulation capacity" (De Sitter, 1986). Spenner (1988) stresses autonomy/control as an important dimension of job skills.

Another type of task-centred strategy is followed by methods for task description and job analysis (Nijhof and Mulder, 1986; Brandsma et al., 1989). These methods follow a similar pattern: a list of possible tasks and job-elements is drawn up, the occurrence and importance of specific tasks in actual vocational practice is established, and differences between groups and possible specializations are determined using a taxonomy. After the content, structure and order of job structures are established, they are then translated into skill requirements. Romiszowski's (1981) taxonomy is widely used. It distinguishes between four types of knowledge (factual, conceptual, procedural, principles) and eight types of skills: reproductive and productive kinds of cognitive, psychomotor, reactive, and interactive skills. These kind of approaches, however, tend to limit job analysis to isolated tasks and qualifications, while variables such as process characteristics, social dimensions, and "subjective" performance competences receive relatively less attention (Laur-Ernst, 1990; Moerkamp and Onstenk, 1991).

Worker-centred Skills Analysis

The "subjective", worker-centred approach to skills analysis is implicated in concepts such as basic skills (Carnevale et al., 1990a) core skills (Levy, 1987), and key qualifications (Reetz, 1989). These concepts refer to the skills people require, independently of their specific job or job level. They may include basic skills such as computing, reading and writing, general cognitive abilities (e.g., problem solving), and social or communicative skills. The growing attention given to learning styles in company training (Thijssen and De Greef, 1989; Bomers, 1991) is another feature of the worker-centred approach.

Whereas objective, task-centred analysis concentrates mainly on job specific skills, the subject-centred approaches mostly refer to organizational and cultural dimensions of jobs and to the basic skills that are shared by many workers. Objective task-analysis puts an emphasis on cognitive demands and the complexity of the job. Subjective approaches pay more attention to the individual as a "bearer" of skills and qualifications. Objective approaches stress moreover the level of autonomy and regulation, whereas the subjective approach emphasizes attitudes and motivation.

The "Activity" Approach

It is argued that skills analysis should take into account both the objective and the subjective dimension. Activity psychology and modern cognitive theory stress that skills should be analyzed as competences or "capacities to act" (Engeström, 1986; Laur-Ernst, 1990), and that these competences are "situated" (Raizen, 1989). This means stressing the relationship between skills and the activities in which they are used. Activity is defined as a meaningful performance of tasks in a situated setting by a competent individual. The starting point remains, as in the objective approach, the content and structure of the tasks to be performed. A broad perspective is taken, however. Activity includes not only the task itself, but also task management and social job context (Levy, 1987; Christis, 1989), and competency refers to all dimensions.

Table 9.2 makes a distinction between *functional* and *motivational* requirements (De Jong et al., 1990; Onstenk et al., 1990a). Functional requirements result from aspects of task performance, such as preparation, execution and control. Three dimensions seem particularly important: task complexity (level of abstraction, complexity, problem solving, improvization), organizational demands, and social-communicative

requirements. Activity as opposed to action not only involves instrumental goals, but also the motives or reasons of the activity (Frei et al.,
1984). In turn, motivational requirements relate to either normative,
strategic, or affective factors required for competent action.

Table 9.2. Typology of occupational requirements

A. *Functional requirements*
    Complexity of tasks
    Organizational demands
    Social-communicative requirements

B. *Motivational requirements*
    Normative
    Strategic
    Affective

Functional and motivational requirements result primarily from the
specific framework of technological and organizational characteristics,
and the division of labour in the firm (Christis, 1989). Changes in skills
are not merely dependent on technological development, but are
explained by a combination of technological change and organizational
renewal. To realize potential influence on decision making, workers need
innovative qualifications, directed to improving the quality of work and
the production process (Fricke, 1975). These qualifications are therefore
part and parcel of the occupational requirements.

Contextual developments also influence occupational requirements.
Norms are very important too, for example those of professional groups
and organizations. Changing conditions on the labour market increase the
need for situational and transfer skills as much as changing demands
from the consumer market. A further determinant of occupational
requirements is the educational system: the differentiation of school
types and educational curricula which not only establishes a variety of
skill patterns but also professional and educational norms. The above
analysis of occupational requirements leads to a multidimensional view
of skills needed in the work place. These are not restricted to job-specific
skills, but also comprise practical competence, situational skills and
transfer skills.

Task performance implies "practical intelligence" (Sternberg and
Wagner, 1986): arithmetic skills, literacy skills, social-communicative
skills, context knowledge, and "tacit" knowledge. Situational skills or

key qualifications are related to task management and organizational context. They are becoming very important in improving the quality and flexibility of production systems. There also is a growing need for methodical, organizational and social skills. Transfer and transferable skills, which are related to job rotation, mobility between jobs or companies, career development and changes in job content as a result of technological and organizational development, are crucial for competent work performance.

Learning In and For the Company

As was stressed above, the learning of new skills is basic to modern concepts of work organization (Simons, 1990). Most of the writings in this field focus on vocational or company training and on learning as a characteristic of specific functions (professionals and managers). It remains to be seen what learning actually means for the "rank and file" workers in the organization.

As mentioned previously the central theme of the Taylorist paradigm is captured by the statement: "The company (or the engineer) thinks for the worker". This does not exclude all learning processes, but they are largely restricted to narrow and precisely defined ways of doing things (Sierksma, 1991). Some critics of vocational education state that the traditional concept of vocation merely reinforces this Taylorist approach, by defining vocation in strictly defined criteria of task performance (Brater, 1987). In terms of autonomy and control this approach may lead to "learned helplessness", especially for unskilled workers (Leymann and Kornbluh, 1989).

By contrast, the new paradigm fosters human resources development, which advocates a worker who thinks for the company. Learning to learn is stated by many employers as the "foundation" for basic skills. Among the other "essential skills (American) employers want" are "communication skills, solving problems, thinking creatively, and managing personal and professional growth" (Carnevale et al., 1990a p. 3). The EURO-TECNET programme, advocating the development of self-learning competency (Nyhan, 1991), and "The Learning Organization" (Development Programme, 1989) claim that the "learning worker" is the most important difference between the Taylorist organizational paradigm and the approach of human resources development. Basic to the new paradigm is the emphasis on information technology.

The concept of self-learning competency (Nyhan, 1991) is strongly prescriptive and stresses the responsibility of the worker for the learning process. This may require that the worker knows how to "apply knowledge gained in one situation to other situations" and "to puzzle out problems without giving up, or becoming too frustrated" (op cit). Learning competency is, according to this paradigm, dependent on self-motivation, self-awareness and self-control. This concept tends, just like other subject-centred approaches (e.g. Carnevale et. al., 1990b), to under-play possible contradictions between the old and new paradigm during the transition. Moreover, the coexistence of different models is neglected. The importance of the work environment as a learning environment is not thoroughly analyzed either. The Swedish programme, by comparison, stresses organizational renewal as a precondition as much as a consequence of developing learning possibilities for all or most workers in the organization (Development Programme, 1989).

Much research has been carried out on promoting people's abilities and motivation to learn (see the several contributions in this volume). In order for learning to take place it is not enough to have workers who are capable and motivated to learn, however. They must also have opportunities to learn both on and off the job. The work site as learning environment has to fulfil specific conditions. This can be analyzed in terms of the *learning potential of jobs* (Baitsch and Frei, 1980; Onstenk, 1992a). Learning processes and the development of competences result from specific combinations of skills and qualifications of the worker (formal education, work experience, learning skills); learning possibilities on site such as co-operation, control, autonomy, training policies and organizational change; and the ability and willingness of the workers to learn and develop their competence. The challenge for management is to create a learning organization that may enlarge this learning potential. To accomplish this all three dimensions (e.g., worker skills, learning possibilities, and worker willingness) must be taken into account. Many companies in fact only attempt to change the first dimension, hoping that the other two may be affected as a consequence. So they try to screen new employees on their trainability and willingness to learn. As this is very difficult, they tend to use school career and attained educational level as indicators. It is supposed that in higher education more learning skills, communicative and problem-solving skills are learnt. This does not make an active policy of on-the-job training superfluous, however, as Japanese firms show (Dore and Sako, 1988). If human resources management concentrates for its skill supply on formal task-related training it chooses a strategy which is limited to only one dimension of the learning potential.

To create a successful learning environment it is necessary to improve opportunities for learning and to enhance the willingness of workers to learn. Learning possibilities include both job-related dimensions and more specific learning directed measures. Barriers to learning, such as the lack of job quality, unrewarding pay systems, lack of career possibilities and appropriate training, have to be removed (Baitsch and Frei, 1980; Onstenk, 1992b).

The identification and recognition of prior learning is becoming more important in this respect. People with little formal education or a weak labour market attachment depend heavily on experience as a major source of occupational knowledge. Experience changes meaning as a consequence of new information technology, however. It is no longer enough to be experienced, but it becomes necessary to "have experiences": to recognize something new, to cope with uncertainty, to interpret and learn from experience (PAQ, 1987). This can be very threatening especially for people with few educational credentials. The recognition of previously acquired knowledge and skills is a prerequisite for further learning. Learning involves an investment of workers — hence it is essential that they also benefit.

Learner-worker interests can be defined in terms of income, quality of labour, and career opportunities. These are to be realized at the level of the company. The assessment and certification of skills which are acquired out of school is very important. As skills become increasingly broader and unspecific, the assessment of content and levels of skills gains in significance. This is especially true for practical skills, which, in many cases, were previously taken for granted. The lack of certification possibilities is seen as a major reason for underinvestment in learning on the job by workers.

Learning and learning to learn cannot be analyzed independently from actual contexts of jobs and occupations. This limits the value for vocational education of general concepts of learning skills (Smith, this volume), transfer skills (Nijhof and Remmers, 1989), self learning competency (Nyhan, 1991) or key qualifications (Reetz, 1989). It is necessary to analyze learning, and learning skills, in relationship to several dimensions of vocational skills.

Practical Competence

As previously mentioned, job competence involves three dimensions: tasks, task management, and job environment (Levy, 1987). These can also be referred to as task competence, methodical competence and social competence (Laur-Ernst, 1990; Kloas and Puhlmann, 1991). From a theoretical viewpoint task-related skills, which enable a worker to perform the job properly, seem to be the least problematic. Most analyzes of job competence concentrate on these skills, which are considered occupation-specific. On closer inspection things are not that simple, however. As previously stated many methods use a listing and adding approach, which tends to underplay important characteristics of practical competence (Moerkamp and Onstenk, 1991; Laur-Ernst, 1990). The definition of occupation itself leans on strict definitions of tasks and product outcomes. This is more straightforward in technical occupations compared with service occupations (Brater, 1987). So traditionally job analysis for technical occupations is more detailed and differentiated than for administrative or service occupations. The new paradigm leads to more emphasis on open task structures, flexibility, and problem solving in technical occupations (Laur-Ernst, 1990). New ways of determining practical competences in administrative and service occupations are needed (Benner, 1984; Buck, 1987).

Recent research based on activity theory and cognitive theory has contributed new views on the nature of practical competences. Raizen (1989, 1991), who gives an overview of research carried out in the United States, analyzes practical skills as a combination of declarative and procedural knowledge. Practical competence is characterized by a combination of a specific domain of knowledge with a specific organization of knowledge. It includes the capacity to use the environment in doing the job: tools and physical environment, other actors (supervisors, co-workers, clients), conceptual tools and the professional culture can contribute in coping with the key problems of work. But by using the environment, these skills are also learned. This is true for unskilled work (Scribner 1986) but also for learning processes in automation or complicated repair jobs (Raizen, 1991). Experts act immediately by recognizing complex problem situations. According to Raizen, effective workers can:

(a) simplify the task, using short cuts and developing least effort strategies;
(b) redefine, when necessary, externally defined problems into personally constituted problems;
(c) use flexible strategies as they depart from the literal framework and reorganize the assigned task to 'fit' with the available social, symbolic, technical and material resources at their disposal;
(d) develop tentative 'gap-closing' or intermediate solutions;
(e) collaborate to develop situated solutions, examine contradictions, explore procedural possibilities and discuss alternative solutions;
(f) produce accurate task completion solutions; and
(g) continue to develop competence (Raizen, 1989 p. 53).

Task oriented as well as social-communicative and learning aspects can be recognized in this description of an effective worker. As the "one best solution" approach of classic Taylorism loses its dominance this type of effective worker is increasingly in demand. This is also true for service and administrative jobs (Benner, 1984; Dreyfus and Dreyfus, 1986). This process can be accelerated by structuring learning tasks and fostering feedback and reflection.

Research findings suggest that it is not fruitful to limit analysis of skill requirements to directly task related skills. Attention must also be given to the development of competences and "action programmes which are objectively and subjectively necessary or desirable for accomplishing tasks and solving problems in the job" (Frei et al., 1984 p. 53). The concept of competence development (Engeström, 1986; Frei et al., 1984) defines competence in terms of its extension (which tasks); reflection (how complicated) and intention (which meaning). Both activity theory and cognitive science stress the importance of "core problems" (see below), such as taking decisions, considering different action possibilities, weighing up alternatives, not only as an essential characteristic of vocational competence, but also as an important way of learning. Theories on situated learning (Brown et al., 1989; Raizen, 1989; Scribner, 1986) and activity theory (Laur-Ernst, 1990) strongly suggest that learning through the work process itself is the best way to acquire this kind of work-related knowledge. Immanent learning processes of this kind are not structured by pedagogical settings in schools or training courses but by the actual activities in and by which people learn.

Situational Skills

Apart from practical competence, task management and organizational roles also require methodical and social competences (Laur-Ernst, 1990; Kloas and Puhlmann, 1991). For expert performance it is necessary to be able to handle the material, symbolic and social context in which skills and knowledge are to be used (De Jong et al., 1990). Learning processes imply acquiring these competences, including changes in the goals and intentions of work activities (Argyris and Schön, 1978). This is especially important in the modern company.

Different concepts are proposed in different countries. In Germany the concept of key qualifications (Reetz, 1989) has been the subject of a lively discussion, in which concepts like innovative qualifications (Fricke, 1975), situation-oriented social and strategic skills (Buck, 1989), and process knowledge (Laur-Ernst, 1990) are also proposed. In the Anglo-Saxon world these skills are discussed in terms of work place basics or essential skills (Carnevale et al., 1990a), core skills (Levy, 1987) or tacit skills (Manwaring and Wood, 1985). In the Netherlands both social-normative qualifications (Van Hoof and Dronkers, 1980) and Anglo-Saxon inspired concepts such as basic skills (Nijhof and Mulder, 1986) or transferable skills (Nijhof and Remmers, 1989) are advanced.

Some of these concepts remain within the realm of task-related skills, which are defined as broad and transferable because they are needed for or can be applied in different tasks and functions within or across occupational domains. These will be discussed further in the next section. Another group stresses the importance of organizational and social contexts of tasks and jobs: organizational, social, communicative, improvisational, strategic, emotional or interest-protecting qualifications. These approaches include processes of socialization and the development of attitudes or a vocational "habitus" (Windolf, 1986). The notion of broadly applicable occupational qualifications or situational skills, which is elaborated in this section, deals with these type of skills.

But first attention needs to be given to the situational dimension of core problems. The importance of such problems has already been briefly discussed.

Table 9.3 presents some characteristics of core problems. These occur regularly as part of occupational practice and are characteristic for the profession. Expert workers are expected to find efficient and effective approaches and solutions for the core problems of their job. The degree to which they can make decisions and choices and deliberately apply knowledge and skills determines the degree of expertise. Core problems refer to occupational situations in which complex problems are solved and in which the specific characteristics of the situation and the social context are of central importance. This implies uncertainty and the need to balance different, sometimes contradictory, considerations and interests. Changes in task structure as a consequence both of information technology and organizational renewal lead to greater occurrence and weight of core problems in a growing number of jobs. A distinction must be made between the level of complexity of tasks and the situational dimension of core problems.

Table 9.3. Characteristics of core problems

- Central to the occupation
- Complex combination of knowledge and skills
- Making decisions
- Coping with uncertainty
- Comparing and choosing among alternatives

Complexity refers to complexity of required activities, handling different kinds of information at the same time, recognizing different dimensions of a problem, possible contradictions, differences in importance, the need for deliberate reasoning and choices as part of the job or task itself.

Cognitive theories on complex or transfer skills (Nijhof and Remmers, 1989; Simons, 1990) refer mainly to this domain. These theories deal mainly with methods of improving the transition from partial observation and concrete training to more abstract and complex insights and procedures. Only marginal reference is made to social skills for handling conflicts.

Yet these aspects are of central importance in the "situational" dimension of labour activities in "real life" situations. Actual occupational practice is characterized by both strategic and social dimensions (Buck, 1989). Strategic action relates to task management and structure of regulation, inasmuch as these are characterized by a certain amount of internal and/or external regulation autonomy (De Sitter, 1986) or freedom of action (Frei et al., 1984). Each task and work environment is characterized by a degree, however small, of uncertainty, uniqueness or conflict (Buck, 1989). Action oriented towards people leads also to a certain amount of uncertainty and informality in tasks, especially in jobs in which social interaction is a part of occupational practice itself, because it involves "working with people", such as in the service professions (Buck, 1989).

The concept of broadly applicable skills distinguishes, following Buck (1989), two important levels of situational skills needed for effective performance in the work place: strategic effectiveness, and social and communicative performance. Strategic effectiveness involves problem-solving skills, organizational skills, versatility (multiskills and procedural knowledge), and leadership skills. Social performance refers to the social character of the work place, both as a working environment and a social context. It implies cooperative, communicative and cultural skills. Both strategic and social competence imply commitment and motivated activity. Table 9.4 distinguishes between strategic, social, and motivational dimensions of the work task.

Carnevale et al. (1990a, 1990b) carried out a large-scale research project on "the essential skills employers want". The authors distinguish seven categories of skills, of which the most important is "learning to learn". Table 9.5 indicates that these categories are not only remarkable because of their generality, but also because the skills are described and analyzed without reference to a specific set of tasks. This may make it difficult to see which group of workers is implicated. On some occasions the authors suggest that the entire labour force is involved, whereas in other places they explicitly refer to managers and professionals. Also the actual content of skills is not defined.

Table 9.4. Typology of situational skills

A. *Strategic effectiveness*
   Problem solving skills
   Organizational skills
   Versatility (multiskills; procedural knowledge)
   Leadership skills
   Methodical skills

B. *Social dimension*
   Cooperative skills
   Social-communicative skills
   Cultural skills

C. *Motives of activity*
   Professional attitudes
   Motivation, commitment
   Flexibility
   Responsibility, normativity
   Handling emotions, fear, uncertainty

Skills should be defined in terms of activities to be performed in a specific technological and organizational context. Thus "general" skills need to be specified for specific types of jobs. This need is recognized in Germany, where new occupational profiles refer not only to technical but also to social and methodical competences (Laur-Ernst, 1990). The same development can be seen in administrative and service occupations (Buck, 1987). Attempts are being made to include these skills in training programmes (Reetz, 1989; Kloas and Puhlmann, 1991). As a result of changes in organization, product quality, and consumer demands these skills also become more important for unskilled production workers, as can be seen from training programmes developed in Dutch industry, which concentrate on fostering communicative skills and enhancing motivation and responsibility, sometimes combined with technical skills.

Transferable and Transfer Skills

Practical, task-related competence and situational, methodical and social skills are required to perform a job. But, as stressed before, change and mobility in and between jobs is becoming the rule rather than the

Table 9.5. Work place basics

Learning to learn
The three R's: reading, writing, computation
Communication: listening and oral communication
Creative thinking and problem solving
Self-esteem; goal setting motivation; employability; career development
Interpersonal; negotiation; teamwork
Organizational effectiveness; leadership

Source: Carnevale et al. (1990a)

exception. The transition value of skills (development in time) is becoming more important on the labour market. This is reflected in the growing attention for concepts such as transferability of skills and transfer or transition skills (Moerkamp and De Bruijn, 1991). The distinction between these two notions is indicated in Table 9.6.

Table 9.6. Dimensions of transfer

Transferability of skills
    Application in different functions (within occupational domain)
    Transformation of skills (from one occupation to another)
    Recognition and accreditation

Transition/transfer skills
    Learning to learn
    De- and recontextualization
    Development of competence

Transferability of Skills

Transferability of skills refers to the application of skills in different functions within the same occupational domain, or to the transformation of skills from one occupation to another. Because skills are activity-related, it is necessary to distinguish between the use of skills in similar activities and the "transport" from skills from one occupation to another. Transferability depends on the applicability of skills in different functions (within a broad field of comparable functions). This requires transformation, including recognition of similarities and differences between functions. As stressed before, the lack of certification possibilities is seen as a major reason for underinvestment in learning on the job by workers: "Employees have no way to certify to prospective employers the general knowledge and skills they have acquired from previous employment. Skill and knowledge that is potentially transportable therefore is not transportable in fact" (Stern, 1990 p. 9).

In the United States there are some attempts on a local level to accredit prior experience, usually by portfolio techniques. In the United Kingdom the new system of National Vocational Qualifications establishes a sector-specific, nationwide solution for this problem (Jansen et al., 1990). The core skills project (Levy, 1987) also provides a useful tool for recognizing skills. The method is being applied to both assessment and selection procedures. The core skills project states as its central goal "linking learning to the work role". This includes the development of job competence at all three levels distinguished before: tasks, task management and job environment. Levy distinguishes a set of 113 core skills, divided in 13 groups and four kinds of skills: number, communication, problem solving and practical skills. These are summarized in Table 9.7.

Assessment and certification of experience-based knowledge and skills can be achieved by using an "experience chart" constructed from the core skills list. The list of 113 core skills is formulated so as to be able to function as a "common language" for comparing concrete skills from different fields. Just like cognitive scientists who recognize arithmetic or problem solving skills in the daily practices of warehouse workers, or copier repairers (Scribner, 1986; Raizen, 1989), the core skills project tries to identify skills in all kinds of experience and to translate them to required skills (Levy, 1987).

Transfer Skills

Transfer occurs only if the worker has specific skills which foster transfer. People need in most cases more than comparable skills to be able to use them in another work setting. In order to do so, they need to recognize them, to be able to perform complex processes of de-contextualization and recontextualization, and to be able to respond flexibly. This is in many respects what people refer to when they stress the necessity of learning to learn (see Nyhan, 1991).

It is relevant to distinguish transfer or transition skills from transferability of skills (Simons, 1990; Moerkamp and De Bruijn, 1991). Transfer or transition skills are skills which enable workers to transfer and use declarative and procedural skills, which they have learned, in

Table 9.7. The core skills list

Numeracy:
    operating with numbers
    interpreting numerical information
    measuring and marking
    recognizing cost and value

Communication:
    finding out information and interpreting instructions
    providing information
    working with people

Problem solving:
    planning: determining and revising courses of action
    decision making: choosing between alternatives
    monitoring: keeping track of progress and checking

Practical:
    preparing for a practical activity
    carrying out a practical activity
    completing a practical activity

Source: Levy (1987)

changing situations. It is not an inherent generality of skills which determines their transfer value, but the specific way in which the worker uses them. Transfer skills are directed to integration (integrating knowledge and skills to a personal "set"), self regulation, reflection, and generalization (Moerkamp and De Bruijn, 1991; De Corte, this volume).

The development of competence as defined in the activity approach can be described as a combination of transferability of skills and transfer skills. Competence is defined as a potential to perform a structured set of activities. The development is related to transfer and career development in and between functions and careers. Learning through core problems contributes not only to the development of practical competence and situational skills, but also to the development of transfer skills. By learning how to handle series of core problems, more general learning, problem solving and metacognitive skills are developed (Moerkamp and De Bruijn, 1991). People learn to deal with complexity, strategic thinking, contradictions and uncertainties (De Jong et al., 1990). They also learn to recognize patterns and differences in importance and urgency (see Benner, 1984; Brater, 1987).

Summary and Conclusions

Skills needed in the work place were analyzed in this chapter. It is proposed that jobs should be considered as competent activities in occupational practice, and that job competence is seen as including three dimensions: tasks, task management and job environment. Required skills are deducted from content and structure of tasks to be performed, which include skills needed to perform the task, to manage or regulate the task, and to perform the task in the organizational and social job context. This leads to a multidimensional interpretation of needed skills, which goes beyond the level of "technical" job-specific skills.

Three skill dimensions were discussed: practical competence, procedural and methodical skills; situational and social skills; and transfer skills. Their development is a challenge both to vocational education and companies. These skills can only be learned through cumulation of specific skills and by reflection on experience. This requires a specific structuring of experience and learning processes. Knowledge and skills should not be learned out of context. Practical learning should be a part of vocational curricula. Complex, procedural vocational qualifications can be effectively learned in other forms than traditional on-the-job-training, for example, in simulation or learning sites. Social and strategic situational skills are more bound to actual work settings. But students must also be helped to expand and generalize specific knowledge or to de- and recontextualize experience. To achieve this, in-school techniques and methods such as problem oriented teaching and learning; cooperative learning and self-directed learning can be very important, as is stimulating reflection on other experiences. To incorporate complex and situational skills in the curriculum, a growing integration of vocational and "general" subjects in vocational education is necessary. These skills cannot be described as general new goals for vocational education, but are to be connected to a new definition of vocational education, including new ways to teach and learn technical or administrative skills.

Developments directed towards integration should be supported, without breaking down this structural advantage. Vocational education should not be satisfied with teaching knowledge and "technical" skills, but should concentrate on preparing pupils and apprentices for competent action in occupational practice. To this end changes both in content and didactics are necessary. The contents should be structured according to key problems of occupational practice. Key problems can be handled better if the professional has broadly applicable qualifications. But also pupils and apprentices (and beginning professionals) learn these qualifications better by dealing with complex and realistic occupational problems. Didactic changes, on the other hand, should be directed at stimulating self directed learning, problem solving, problem formulation, and learning to learn

References

Argyris, Ch., & Schön, D.A. (1978). *Organizational learning: A theory of action perspective*. Reading, Massachusetts: Addison-Wesley.

Baitsch, C., & Frei, F. (1980). *Qualifizierung in der Arbeitstätigkeit*. Bern: Verlag Hans Huber.

Benner, P. (1984). *From novice to expert. Excellence and power in clinical nursing practice*. Menlo Park, California: Addison-Wesley.

Bomers, G.B.J. (1991). De lerende organisatie. In J. Peters et al. (Eds.), *Gids voor de opleidingspraktijk* (pp. 1-25). Houten, The Netherlands: Bohn, Stafleu and Van Loghum.

Brandsma, T.F., Nijhof, W.J., & Kamphorst, J.C. (1989). *Kwalificatie en curriculum. Een internationaal vergelijkende studie naar methoden voor de bepaling van kwalificaties*. Lisse, The Netherlands: Swets and Zeitlinger.

Brater, M. (1987). Dienstleistungsarbeit und berufliche Bildung. Thesen zur Problematik berufsförmig organisierter Dienstleistungsarbeit. In B. Buck (Ed.), *Berufsbildung in Dienstleistungsbereich* (pp. 9-20). Berlin: BIBB.

Brown, J.S., Collins, A., & Duguid, P. (1989). Situated cognition and the culture of learning. *Educational Researcher 18*, 32-40.

Buck, B. (Ed.) (1987). *Berufsbildung in Dienstleistungsbereich*. Berlin: BIBB.

Buck, B. (1989). Technologie oder Praxis? Berufsbildungsverständnis und seine Auswirkungen auf Vermittlungsformen. In BIBB (hgst.), *Neue Entwicklungen in den Kaufmännische Berufen* (pp. 213-220). Berlin und Nürnberg: BW Verlag GmbH.

Carnevale, A.P., Gainer, L.J., & Meltzer, A.S. (1990a). *Work place basics. The essential skills employers want*. San Francisco: Jossey Bass.

Carnevale, A.P., Gainer, L.J., & Villet, J. (1990b). *Training in America. The organization and strategic role of training*. San Francisco: Jossey Bass.

Christis, J. (1989). Arbeidsprocesdiscussie en sociotechniek. *Tijdschrift voor Arbeidsvraagstukken 5* (2), 43-59.

De Sitter, U. (1986). *Het flexibele bedrijf*. Deventer, The Netherlands: Kluwer.

Development Programme (1989). *Towards a learning organization*. Stockholm: SAF-LO-PTK Council and Swedish Employers Confederation.

Dore, R., & Sako, M. (1988). *How the Japanese learn to work*. London: Routledge.

Dreyfus, H.L., & Dreyfus, S. (1986). *Mind over machine: the power of human intuition and expertise in the era of the computer*. New York: Free Press.

Frei, F., Duell, W., & Baitsch, C. (1984). *Arbeit und Kompetenzentwicklung. Theoretische Konzepte zur Psychologie arbeitsimmanenter Qualifizierung*. Bern: Verlag Hans Huber.

Fricke, W. (1975). *Arbeitsorganisation und Qualifikation. Ein industriesoziologischer beitrag zur Humanisierung der Arbeit*. Bonn: Neue Gesellschaft GmbH.

Hoof, J.J. van (1991). Balanceren tussen prestaties en tegenprestaties. *Tijdschrift voor Arbeidsvraagstukken 7* (3), 56-63.

Hoof, J.J. van, & Dronkers, J. (1980). *Onderwijs en arbeidsmarkt*. Deventer, The Netherlands: Van Loghum Slaterus.

Jansen, J.E.M.B., Justino, R.C.M., & Dersjant, N.J. (Eds.) (1990). *Technological change and human resources development: The service sector*. Assen and Maastricht: Van Gorcum.

Jong, M. de, Moerkamp, T. Onstenk, J.H.A.M., & Babeliowsky, M. (1990). *Breed toepasbare beroepskwalificaties in leerplan en beroepspraktijk.* Amsterdam: SCO, University of Amsterdam.

Kloas, P.W., & Puhlmann, A. (1991). *Arbeit qualifiziert — aber nicht jede.* Berlin: BIBB.

Kochan, T.A., & Osterman, P. (1991). *Human resources development and utilization: Is there too little in the U.S.?* Report for the Time Horizons Project of the Council on Competitiveness. Cambridge, Massachusetts: MIT.

Laur-Ernst, U. (Ed.) (1990). *Neue Fabriksstrukturen — veränderte Qualifikationen.* Berlin: BIBB.

Levy, M. (1987). *The core skills project and work based learning.* London: FESC/MSC.

Leymann, H., & Kornbluh, H. (1989). *Socialization and the world of work.* Aldershot: Gower.

Manwaring, T., & Wood, S. (1985). The ghost in the labour process. In D. Knights, H. Willmott and D. Collinson (Eds.), *Job redesign* (pp. 171-196). Aldershot: Gower.

Mickler, O., Dittrich, E., & Neumann, U. (1976). *Technik, Arbeitsorganisation und Arbeit.* Frankfurt: Aspekte.

Moerkamp, T., & Bruijn, E. de (1991). *Transitievaardigheden in het onderwijs.* The Hague: OSA.

Moerkamp, T., & Onstenk, J.H.A.M. (1991). *Het ontwikkelen van beroeps- en opleidings-profielen.* Utrecht: RVE.

Nijhof, W.J., & Mulder, M. (1986). *Basisvaardigheden in het beroepsonderwijs.* Enschede: OCTO, University of Twente.

Nijhof, W.J., & Remmers, J.L.M. (1989). *Basisvaardigheden nader bekeken.* Enschede: OCTO, University of Twente.

Nyhan, B. (1991). *Developing people's ability to learn.* Brussels: Eurotecnet/EIP.

Onstenk, J.H.A.M. (1992a). *Deelname aan scholing door laag opgeleide werknemers.* Amsterdam: SCO, University of Amsterdam.

Onstenk, J.H.A.M. (1992b). *Leren en opleiden op de werkplek.* Utrecht: RVE.

Onstenk, J.H.A.M., Moerkamp, T., & Dronkers, J. (1990a). Broadly applicable vocational qualifications: A challenge for vocational education. Paper for the international experts conference on vocational education and training, Boekelo, The Netherlands.

Onstenk, J.H.A.M., Moerkamp, T., Voncken, E., & Van Den Dool, P.C. (1990b). *Leer-cessen in stages.* Amsterdam: SCO, University of Amsterdam.

PAQ (Projektgruppe Automation und Qualifikation) (1987). *Widersprüche der Automationsarbeit.* Berlin: Argument Verlag.

Raizen, S. (1989). *Reforming education for work: A cognitive science perspective.* Berkeley, California: National Centre for Research in Vocational Education.

Raizen, S. (1991). *Learning and work: The research base.* Paris: OECD.

Reetz, L. (1989). Zum Konzept der Schlüsselqualifikationen in den Berufsbildung. *BWP, 5/6,* pp. 3-10 and 4-10.

Romiszowski, A.J. (1981). *Designing instructional systems.* London: Kogan Page.

Scribner, S. (1986). Thinking in action: Some characteristics of practical thought. In R.Sternberg and R.K. Wagner (Eds.), *Practical intelligence: Nature and origins of competence* (pp. 13-30). Cambridge: Cambridge University Press.

Sierksma, R. (1991). *Toezicht en taak. Pragmatisme, Taylorisme en het beheer van arbeid.* Amsterdam: SUA.

Simons, P.R.J. (1990). *Transfervermogen.* Oratie. Nijmegen: University of Nijmegen.

Spenner, K.I. (1988). Technological change, skill requirements, and education: The case for uncertainty. In R.M. Cyert and D.C. Mowery (Eds.), *The impact of technological change on employment and economic growth* (pp. 131-184). Cambridge: Cambridge University Press.

Stern, D. (1990). U.S. employers' investment in human resources. In *Report of the conference "Investing in human resources: Adult education and training in the Netherlands"*, Amsterdam, December 10-11, 1990 (pp. 37 - 53) Utrecht: RVE.

Sternberg, R.J., & Wagner, R.K. (Eds.) (1986). *Practical intelligence: Nature and origins of competence in the everyday world.* Cambridge: Cambridge University Press.

Thijssen, J.G.L., & De Greef, I. (1989). Het leren van volwassenen: theorieën en grondprincipes. In J.W.M. Kessels and C.A. Smit (Eds.), *Handboek opleiders in organisaties* (pp. 97-117). Deventer, The Netherlands: Kluwer.

Windolf, P. (1986). *Berufliche Sozialisation. Zur Produktion des beruflichen Habitus.* Stuttgart: F. Enke Verlag.

Part 4

Learning to Learn in the Lifespan

Chapter 10

THEORIES AND PRINCIPLES OF LEARNING TO LEARN

P. ROBERT-JAN SIMONS
University of Nijmegen, The Netherlands

The subject of this chapter is learning to learn. A theory is presented concerning learning functions and media that can be fulfilled either by teachers, books, or computers, or by the students themselves. From the viewpoint of learning to learn it matters who initiates and controls the learning functions. Interaction among teachers, expert systems, and adult learners influences the development of thinking and learning skills. In many situations, however, the desired patterns of interaction do not occur. If the goal is to increase the number of people who know and can apply the principles of learning how to learn then the fostering of learning skills and habits should form part of all teaching and learning situations. The main purpose of this chapter is to discuss some principles of an integrated approach to learning to learn.

Learning Functions

Shuell (1988) has defined learning functions as psychological functions to be performed by the learner. In his view it is not so much how the function is performed that is important, but that it is accomplished. There are, for instance, different ways of attracting the attention of students: by physically pointing, by using different colours, or by means of a verbal prompt. Furthermore, learning functions can be initiated by the teacher or by the learner. Expectations concerning learning outcomes, for example, can be specified by the teacher through instructional objectives or they can be initiated by the learner. Shuell distinguishes between 10 functions: expectations, attention, encoding, comparison, hypothesis generation, repetition, feedback, evaluation, monitoring, and what is termed "combination/integration synthesis".

Shuell's ideas considerably resemble those developed in this chapter. As can be seen from Table 10.1, his list of functions overlaps with our categorization of self-regulatory abilities. Expectation and attention correspond to our preparatory abilities. Encoding, comparison, hypothesis generation, repetition and combination/integration synthesis come close to our notion of learning steps to be achieved. Feedback, of course, corresponds to our performance and feedback category. Evaluation and monitoring fit into our regulation processes category.

Table 10.1. List of learning functions

Main Category	Subcategories	Shuell's category
1 Preparation of learning	orientation on goals and action	Expectation
	choice of goals	---
	relevance of goals	Expectation
	self-confidence	Expectation
	planning of learning activities	---
	motivating students to learn	---
	getting started	attention
	getting attention	attention
	recalling prior learning	---
2 Learning steps	comprehension	encoding
	integration	comparison/repetition hypothesis generation combination/integration synthesis
	application	---
3 Regulation processes	monitoring	evaluation/monitoring
	testing	evaluation/monitoring
	revision	---
	reflection	---
	evaluation	---
4 Performance judgement and feedback	feedback	feedback
	judgement	---
5 Motivation and concentration management	---	---

Even though the two approaches show some agreements, there are some important differences too. It can be inferred from Table 10.1 that our list may be more comprehensive and more differentiated than Shuell's categorization of learning functions. In our system the two phases of learning (i.e. before and during the activity) are better distinguished. Our system also accomodates the motivational, volitional and emotional aspects of learning to a greater extent (cf. Paris, 1988; Keller and Kopp, 1986). On the other hand, the concept of learning function seems useful and can easily be incorporated in our approach. Therefore, Table 10.1 presents the learning functions considered to be essential elements of any learning situation.

Table 10.2. Examples of the categories, when initiated by the teachers

Category	Teacher action:
Orientation on goals and actions	Presents information on goals
Choice of goals	Chooses goals for students
Relevance of goals	Explains why goals are relevant
Self-confidence	Reassures students that the goals are within their reach
Planning of learning activities	Chooses learning activities and their sequence
Motivating students to learn	Makes learning appear interesting, for example through story telling
Getting started	Gives the sign to start
Getting attention	Attracts students' attention through voice raising
Recalling prior learning	Gives an overview of prior learning that has relevance
Comprehension	Presents information in a structured way
Integration	Relates new information to old; presents a scheme
Application	Demonstrates how one can apply a certain principle in practice
Monitoring	Observes whether students understand
Testing	Poses a question
Revision	Presents information a second time in a new way
Reflection	Tells students why they learned in a certain way
Evaluation	Judges the process of learning
Feedback	Gives feedback on student response
Judgement	Judges students performance
Motivation	Promises a reward
Concentration management	Stimulates students to keep on

Table 10.3. Examples of the categories, when initiated by learners

Category:	Learner action:
Orientation on goals and actions	Thinks of possible goals and activities
Choice of goals	Chooses personal learning goals
Relevance of goals	Realizes why goals are relevant
Self-confidence	Is self-confident; promotes self-confidence
Planning of learning activities	Plans and chooses learning activities
Motivating students to learn	Is motivated to learn; promotes motivation
Getting started	Has an adequate starting strategy
Getting attention	Pays attention
Recalling prior learning	Recalls prior learning
Comprehension	Reads, listens, analyzes
Integration	Relates, makes a scheme
Application	Applies to a new situation, thinks of possible applications
Monitoring	Consults feeling of knowing
Testing	Paraphrases in order to test compehension
Revision	Tries a new strategy
Reflection	Thinks of possible reasons for succeeding this time
Evaluation	Evaluates the process of learning
Feedback	Uses external feedback possibilities
Judgement	Judges own performance
Motivation	Thinks of future rewards
Concentration management	Takes a break

The learning functions indicated in Table 10.1 can be initiated and accomplished either by the teacher or by the learner. Table 10.2 presents examples of actions initiated by the teacher and shows how these correspond to the main categories of the theoretical model. Table 10.3 lists similar examples indicating how various actions initiated by adult learners may fit in with the model.

There is of course a third possibility, namely of shared control of teachers and students. In this case the teachers will give specific assignments in order to give meaning to the various learning functions. An example of this type of learning activation is when teachers ask students to choose some learning goals from a list of possible goals, or when they ask students to study a given text in a specified way, for example, using paraphrasing or underlining.

The examples listed in Table 10.3 constitute learner initiations of the learning functions. These can occur in all kinds of teaching-learning situations. In some, however, they occur more readily than in others. If teachers fully control the activation of the learning functions, then the students will be less active than when they are given opportunities for self-regulation. When teachers do not assume responsibility for one or more of the functions, then the students are forced to do it on their own. Formulated somewhat differently, the categories presented in Table 10.3 can be seen as the skills and habits of self-regulated or independent learning. Thus independent learning skills comprise, for instance, the ability to think about learning goals and activities, the capacity to choose learning goals, and to understand the relevance of these goals.

Interaction Among Teachers and Students

Shuell (1988) stated that it does not matter who fulfils the learning functions discussed above as long as they are adequately fulfilled. On this point one may disagree. Although it is true that all of the functions should indeed be accomplished in one way or the other, it does matter who is the initiator. This may not be so important in the short as the long run. If teachers initiate and control all of the learning functions, then students will not learn how to fulfil them on their own. They will rely on teachers more and more. They will even come to believe that teachers are persons who are there to make you learn: to motivate you, to inform you, to give you assignments and to control and evaluate your learning. In other words, if teachers initiate and control all of the learning functions, then students may come to believe that this is the only feasible division of tasks between teachers and learners, and that their role in learning is a passive one. They do not develop their independent learning skills and they will not be able to fulfil the learning functions independently. It is our experience that interactive patterns in many schools, including the institutions catering for adult students, are organized so that teachers are the principal initiators and controllers of almost all activities that are of relevance to learning. Therefore many people, and especially those adults who have a negative recollection of their previous encounter with school, develop passive ideas about learning in line with the examples discussed above.

The interaction among teachers and students can also be examined from a teacher's perspective (cf. Larsson 1983). On a theoretical level many teachers believe that it is important to teach students how to learn independently. In one of our studies over 80 per cent of a group of teachers agreed with statements that independent learning is an important goal to be achieved. Many teachers also attempt to draw upon independent learning abilities, at least now and then. However, more often than not they become disappointed in the results of these endeavours, since many students apparently are not able to fulfil the necessary learning functions on their own. This is a result of the ideas about learning that adults develop in school situations. The teaching-learning processes commonly used in school inhibit the development of independent learning abilities, or the students unlearn how to apply them. If schools do not offer the opportunity to practise these skills, and students come to believe that they are no longer needed, then this development does not come as a surprise. Teachers tend to find a rather curious solution to this problem. Instead of trying actively to teach their students how to learn, they are more likely to decide that learning can be optimalized if they take full control of the situation and fulfil most of the learning functions themselves.

In school situations, then, few students are taught how to learn. Yet many students master the principles of how learning can be accomplished. In a recent study, Leseman (1989) concluded that children learn these skills not in school but through interactions with adults that largely take place before they even attend school. Some children, especially those coming from homes with low socioeconomic status, do not learn how to think and learn independently. This finding has led some authors to conclude that parental training programmes are the only solution. In this chapter this conclusion is challenged on several grounds, although it is agreed that small-scale interactions with experts are indeed very important for the development of thinking and learning skills in children. This has been shown by experimental studies carried out by, for instance, Palincsar and Brown (1984), Scardamalia et al. (1984) and Schoenfeld (1985).

We disagree, however, with the conclusions drawn as to the necessity of parental training. First, the studies mentioned above are all performed in school settings. Thus the interactive patterns among adults and students that are conducive to learning to learn can also take place in school, and these interactions can have lasting effects. Secondly, we can not conclude from the fact that certain patterns between teachers and students fail to occur, that they can not be organized in schools. Aarnoutse (1989) and Moely et al. (1986) show that only a very small portion of school time and energy is devoted to learning to think and learning to learn. When teachers do not even try then they cannot expect to achieve the desired results. Finally, it cannot be concluded from the fact that certain interactive patterns which occur in families when children are very young have lasting effects, that these interactions cannot and will not take place again at a later stage in the lifespan. It is our belief that interaction between parents and children concerning homework, motivation to learn, and so on, which occur when children are between about seven and 14 years of age, are as important as adult-child interaction during early childhood. Moreover, interactions between experts and novices are important for all learners. Relevant research is scarcely available, however. Consequently it is not known whether schools can and should aim at organizing the relevant interactive patterns.

In conclusion, many people do not learn how to learn because the necessary interactive patterns do not occur during early childhood. Moreover, schools fail in compensating for this handicap because the interactive patterns between teachers and students, which are discussed above, inhibit learning to learn. However, there is some evidence that the required patterns can be organized in school settings, even at a late age, and that this can be effective.

Aspects of Teaching How to Learn

From the perspective of lifelong learning it seems very important that as many people as possible will develop the skills of independent learning. It is of course impossible to educate all adults who want or need to change in some respects in the same way school-aged children are educated. Hence new ways of fostering learning to learn have to be found, both in school and subsequently. The following ideas may be helpful in this respect.

First, it is important that all teaching and learning situations be evaluated in terms of the short- and long-term consequences they may have for the development of independent learning skills. A second challenge is to agree on a set of essential learning skills that may be focussed on. The categories listed in Table 10.3 may be considered a starting point. A third aspect is to define the goal of imparting learning skills in a developmental context. The position at present seems to be that children forget the independent learning skills they mastered in elementary school once they attend secondary school. It needs to be established when children should be able to fulfil certain learning functions on their own and at a specified level. Our approach to teaching and learning should be adjusted accordingly.

An important implication of the discussion so far is that individuals are never too old to learn how to learn. Hence it is not entirely fair to blame the school for failing to instill the appropriate learning skills in their students, since adults can acquire these skills as well. It may be more difficult to foster independent learning skills in older adults, in part because they have already developed fixed ideas that may be in the way of independent learning. Yet this is no excuse for not trying. Finally, it means that attempts should be made to organize educative situations in such a way that emphasis is put on those interactive patterns between teachers and learners that are known from research to be important for the development of independent thinking and learning skills

An Approach to Teaching How to Learn

Some general principles constituting a teaching how to learn approach are presented in the paragraphs that follow. Two general features characterize this approach. First, it takes both existing learning skills and habits as well as a developmental perspective as its two main points of departure. Second, it attempts to reach both domain specific learning goals and goals associated with learning to learn. This means calling upon the learning skills and habits that are available to children and adults, and providing opportunities to practise them. A next step can be taken only after new skills and habits have developed. In this way the vicious circle discussed before can be broken.

The principles constituting a teaching how to learn approach can be divided in two sets. First there are four principles that concern the way learning should proceed in ideal cases. Shuell (1988) formulated this as follows:

> ... learning is an active, constructive, cumulative and goal directed process.... . It is *active* in that new information must be elaborated and related to other information in order for the student to retain simple information and to understand complex material. It is *cumulative* in that all new learning builds upon and/or utilizes the learner's prior knowledge in ways that determine what and how much is learned. It is *goal oriented* in that learning is most likely to be successful if the learner is aware of the goal (at least in a general sense toward which he or she is working and possesses expectations that are appropriate for attaining the desired outcome (Shuell, 1988, pp. 277-278).

Then there is a set of principles that prescribe how one can organize learning to learn or, in other words, how the learning of students can be made more active, cumulative, constructive, goal-directed and diagnostic.

Four Principles for Successful Learning

1. Activity principle
Instruction is designed in such a way that there is an optimal balance between the quality and quantity of learning activity.

One aspect of learning skill that is stressed by many researchers is that it should be active. Students should think while learning, they should make decisions about their learning, and so on. Thus in instruction that aims to develop learning-to-learn behaviour, opportunities should be given for active learning by the students themselves. Nobody, however, can be active all the time. Therefore, an adequate balance should be found between more active and more passive learning periods. It is in other words not the quantity of learning activity (such as the amount of effort), but its quality (e.g., the kind of questions posed, or the way one is active) that counts (see also Corno and Snow, 1986).

2. Constructivist principle
Higher cognitive learning goals requiring deep processing are stressed.

Instead of memorization and learning by heart, constructive learning is stimulated. Students are encouraged to think while learning and to find meaningful relations (cf. Simons, 1992; Simons and Verschaffel, 1992). Some of the techniques that can be used to develop constructive learning in students are: posing higher level questions, discussing memory organization, activating all kinds of integration processes, helping students to find memory aids, stimulating problem solving, and contextualizing learning by relating knowledge and skills to possibilities for application.

3. Cumulativity principle
New subject matter becomes anchored to existing preknowledge and pre-conceptions of students.

Relations between the information to be learnt and the existing preconceptions of students should be stressed and students should be activated to search for these relations themselves (see De Klerk et al. 1991).

4. Goal principle
The students know what they are learning and why it is considered important.

In many school situations students do not know why they have to learn certain information or skills. This is neither good for motivation nor for learning to learn. Instead, learning should be functional in the sense that students are informed of its short- and/or long-term relevance. Students should know where there are going and why (see also Shuell, 1988; De Klerk, 1990).

Nine Principles for Learning to Learn

1. Process principle
Learning activities and processes are stressed instead of learning outcomes.

Because students should learn the thinking and learning skills at the same time as they are using them, they should receive explicit attention. The covert processes of learning and thinking should become overt. This can happen at all phases of learning (the embedding approach) or afterwards, when looking back at the learning process (the immersion approach). The advantage of the immersion approach is that less confusion and interference will occur (Prawat, 1991).

2. Reflectivity principle
Learning is "thematized" and students become aware of learning strategies, self-regulation skills, and their relations to the learning goals.

One reason why learning skills and habits do not develop is because they are taken for granted. Students do not think about learning. They automatically tend to assume that everybody learns in the same way and that there is only one way to learn. Students can be expected to learn how to learn only if they are aware of and can think about the different forms of learning, the various learning goals and the several ways to reach these goals.

3. Affectivity principle
The interaction of cognitive, metacognitive and affective/motivational aspects is central.

Learning as a process is closely connected to personality. It is related to self-concept (of ability). People have fears of changing their learning approach. Learning can give rise to stress. We cannot change peoples' cognitions and metacognitions when we do not take their emotions, motivations, and desires into account.

4. Transfer principle
Explicitly one strives for transfer and generalization, without expecting these to occur without practice in a concrete context.

Learning skills and habits, like other skills and habits, will not automatically transfer from one situation to another. Many studies on the phenomenon of transfer have made clear that spontaneous transfer is rare, but that it is possible to reach it when adequate measures are taken (Simons and Verschaffel, 1992). This means that learning skills and habits learned in one situation or domain will not automatically be used in another situation or domain. They should be practised and integrated in different situations and domains. Separate learning-to-learn courses cannot be expected to be successful in the absence of curriculum led appointments for transfer and generalization.

5. Context principle
Learning skills and habits are practised regularly, during longer times and in context.

One persistent misconception is that learning skills and habits can be learnt easily. It takes a long time to change one's way of learning. Therefore these changes can only be expected to occur if regular education (and feedback) are given in a context in which the learning skills can be used or contexts that closely resemble such actual use.

6. Self-diagnostic principle
Students are taught how they can regulate, diagnose and revise their own learning.

As may be clear from Table 10.3 an important part of independent learning refers to self-regulation and self-diagnosis by students. Thus, self-regulatory skills such as comprehension-monitoring, self-testing, and the revision of learning strategies should also be practised and taught.

7. Scaffolding principle
The responsibility for learning is gradually shifted to the students.

This is perhaps the most important, but also most difficult principle of all. To break the vicious circle that characterizes many teaching and learning interactions, it is essential that students should receive opportunities to develop their learning and self-regulation skills, and that these are called upon when the students reach a sufficient level of learning and self-regulation expertise. Hence the teachers should attempt to construct scaffolds that allow the students to bear responsibility for their own learning. On these learning platforms new scaffolds can be based that eventually will also make other levels reachable.

8. Supervision principle
There are, especially in the case of younger students, good cooperation with parents and others about the supervision of self-regulated learning and thinking activities.

Many adults are involved in guiding the learning of primary and secondary students. Over and above the parents there may be up to 20 different teachers and support staff. If these do not communicate and co-operate in guiding the growth of learning and self-regulation skills (as is often the case, especially in secondary education), students are bound to get confused and to follow their own course. Often this will mean adhering to old habits and skills. Developing learning and self-regulation skills and habits in students therefore asks for effective cooperation and communication between the various actors involved.

9. Cooperation principle
Cooperation and discussions between students, closely supervised by experts, form essential ingredients of instruction.

As stated previously in this chapter certain small-scale interactive patterns between students and adults or experts are very important for the development of learning and thinking skills. By observing the strategies and ways of thinking of other students, teachers, and adults, students can learn how to go about it, and what is essential By discussing these strategies and procedures with peers and adults in small-scale interactions, students are given a chance to compare their approaches with those of others and practise new skills in a guided learning situation. Research shows that reciprocal teaching is effective in this respect (Palincsar and Brown, 1984). The teacher and a small group of students take turns in executing the role of the teacher when discussing and practising thinking and learning skills.

Conclusions

The main argument put forward in this chapter is that learning to learn is an important topic, not only for children but also for adult learners. Learning and thinking skills can develop spontaneously in small-scale interactions between adults (mostly parents) and children even before children enter schools. This does not mean, however, that it is not possible to learn learning and thinking skills within the teaching learning context and at later ages. Learning and thinking skills can be learned within a school-like context, but this asks for a new didactical approach. Such an approach is important for learners of all ages. Even many adult learners are not able to fulfil all of the learning functions themselves. On the one hand this has to do with their school experiences; on the other hand it is because even adult educators do not always aim for independent learning by students themselves. Some may believe that it is too late for learning and thinking skills to develop. Others may think that these skills develop automatically given adequate opportunities for independent learning and thinking.

Adult educators should realize that the best short-term solutions for educational problems are often detrimental for long-term effects on learning and thinking skills. Moreover, they should realize that there is a need for more than just opportunities to learn or think independently. Learning to learn and think asks for an integrated approach with an emphasis on the division of tasks between teachers and learners and on a gradual shift from teaching to learning, giving students responsibility for their own learning when they are ready to bear it. The 13 principles presented above may help teachers in devising learning environments that build the necessary scaffolds that learners need.

This is only possible when interactive patterns between teachers and students change. Typically, teachers fill in the missing learning functions they believe their students cannot handle on their own. By doing this, however, they achieve perhaps short-term effects, but they fail to develop the necessary learning and thinking skills. Learning to learn thus involves the pursuit of two goals at the same time: aiming for the normal learning goals, and aiming for learning-to-learn type of goals. This chapter has contributed some insights into the kinds of learning and thinking skills that may be important as well as into a possible didactic approach.

References

Aarnoutse, C. (1989). Reading comprehension instruction: Where is it and how to improve it. Paper presented at the Third European Conference on Research on Learning and Instruction, September 4-7, Madrid.

Corno, L., & Snow, R.E. (1986). Adapting teaching to individual differences among learners. In M.C. Wittrock (Ed.), *Handbook of research on teaching, third edition* (pp. 605-629). New York: MacMillan.

De Klerk, L.F.W. (1990). Een metacognitieve benadering van de doelstellingen-problematiek in het onderwijs. [A metacognitive approach of the problem of instructional objectives]. *Pedagogisch Tijdschrift, 15*, 152-161.

De Klerk, L.F.W., Ali, K.S., & Simons, P.R.J (1991). Activating preconceptions through a computer assisted strategy. Paper presented at the fourth Meeting of the European Association for Research on Learning and Instruction, August 23-29, Turku, Finland.

Keller, J.M., & Kopp, T.W. (1986). An application of the ARCS model of motivational design. In: C.M. Reigeluth (Ed.), *Instructional theories in action* (pp. 289-320). Hillsdale, New Jersey: Erlbaum.

Larsson, S. (1983). Paradoxes in teaching. *Instructional Science, 12*, 355-365.

Leseman, P.P.M. (1989) *Structurele en pedagogische determinanten van school-loopbanen [Structural and didactic determinants of school careers]*. Rotterdam: Schooladviesdienst.

Moely, B.E., Hart, S.S., Santulli, K., Leal, L., Johnson, T., Rao, N., & Burney, L. (1986). How do teachers teach memory skills? *Educational Psychologist, 21*, 55-71.

Palincsar, A.S., & Brown, A.L. (1984). Reciprocal teaching of comprehension-fostering and comprehension-monitoring activities. *Cognition and Instruction, 1*, 117-175.

Paris, S. (1988). Fusing skill and will: The integration of cognitive and motivational psychology. Paper presented to the Annual Meeting of the American Educational Research Association, New Orleans, April 5-9.

Prawat, R. (1991). The value of ideas: The immersion approach to the development of thinking. *Educational Researcher, 20*, 3-10.

Scardamalia, M., Bereiter C., & Steinbeck, R. (1984). Teachability of reflective processes in written composition. *Cognitive Science, 8*, 173-190.

Schoenfeld, A.H. (1985). *Mathematical problem solving*. New York: Academic Press.

Shuell, T.J. (1988). The role of the student in learning from instruction. *Contemporary Educational Psychology, 13*, 276-295.

Simons, P.R.J. (1992). Constructive learning: The role of the learner. In T. M. Duffy and D.H. Jonassen (Eds.) *The design of constructive learning environments: implications for instructional design and the use of technology*. New York: Springer Verlag.

Simons, P.R.J., & Verschaffel, L. (1992). Transfer: onderzoek en onderwijs. *Tijdschrift voor onderwijsresearch, 17*, 3-16.

Chapter 11

IMPLEMENTING THE LEARNING TO LEARN CONCEPT

ROBERT M. SMITH
Northern Illinois University, U.S.A.

This chapter begins with a synthesis of some of the existing knowledge concerning the concept and process of learning to learn. The effective learner is described as active and self-aware, in possession of a variety of learning strategies, knowledgeable about resources for learning, and capable of accurate self-monitoring and reflection on learning experience. It is concluded, however, that current programming and instruction at all levels of education inadequately contribute to the acquisition of such dispositions and capacities. Yet research and development have yielded sufficient information concerning learning to learn to warrant making the systematic pursuit of helping people to develop and improve their abilities, dispositions, and strategies for learning, a major goal of education at all ages. Many of the facilitative strategies and resources for enhancing learning effectiveness are proving suitable for children as well as young and older adults.

Developments Relevant to Learning to Learn

In recent years several developments have fueled a great deal of interest in learning to learn. Vast increases in knowledge production prompted interest in efficiency in learning. Rapid acceleration of social change made lifelong education a necessity. Issues of school reform and educational accountability came to the fore in many nations. A proliferation of institutional forms and delivery systems occurred, each requiring contextual learning strategies. Group dynamics research and applications demonstrated the feasibility of training in collaborative learning strategies (Benne, 1975). Naturalistic inquiry demonstrated the utility of investigating learning and learning to learn as interrelated processes. Research in student learning and metacognition provided a conceptual basis for efforts to increase learning effectiveness in secondary and higher education. Investigations of self-planned learning yielded useful information for enhancing self-directedness in learning and improving the quality of personal learning projects (Knowles, 1975). The business and corporate world came to value employee learning ability as a resource for increasing flexibility and productivity.

The Learning to Learn Concept

Much is now known about how people experience learning and the foundations of competence in learning. Relationships between teaching, learning, and learning to learn are becoming clearer. The central importance of context in learning to learn has been demonstrated. And numerous useful approaches and resources for appropriate facilitation and training have been developed. Learning to learn involves the acquisition and facilitation of dispositions, capacities, and strategies for learning effectively whatever the setting and context.

Learning to learn represents a complex, multifaceted concept, involving intrapersonal and interpersonal processes and strategies, and training intervention processes and strategies. It is a developmental process — a matter of becoming rather than being — when one, for example, learns to set more realistic learning goals, or cope with anxiety, or read text for in-depth understanding. Instruction, learning, and learning to learn are inextricably bound together. As we learn, we learn how to learn, and often how not to learn. People can be set up for failure when curriculum or instruction call for strategies that they lack and are not supported in obtaining.

Generic Foundations of Competence

The foundations for learning effectively include self-awareness and the ability to accurately monitor and usefully reflect on learning-related activity and experience. Self-aware people exhibit knowledge of their learning style — characteristic ways of feeling, behaving, and processing information in learning situations. They are sensitive to their motives, strategies, and goals for learning. They tend to know what they know and can reasonably expect to learn. They are aware of personal myths concerning education and learning and some of the ingrained principles and rules that govern their study and learning-directed behaviour, and of the distinction between learning to learn and learning to be taught.

Self-aware learners exhibit sophisticated conceptions of learning and of knowledge. They have come to the awareness that to learn something may be variously to memorize pieces of information, to acquire knowledge for practical application, to abstract meaning from experience, or even represent an interpretive process directed to understanding reality. An elaborated concept of knowledge acknowledges that more than one solution to a problem may be correct and that several conflicting themes may have utility. It is important to understand that there are different histories or psychologies and that one has a right (obligation?) to question official knowledge — and that knowledge can be played with, scaffolded, and integrated through mental models, conceptual frameworks, principles, and metaphor. Finally, it is useful to know that one possesses personal knowledge in the form of intuitions, insights, dreams, and fantasies that have content that can be validated through rational processes.

Awareness, monitoring and reflection interact and inform one another. As we engage in learning-directed behaviour we monitor ourselves for physical responses (muscle tension, fatigue), and psychosocial factors (anxiety, blocks). Effective self-monitoring also requires paying attention to such matters as comprehension, progress and the utility of learning resources and strategies. It is the "quality of our reflection" (Boud et al., 1985) that determines the extent to which we gain the insights for improving learning performance (Mezirow, 1990). We may reflect on a specific learning task or event or on larger amounts of educational experience. When reflecting on a specific event, we tend to extract instrumental inferences related to similar upcoming events (e.g., "I need to read the examination questions twice before I begin to write" or "I need to listen more actively"). When large blocks of experience are involved — a professional conference or workshop, the first year of college — reflection will often have major financial and career implications as well as effects on motivation or confidence for further learning (Smith, 1990).

Experience, instruction, and training that directly or indirectly support these foundations of effective learning are especially valuable.

Contextual Considerations

Recent research has confirmed that context impacts learning to learn more than was formerly apparent and precludes the possibility of providing people with generic training that yields adequate understandings and strategies for all occasions of learning and, of course, all life stages. Two major contexts are institutional setting and subject matter.

Each subject area represents a particular, often formidable, challenge to the learner. It has its "grammar of study", particular norms, principles, academic methods of discourse and analysis that tend to involve characteristic ways of thinking. Mathematics and science emphasize problem solving; economics and philosophy require analytical thinking; the arts stress imagination and creativity. Methods of teaching can be said to represent modes of thinking that become part of the content learned. Approaches to curriculum and instruction reflect a wide variety of emphases: problem solving, inquiry, critical thinking, competition, negotiation, democratic process, experiential discovery, imaging, behaviour modification, self-understanding. In the context of a course or subject, the individual must accommodate to the nature of the content, the instructional methods employed, and the ways of demonstrating what is learned. In many respects it is the instructor who is best positioned to assist in enhancing learning abilities, although few instructors have the requisite interest and preparation to take full advantage of this opportunity.

In addition to schools and colleges, people obviously learn in and through participation in such institutions as home, church, club, work place, labour union, prison, and professional association. Successful implementation of learning-to-learn activity in an organization is aided by identifying how the organization affects learning opportunities, the climate for learning, desired learning outcomes as well as people's development as effective learners. Certain competencies and strategies stand out as especially desirable or essential and often in need of enhancement if the individual is to learn effectively in a given context.

Young Children

For the young child a learning-to-learn perspective sees the home, club and school as environments in which to explore interests, to begin to develop self-discipline, and collaborate with peers. An accepting but stimulating climate that encourages self-expression and active learning needs to be maintained. The development of a spirit of inquiry and openness to knowledge can begin. Activeness in learning can be encouraged, along with the ability to "make connections" and apply what is learned. It is not too early to introduce personal goal-setting and self-managed learning projects. While basic subjects are important, they are not more important than laying the foundations for school-based and out-of-school learning. Parent-teacher cooperation is believed to be almost essential. In the literature, elementary school teachers and parents are encouraged to think aloud and to model strategic thinking. Upper-level elementary students can be involved in concept mapping and the keeping of learning diaries.

Secondary Education

Here education is seen as an environment to build on the initiatives of early childhood, to foster genuine intellectual inquiry, and, of course, to acquire basic knowledge in a variety of academic subjects. A growing number of theorists see it as an excessively competitive environment focussed on reproduction by the student of the information presented: the "bitting" of information and standardized testing. Learning-to-learn applications include compensatory training for inadequate metacognitive skills and learning disabilities, helping students accept greater personal responsibility for learning, and the acquisition and refinement of self-management strategies (Hunter, 1985).

Recently, a "thinking curriculum" has been proposed as an alternative or supplement to the prevailing curriculum that seeks to cover ever-expanding amounts of traditional subject matter and evaluate this with the help of standardized tests. Here the emphasis is often on challenging students through action and reflection projects, goal setting, cooperation in learning (Slavin, 1983), self- and criterion-referenced evaluation, linking school-based and out-of-school learning, and facilitating the transition from secondary school to higher education or work. So-called interactive teaching that focusses on meaning and understanding is recommended. The teacher tries to lead learners to the limits of their knowledge and find aspects of the subject that are especially interesting and meaningful. The teacher helps the student to understand the structures of knowledge, to interact with it, and to anchor new knowledge in prior knowledge. The teaching and learning of concepts and principles and the examination of issues becomes important and the retention of details becomes somewhat less important than learning how to access them (Biggs, 1987; Nisbet and Schucksmith, 1986).

Higher Education

Learning in the higher education setting has been compared to trying to drink from a fire hose: a figure of speech that suggests colleges and universities are by far the most content centered (and least learning and learning-to-learn centered) of the formal education environments (Cell, 1984). In many instances they do constitute highly competitive, impersonal environments with little support for the learner with problems beyond what might be available from the odd instructor and an under-funded student development office. But a growing number of institutions are beginning to do more. Responses range from comprehensive, institution-wide efforts to provide support for the student from entry to graduation to more modest undertakings in the form of initial orientation experiences for undergraduates, or elective courses on study strategies (Schlossberg et al., 1989).

Getting through college and university requires a relatively high level of basic self-management skills, the ability to adapt to different teaching styles and subjects, and such survival skills as coping with examination anxiety. Getting the most from the experience requires competence in understanding complex content and being able to use the entire institution as a resource for learning. One recent development is the introduction of academic support services into postgraduate professional programmes, including medicine and pharmacy; among the methodological innovations are problem-based learning, contract learning, and mentoring by volunteer peers and faculty (Knowles, 1986).

Work Place

The work place now enjoys considerable attention as a learning environment. Problem solving and direct application of what is learned seem to lie at the heart of "work place learning". Individuals and groups learn on the job; the entire organization can be said to learn as well. Almost every organization has a stake in problem solving, accommodating to change, and renewal. Many organizations invest heavily in on- and off-site training and education (Carnevale et al., 1990).

The concepts of action learning, organizational learning, and the learning organization have emerged to help provide a theoretical basis for thinking and activity concerning learning to learn in this context. One writer has suggested adapting the learning-to-learn concept to the no-nonsense environment of corporate life by labeling it "learning management", a term presumed less likely to suggest a potentially costly frill (Cheren, 1987). He sees learning to learn applications in the work place as processes to be built into the formal training activities (e.g., enhancing strategies required for a training course) and, perhaps more important, a dimension of day-to-day-activity. Human resource and training professionals are urged to take the lead in improving problem solving by individuals and work-station groups (Barrows and Tamblyn, 1980), establishing in-house learning resource centres, supporting the employee's personal development plans, and designing record keeping and evaluation systems that credit and reward informal and formal efforts to learn.

Action learning is an approach that involves problem solving, alternating episodes of action and critical reflection, and the examining of norms and assumptions. It focusses on real life problems and consequences (Marsick, 1987). Effective organizational (or "double-loop") learning requires training people to be willing to acknowledge uncertainty, admit error, respond to the future, and acquire such skills as listening, problem posing, and nurturing (Bennis and Nanus, 1985). Less demanding learning-to-learn efforts in so-called "human resource organizations" include study strategy workshops, orientation to in-house and outside educational opportunities, and the establishing of corporate learning centres for help with personal learning projects, self-assessment, and answers to reference questions. IBM Corporation recently made available system-wide a 14-hour interactive video programme to enhance the employee's learning strategies; it is directed to the employee involved in academic study but available to all.

Home/Community

In addition to elementary, secondary, higher and work place education, the home and community also represent a context for learning with implications for enhancing people's effectiveness in learning. Leaving aside the immense amount of random learning that goes with the normal business of living, most people are in the habit of undertaking self-teaching or self-directed learning projects. Success with such endeavours is associated with realistic goal-setting, sustaining one's motivation, obtaining accurate feedback, and accessing resources for learning, with the latter two often proving to be especially problematic.

Progress has been made in identifying learning-to-learn applications of transpersonal psychology and nonrational thought processes by such means as teaching people to learn systematically through dreams, intuition, fantasy, meditation, and the like; manage anxiety through relaxation techniques; and employ imagistic and metaphoric thinking processes (Maxfield, 1990). Some persons have learned by trial and error to employ nonrational processes, but there is interest in the provision of training for competence in these matters through higher education institutions, public libraries, and learning centres. It is also envisioned that training for group problem solving and discussion skills, assessment of learning styles, mentoring, and the like, could be made more readily available to autonomous groups and nonprofit agencies

Adult Basic Education

Potential applications of the learning-to-learn concept have been identified in two other contexts: adult basic education and education of the elderly. A comprehensive study of essential skills needed for successful living in Alberta, Canada, yielded a taxonomy of learning-to-learn competencies for participants in adult literacy or basic education programmes. Among the prominent areas of need were self-confidence, ability to use community resources, self-management, and practical thinking skills. Some writers have considered the possibility of helping people to learn more effectively from everyday experience and a few have undertaken to provide assistance through analysis of the obstacles (e.g., dogmatism and the tendency to confuse what one has learned with what one has experienced) and guided collaboration in the examination of experience (Miller, 1964).

Older Learners

In this connection, a primary educational need of the older person seems to lie in making meaning of experience — to validate a life. Reminiscing represents an almost universal technique for extracting meaning from experience with potential value for learning in the later years, one that offers possibilities of enhancement through training. The older person is also likely to need support in overcoming doubts about ability to learn and the need to stay involved in educational activities — especially those that require challenge and active participation, although these are felt to be too infrequently offered by programming agencies.

Summary

Some of the more salient competencies believed to be essential for success in learning in most of these contexts are depicted in Table 11.1 Rough estimates of their relative importance are also indicated. Reflection, self-awareness, and confidence are not included since they are believed to be of high importance in almost all contexts.

Facilitation and Training

A growing body of information is available concerning the facilitation of activities to improve people's effectiveness in learning. There are guidelines for successful training design. There are comprehensive approaches directed to specific audiences and also collections of resources and activities that can be adapted to various purposes and contexts. Electronic media applications are proliferating, such as the previously mentioned IBM package, a computer-assisted simulation game developed in Britain to assist students in making the transition from secondary to higher education, the JSEP Basic Learning Skills Curriculum, and repertory grid technology (Thomas and Harri-Augstein, 1985).

Comprehensive learning-to-learn programmes tend to gain acceptance to the extent that they:
1. include a credible theoretical base;
2. undergo field testing and evaluation;

3. provide the learner with relevant experience, practice, application, and reinforcement in the use of new behaviour;
4. make available the required materials for both the learner and the facilitator;
5. make provision for facilitator training (if required); and
6. implement a systematic approach to dissemination.

Table 11.1 Relative importance by context of selected competences

Strategies/ Competencies	Preschool/ Elementary	Secondary/ Higher	Home- Community	Work Place
Basic skills	M	H	M	M
Academic study strategies	M	H	L	M
Structures of knowledge	M	H	L	M
Negotiate educational institutions	L	H	M	M
Collaborative learning strategies	M	M	H	H
Create learning environment	L	M	H	M
Holistic/trans- personal strategies	M	M	H	M
Locate/access resources	M	M	H	M
Obtain feedback	M	M	H	H

L = low
M = medium
H = high.

Table 11.2 Foci and approaches for the facilitation of training

Facilitation/training for . . .	Useful resources/approaches	References
Self-awareness and understanding as learner	Learning style profiling Analysis of prior learning Repertory grids Keeping diaries and logs	Smith, 1982 Gibbs, 1981 Thomas & Harri-Augstein, 1985
Reflection and monitoring	Composing educational biographies Reflection exercises Process reports, diaries, logs	Mezirow, 1990 Cell, 1984 Boud et al., 1985 Gibbs, 1981
The nature of knowledge and more meaningful learning	Concept mapping Vee diagramming Interactive teaching Reciprocal teaching	Novak & Gowin, 1984 Smith, 1990 Baird & Mitchell, 1987
Study and self-organizing strategies	Exercises, checklists, Diagnostic instruments Assessment techniques SQ3R system	Nisbet & Schucksmith, 1986 Biggs, 1987 Bowden, 1986 Weinstein et al., 1988 Joyce & Weil, 1986

(continued)

Table 11.2 Continued

Self-directedness and proactiveness	Diagnostic instruments, Learning contacts, exercises to analyze learning projects Valuing out-of-school learning accomplishments	Candy, 1991 Knowles, 1975, 1986 Smith, 1982, 1990
Collaboration in learning and problem solving	Problem-based learning Cooperative learning T-group - laboratory learning Participation training	Barrows & Tamblyn, 1980 Slavin, 1983 Benne, 1975 Bergevin & McKinley, 1967
Institutional Learning	Basic skills training Action learning Double-loop learning Workshops, consultation Coaching and mentoring	Carnevale et al., 1990 Marsick, 1987 Bennis & Nanus, 1985 Cheren, 1987 Smith, 1990

Facilitators are advised to expect resistance and difficulties in helping people to externalize, examine and modify assumptions and habits related to learning, study, and knowledge (Bowden, 1986). They are enjoined to: (a) find ways to make process training palatable and understandable; (b) maintain a climate conducive to behavioural change; (c) carefully adapt approaches and materials to different audiences, and (d) seek ways of continually strengthening what were earlier referred to as the foundations of competence.

Since it is difficult to change behaviour through merely presenting information about learning to learn, most approaches stress active participation through practice activities, simulation, postexperience critiques, keeping logs, writing process reports, learning style profiling, concept mapping, and the like (Smith, 1982; Mezirow, 1990).

Despite growing acceptance of the view that academic learning skills are best fostered in conjunction with instruction in subject matter and the availability of useful tools (Gibbs, 1981; Novak and Gowin, 1984), there is still a dearth of information about how to do this effectively and how to prepare and support faculty in the effort. One outstanding exception is the case study of an experiment in an Australian secondary school contained in Baird and Mitchell (1987). Firm evidence concerning the positive impacts of training is available. For example, long-term experimental research at the universities of Michigan and Texas have found that semester-long learning-to-learn courses produce significant gains over control groups in reading achievement, grades, and retention (McKeachie et al., 1985; Weinstein et al., 1988). Table 11.2 summarizes information about facilitation and training for learning to learn.

Further Implications for Policy and Practice

Knowledge about learning to learn greatly exceeds dissemination and application. The personal and social costs are considerable in terms of such matters as unfulfilled potential, inadequate responses to change, and programme dropouts. To be sure learning to learn represents no panacea, but recent research and development provides concepts, rationales, and tools to help make learning in and out-of-school more efficient and meaningful, less mysterious and forbidding. People can be helped to develop and use wider repertoires of strategies and make better educational decisions. They can be taught to take more responsibility and control of learning and also to collaborate more effectively in learning (Bergevin and McKinley, 1965; Candy, 1991). They can be given the tools to negotiate with educational bureaucracies. They can be groomed for success when encountering an unfamiliar teaching methodology or content area.

The implication is clearly that educational leaders and policy makers have a responsibility to see that more energy and resources go into activity directed toward learning to learn. Three kinds of activity suggest themselves:

1. *Stimulate programming and instruction from a learning to learn perspective.*

This will require new ways of looking at needs analysis and assessment. Process needs become almost as important as content needs. People receive preparation and support when unfamiliar instructional methods are employed. Programmatic effects on the participants as learners come under review become relevant, as do such questions as: Does the programme diminish, maintain, or enhance the disposition and ability of the participants for further learning and taking control of learning-related activity? Does it encourage and reward meaningful learning, as opposed to the rote acquisition of undigested information? Does it adequately prepare the participant for the next level of education or life phase? Models for informing an entire curriculum or organization with a learning-to-learn dimension have been proposed by Gibbons and Phillips (1982) and Lindsey (1988) for elementary-secondary education; by Schlossberg et al. (1989) for higher education; and by Cheren (1987) for human resource organizations.

2. *Encourage and support appropriate preservice and in-service education for educational personnel.*

Preservice education will need to become more process-centered, directed toward self-awareness, reflection, and greater openmindedness. Would-be teachers will need more than knowledge *about* the learning-to-learn concept. They will need to have confirming experiences such as positive changes in their own learning-related behaviour if they are to be expected to teach from a learning-to-learn perspective. Practising teachers will need to acquire new perspectives on the teaching-learning process and in a sense acquire commitment to the learning-to-learn idea along with their students.

Success in pre and in-service education related to learning to learn is associated with the following (Smith, 1990):
1. Directing instruction to self-examination of assumptions and reflection upon practice by the participants;
2. Maintaining an orientation to learning to learn as a change process, involving learner change, staff change, and organizational change;
3. Recognizing that both facilitator and client need experiences that confirm the utility of learning-to-learn activity;
4. Enabling participants to acquire both generic and contextually appropriate procedures and strategies;

5. Providing adequate support and rewards to participants as they make applications of their newly acquired knowledge.

3. *Support research-to-practice activity and make dissemination more systematic.*

Learning-to-learn knowledge is not particularly easy to package and disseminate. It stems from experience and research conducted in a variety of nations and academic disciplines and is anchored in various settings and contexts. It involves instruction and learning about processes, metaprocesses, and thinking clearly about multiple realities. The information is organized under various descriptors — for example, learning how to learn, metacognition, learning strategy training, heuristics, student development — and much of it is dispersed research reports, dissertations and journals. The people who do the basic research are not necessarily disposed or well-equipped to convert their findings into practical applications. Faculty reward systems often discourage research-to-practice activity.

Conclusions

A number of conferences have been held in various countries and a significant number of articles and books about learning to learn have now been produced. But major impacts on practice through the usual processes of diffusion appear to be unlikely and the gains of the past two decades are in danger of erosion unless better ways are found to influence policy, exchange information, encourage demonstration projects, produce the necessary materials, and train trainers.

An approach worth experimenting with is the dissemination centre. Such an organization could serve as a demonstration project for the development of an appropriate dissemination model. It could establish a newsletter and a data base on learning to learn and provide an information clearinghouse. It could evaluate existing and emerging materials, encourage appropriate action research and development, and put researchers and practitioners in touch with each other. It could sponsor workshops on such topics as electronic media applications of learning to learn and the production and marketing of learning-to-learn materials, and provide technical assistance and consultation for local learning-to-learn initiatives (Smith, 1988).

If such a centre were located in a university, faculty and graduate students from various academic disciplines could be involved and research-to-practice activity stimulated. Maintaining a dissemination emphasis, however, might be difficult because of the reward system and multiple demands on faculty time and energy. In a country such as the

Netherlands, it might be feasible to establish a network of centres that serve different clientele: parents, preschool and primary school teachers; secondary and higher education personnel; adult, workplace, and community educators. Community centres might direct training activity toward citizens at large, especially people embarking on educational leave.

References

Baird, J., & Mitchell, I.J. (1987). *Improving the quality of teaching and learning: An Australian case study — the Peel project.* Melbourne: Monash University Printery.

Barrows, H.S., & Tamblyn, R.M. (1980). *Problem-based learning: An approach to medical education.* New York: Springer.

Benne, K. (1975). *The laboratory method of changing and learning.* Palo Alto, California: Science and Behavior Books.

Bennis, W., & Nanus, B. (1985). *Leaders.* New York: Harper and Row.

Bergevin, P.E., & McKinley, J. (1965). *Participation training for adult education.* St. Louis, Missouri: Bethany Press.

Biggs, J.B. (1987). *Student approaches to learning and studying.* Melbourne: Australian Council for Educational Research.

Boud, D.J., Keogh, R., & Walker, D. (1985). *Reflection: Turning experience into learning.* London: Kogan Page.

Bowden, J.A. (1986). *Student learning: Research into practice.* Proceedings of the Marysville symposium. Melbourne, Australia: University of Melbourne Center for Higher Education.

Candy, P.C. (1991). *Self-direction in lifelong learning.* San Francisco: Jossey-Bass.

Carnevale, A.P., Gainer, L.J., & Meltzer, A.S. (1990). *Workplace basics: The essential skills employers want.* San Francisco: Jossey-Bass.

Cell, E. (1984). *Learning to learn from experience.* Albany: State University of New York Press.

Cheren, M.E. (Ed.). (1987). *Learning management: Emerging directions for learning to learn in the workplace.* Information Series No. 320. Columbus, Ohio: NCRVE, The Ohio State University.

Gibbons, M., & Phillips, G. (1982). Self-education: The process of lifelong learning. *Canadian Journal of Education, 7* (4), 67-86.

Gibbs, G. (1981). *Teaching students to learn.* Milton Keynes: The Open University Press.

Hunter, M. (1985). *Mastery teaching.* El Segundo, California: TIP Publications.

Joyce, B., & Weil, M. (1986). *Models of teaching.* Englewood Cliffs, New Jersey: Prentice-Hall.

Knowles, M.S. (1975). *Self-directed learning.* New York: Association Press.

Knowles, M.S. (1986). *Using learning contracts.* San Francisco: Jossey-Bass.

Lindsey, C.W., Jr. (1988). *Teaching students to teach themselves.* New York: Nichols.

Marsick, V.J. (1987). *Learning in the workplace.* New York: Croom Helm.

Maxfield, D. (1990). Learning with the whole mind. In R.M. Smith (Ed.), *Learning to learn across the lifespan* (pp. 98-122). San Francisco: Jossey-Bass.

McKeachie, W.J., Pintrich, P.R., & Lin, Y. (1985). Learning to learn. In G. d'Ydewall (Ed.), *Cognition, information processing, and motivation* (pp. 601-618). Amsterdam: Elsevier Science Publishers.

Mezirow, J. (Ed.) (1990). *Fostering critical reflection in adulthood.* San Francisco: Jossey-Bass.

Miller, H.L. (1964). *Teaching and learning in adult education.* New York: Macmillan.

Nisbet, J., & Schucksmith, J. (1986). *Learning strategies.* New York: Routledge.

Novak, J.D., & Gowin, D.B. (1984). *Learning how to learn.* New York: Cambridge University Press.

Schlossberg, N.K., Lynch, A.Q., & Chickering, A.W. (1989). *Improving higher education environments for adults: Responsive programs and services from entry to departure.* San Francisco: Jossey-Bass.

Slavin, R.E. (1983). *Cooperative learning.* New York: Longmans.

Smith, R.M. (1982). *Learning how to learn: Applied theory for adults.* New York: Cambridge University Press.

Smith, R.M. (1988). Improving dissemination of knowledge about self-directness in education. In H.B. Long (Ed.), *Self-directed learning: Application and theory* (pp. 149-167). Norman, Oklahoma: Oklahoma University Center for Continuing, Professional, and Higher Education.

Smith, R.M. (Ed.) (1990). *Learning to learn across the lifespan.* San Francisco: Jossey-Bass.

Thomas, L.F., & Harri-Augstein, E.S. (1985). *Self-organized learning.* London: Routledge and Kegan Paul.

Weinstein, C.E., Goetz, C.E., & Alexander, P.A. (1988). *Learning and study strategies: Issues in assessment, instruction and evaluation.* Orlando, Florida: Academic Press.

Part 5

Implications for Initial and Adult Education

Chapter 12

EFFECTIVE ADULT LEARNING

MAX VAN DER KAMP

University of Groningen, The Netherlands

Much of the increased knowledge concerning learning, cognition and motivation has found wide application in initial education. In adult education the response has generally been less marked. If learning across the lifespan is taken seriously, then it will be necessary to develop theories of learning and instruction that can be used to design powerful learning environments suitable for adults. Some relevant developments and their applications to adult education will be discussed in this chapter.

The main factors enhancing 'effective' adult learning are summarized, but also the barriers to learning are dealt with. Next, the principles guiding two practical approaches to adult learning are examined and the educational implications reviewed. Some innovations that possibly hold promise as "new pathways to adult learning" are subsequently described. Finally, some important conclusions are drawn.[1]

Factors Enhancing Effective Adult Learning

Many insights into the factors enhancing effective adult learning can de derived from reviews of the literature on specific themes in adult education (e.g., Darkenwald and Merriam, 1982; Brookfield, 1989; Van Der Kamp, 1990; Houtkoop and Van Der Kamp, 1992; Tuijnman and Van Der Kamp, 1991). Valuable insights are also offered in the previous chapters of this volume. These can be summarized as follows:

1. All adults have an ability to learn.
2. Adults want to learn and learn effectively when they have a strong

---

[1] Sections of this chapter are drawn from the CERI/OECD study *Effective Adult Learning: Theories and Policies,* by Albert Tuijnman and Max Van Der Kamp (1991).

inner motivation. Intrinsic motivation is a key factor in effective learning.

3.   Adults resist learning when they are told they must learn something.
4.   Adults tend to learn effectively if they consider the material relevant to their needs and interests.
5.   Adults seek to learn what can be applied; they are generally problem-oriented learners.
6.   Adults value information which is meaningful and useful to them: information related to their expectations and previous experience.
7.   Adults have a desire to know the outcomes of their learning efforts; they require positive reinforcement and performance feedback.
8.   Differences in learning abilities are larger within than between age cohorts. Older people tend to learn a little slower, but often learn more meticulously and with more intensity than young people.
9.   Learning abilities are determined more by previous experience of education and experience of work than by age.
10. Different educational needs are associated with different stages in life career.
11. Adults exhibit diverse learning styles, that is, the unique ways and means by which individual learners gather, process, and internalize information.
12. Previous learning experience can influence current learning, both positively and negatively. The readiness of adults to learn depends on their previous learning experience.

As important as the factors enhancing adult learning are the barriers to learning. What is known about these obstacles to lifelong learning?

The learning of initially poorly educated people, who after a long delay return to school or participate in programmes of adult education, can be hindered by anxiety and resistance. Negative school memories may emerge, for example. It is also possible that acquired knowledge gets unsettled, and that this undermines self-confidence. Fear of failing in front of the group is another factor that may lead to lack of initiative, anxiety, and resistance.

These examples show that there are many barriers to adult learning. Lack of time and high costs are often mentioned in research as barriers to learning. Work-specific barriers are also often noted. Drawing on the results of previous investigations, Cross (1984) makes a distinction between three categories of deterrents to participation: situational, institutional, and dispositional.

Situational barriers arise from one's situation in life at a given time. Lack of money and lack of time are prime examples. Others are low personal priority, costs, and unfavourable personal circumstances. Institutional barriers arise from characteristics of the educational establishments, for example accessibility, recognizability and attractiveness. Dispositional barriers arise from psychological characteristics, such as lack of confidence. Darkenwald and Merriam (1982) add a fourth category, namely, information barriers. Lack of relevance may belong to this category. The findings of research (e.g., Blais et al., 1989; Martindale and Drake, 1989) seem to indicate that situational and institutional barriers may be more important than dispositional barriers. Rubenson (1987) suggests, on the basis of a review of previous research, that the most powerful impediment to adult learning is the individual's expectation that participation will not result in a desired outcome, whether enhanced general living conditions, improved labour market position, or some other objective.

Theories in Practice

A coherent and empirically tested theory on adult learning does not exist and, because of the diversity of theoretical orientations, probably never will. The various theories so far developed are to an extent complementary, as the central hypotheses they address tend to be concerned with different aspects of learning. For example, behavioural theories stress learning as an observable behaviour.

Cognitive theories emphasize learning as a mental process. Social interaction theories focus on the interaction between people. Most theories have something to contribute to educational practice. A pluralistic and multidisciplinary perspective on adult learning is therefore recommended.

A theory on the learning styles of adults has been developed by Kolb (1984). The point of departure is a dialectic model of learning. A two-way matrix is hypothesized based on the following dimensions: concrete versus abstract learning, and active versus reflective learning. Learning is assumed to occur in a field of tension formed by these categories which, according to Kolb, are cyclically arranged. The notion of a "learning circle" is at the heart of the theory. It is postulated that learning adults proceed through the four stages of the learning circle. Experience lies at the basis of perception and reflection ("what was good, what was wrong?"). The learner "collects" observations and "translates" them into a "theory". Hypotheses can be derived from this body of ideas, and these are tested in practice by action. This eventually results in new experience. According to Kolb (1984), four kinds of ability are needed for optimal learning. These are in the domains of experience, reflective observation, abstract concept formation and active experimenting. However, people usually do not perform equally well in all four domains. One or two may stand out. Adult learning can be particularly effective if the preferred learning ability or mode is employed. Kolb distinguishes four such learning styles, namely: the diverger, the assimilator, the converger, and the accomodator. Although Kolb's theory seems very relevant, in particular for designing learning environments, it has not yet an adequate empirical basis.

Especially for older employees the "experience concentration theory" could be of importance (Thijssen, 1988). This theory can be summarized in the premise: the quantity of experience grows with age whereas the variety of experience decreases with age. The theory is based on the assumption that adults with a concentration of similar experience have a smaller domain in which they feel confident than people with a broad spectrum of experience. Learning will be easier the smaller the discrepancy between a subject and a "concentration domain" based on previous learning and experience. The willingness and capacity to learn depends to no small extent on the scale of this domain. Thijssen (1988) distinguishes three variables of relevance to a person's capacity to learn at work: professional skills, learning strategy, and social and cultural context.

The professional skills refer mainly to someone's work experience. Many employees who have carried out the same tasks for a long time show job fixation. When great changes of tasks occur, someone might be inflexible. Learning strategy means the experience and capacity to solve problems. An executive, for example, tends to be continually confronted with new challenges, whereas someone working on an assembly line may be more vulnerable when retraining becomes necessary. The social and cultural context is important, because it can encourage the motivation to learn. These three variables determine a worker's domain of concentration. The more the new knowledge and skills someone has to learn in order to perform well on a job task lie outside this domain, the more formal instruction may be needed.

New skills that are close to previous experience may be acquired through informal learning at the workplace. The greater the discrepancy the more important it becomes to organize systematic learning encounters. Programme design and instructional technology are essential ingredients in a strategy of devising learning encounters with subjects that are only remotely related to the previous experience of workers. Some of these educational implications are discussed below.

Some Educational Implications

In order to create powerful learning environments in adult education the educational designer also needs some guidelines based on learning theories. The following is a selection made on the bais of theories, previous research and the insights provided by Roger Hiemstra and other contributors to this volume:

1. The learner must have access to sufficient information.
2. The learner must have enough time and freedom from threat to allow learning to proceed naturally.
3. The learner must have sufficient prerequisite knowledge and an understanding of certain basic concepts and principles.
4. The learner must proceed through an appropriate learning "gradient", that is, the stepwise progression or "pacing" from easy to difficult.
5. Effective learning is linked to an individual's self-concept and self-evaluation as a learner.
6. The learning environment should take account of individual differences in learning abilities and learning styles.
7. Material to be learned should be organized into manageable units.

The implication could be that the preferences adults have with respect to learning styles and the pacing of the learning activity ought to be matched with differences in using "personalized" systems of instruction. Although it is generally assumed that the matching of learning styles with specific instructional methods will enhance both the ability and motivation to learn and, hence, improve learning outcomes, a review of empirical studies by Cohen et al. (1989) found little evidence to support this hypothesis. The apparent absence of a clear link between learning styles, tailored instructional methods and learning outcomes does not necessarily imply that the concept of learning styles is invalid. Knowledge of the preferred learning modes of workers can be useful in the design of training programmes. There is a realization at present that "good practice" in adult education and training often depends on the application of methods that give attention to individual learner needs and match preferred learning styles.

The learning environment and the instructional methods used as a means for promoting transfer may need to be modified in case people have to learn knowledge and skills that lie either completely or partially outside their domain of concentration. Thijssen (1988) suggests several adaptations, among which the following:

1. Stimulate *active* processing of new information;
2. Encourage systematic feedback;
3. Promote the use of recognizable concepts;
4. Put emphasis on the *direct* application of what has been learned;
5. Facilitate the social setting by creating a friendly atmosphere;
6. Facilitate the logistical context.

New Pathways to Learning

Some promising innovations in adult education, which to an extent are based on recent insights into the factors that optimalize adult learning, are described below. Attention is given, first, to the possible applications of new information technology and, second, to the idea of "open learning", which is considered to hold great potential for development.

New Information Technologies in Adult Education

Personalized systems of instruction that allow the learner to pace the learning encounter are generally considered effective; acccording to some sources they may increase retention and the satisfaction of adults with the learning encounter. Computer-based training is a concept being used at present to denote the entire range of information technologies and programmed instruction applied to further education and training.

Training through technology makes use of a variety of approaches (for an overview, see Brainbridge and Quintanilla, 1989). Examples are traditional media such as broadcasting and audio-cassettes and innovative media such as preprogrammed computer-based learning, computer-based communications, interactive video, tutorial systems, and simulation programmes. Interactive videodisk training, for example, is increasingly being used in learning environments where an error in decision making would be too dangerous or costly. Obvious applications are simulation models used in the advanced training of airline pilots or surgeons.

New technologies are important, potentially at least, in enhancing learning at the work place. They not only make further education and training a necessity but also change the context in which training takes place. For example, new information technologies put a demand on the preciseness of the learning task and its objectives, and pose new problems for communication. This also has repercussions on the competence and teaching capacity required of trainers.

According to some sources reviewed in Eraut (1989), the effectiveness of the learning process can be enhanced by means of new information technologies because these:

1. encourage the standardization of learning experience without jeopardizing flexibility;
2. encourage decentralization of training in firms;
3. help save time and equipment;
4. reduce training costs.

The new media are directed towards the individual learner. This offers not only an instructional advantage but may also improve learner feed-back, thus enhancing opportunities for self-assessment and optimalizing learning.

New information technologies have provided an impetus for develo-ping new strategies of effective adult learning. Two examples are "integrated learning" and "accelerated learning". Integrated learning refers to a cooperative approach where instructors work in "corporate classrooms". It is essentially based on complete job analysis, after which learning modules for specific skills are developed. Instructors work together with employees in developing activity guides, job-plan sheets and other instructional materials. Accelerated learning is another innova-tive concept. Some general principles for achieving accelerated learning can be found in the research literature. Among the most important recommendations are:

1. be learner-centered;
2. use mindmaps to organize material and improve retention;
3. use a variety of methods for presenting materials;
4. install cooperative learning exercises;
5. use knowledge bridges often and in different ways;
6. create high expectations about learning outcomes;
7. support learner self-esteem;
8. hook into early positive experience of learning;
9. provide a stimulating and comfortable environment.

Open Learning

Open learning centres have their origins in the concept of open learning, which refers to a principle of learner-centredness and open access to learning opportunities. Open learning, as currently conceived, is associated but not necessarily similar to distance education. According to one source (Paine, 1988), the term refers to "learning which allows the learner to choose how to learn, when to learn, where to learn and what to learn as far as possible within the resource constraints of any education and training provision" (p. ix).

New directions for open learning have opened up as a consequence of the development of educational technology and its application to training provision and the education offered by the open universities and other institutions providing opportunity for distance learning. However, relying only on the applications of educational technology may curtail the contribution the open learning concept can make to the design of routes to effective adult learning.

Before presenting some examples illustrating that the open learning concept can be developed in several different directions, such as media- and network baoed provioiono, and oohool and reoource centre baoed provisions, it may be useful to review briefly the main characteristics of open learning, which are emphasized by writers supportive of the idea (Van Der Zee, 1989):

1. Open learning is learner-centred, rather than institution centred;
2. Open learning provides a means of equipping participants for self-directed learning;
3. Open learning implies informal learning and the use of a wide range of teaching and learning strategies;
4. Open learning helps in removing barriers to learning, particularly those barriers inherent in the established patterns of education and training;
5. Open learning gives the student more choice by creating a diversity of individual opportunity;
6. Open learning is user-friendly, bringing education closer to the client who decides on when and how to engage in the learning task;
7. Open learning is in sharp contrast with a supplier-oriented approach in adult education; hence it has much to offer in designing a learning environment.

The means for learning in this type of provision derives from telecommunications, primarily television and radio but also "traditional media" such as newspapers, books, and magazines. The learning takes place predominantly at home. Media-based learning systems can be worked out in various ways. Examples of provisions that to some extent can be characterized as open learning centres are the *FernUniversität und Gesamthochschule* of Hagen in Germany and TELEAC, a Dutch institution for distance education.

In Limburg, the southernmost province in the Netherlands, three secondary schools for adults are working together in the development of an Open Learning Centre. A major incentive was provided by the construction of a two-way cable in South Limburg. The intention was that this medium could be used not only by the media but also by educational institutions working in accordance with the open learning principle. The Dutch Ministry of Education and Science provided a grant for the development of an Open Learning Centre that would interactively use the cable in bringing educational programmes to the public.

In order to supplement the above discussion with an example of the idea in practice, it may be useful to review briefly some of the relevant aspects of the Open Learning Centre in the Netherlands:

1. Cooperation with the Open University and other educational provisions at the primary level;
2. Splitting the curriculum in different modules;
3. Promoting self-study by the students;
4. More time for development and guidance by teachers;
5. Attention for the personal needs of students;
6. Flexibility in instruction;
7. Flexibility in administering examinations that are, as far as possible, applicable to the learning activity;
8. The use of information technology;
9. The development of the necessary software;
10. The creation of "open" meeting places for students and teachers;
11. Open entry conditions for all adult learners.

An implementation study of the Open Learning Centre is being carried out at present under the auspices of the Dutch Foundation of Educational Research. The preliminary results show that implementation is beset by a variety of problems (De Wolf, 1990). Legal restrictions and the very detailed guidelines provided by the authorities hamper creativity and flexibility. Moreover, many of the teachers are not used to working with the new tasks. The more traditional among them show some resistance to the innovation. The project is faced with organizational and procedural problems, partly due to the fact that there are not many precedents for the institution that is being set up. Some logistic difficulties have also been encountered. However, in spite of these problems, there is much interest in the experience of the Open Learning Centre in the Netherlands. Some regard it as a promising model that sets an example for the further development of adult secondary education in the country.

In contrast to the media-based systems, network-based systems draw interactively on the experience and expertise of the participants. Although the terms "network" and "networking" are currently fashionable, they refer to activities which can hardly be described as new. Contemporary examples that have an open learning potential are exchange and brokerage services like the Gilde (guild) in Amsterdam and self-help groups, of which there are many varieties in Germany and the Netherlands. Other interesting examples are the liberal study circles in Denmark and Sweden, and the work place variants developed in Germany.

A study circle is loosely defined as a group of people united for common and planned studies of a predetermined subject area. The study circle as a method of training, informing and activating the members of a group has a long history in the Nordic countries and in Sweden in particular. In recent years the study circle approach has become an accepted means and method of adult liberal education in countries such as Canada and the United States. In Germany there has been a parallel development. However, an interesting feature of the German position is that the idea of the study circle has been applied to the work place. Workers in many medium-size and large firms meet once a week for one or two hours during worktime in groups of three to 10 people in order to discuss and learn about subjects such as new production technology and communication techniques. "Quality circles", as study circles organized in the firm are usually called, are both economically and socially effective as a means of providing on-the-job training and stimulating work place learning.

While the learning associated with the previously mentioned forms normally occur at home or at work, the learning can of course also take place on site. Students come to the institution instead of the latter to the student. School-based open learning systems are commonly run by professional educators or trainers who design systematic learning encounters in accordance with the philosophy of openness, for example, by designing independent learning packages, so that self-study may be facilitated, or by enabling students to learn whatever they wish, however they please, at the time, place and pace which suits them best.

Cultural institutions such as libraries and museums are examples of resource centres that facilitate open learning. These institutions assemble information for public inquiry and use. They require no examination for entrance, conduct no assessment of the learning outcomes realized by individual users, and offer no credentials. They are available to learners of all ages. Libraries, museums, nature reservations, zoos, festivals, exhibitions all have the potential of providing a stimulating learning environment. An example is La Vilette, a block of futuristic buildings in Paris, which invites the visitor to explore the world of industry, science, and technology. Similar, but more limited in conception and only accessible for own company personnel, are the learning centres of companies such as IBM, Rover, and Lucas industries (Van der Zee, 1989).

The Role of Guidance

The range and variants of learning are increasing in highly industrialized countries. Given the increased diversity, incohesiveness, unstructuredness, and variance of continuing education and training markets and learning options and routes to adult learning, the role that guidance can play in helping the individual learner to make an informed choice among learning options is becoming more important. Bailey (1988, p. 334-5) suggests a range of activities aimed at assisting adults in becoming aware of learning options and helping them in managing learning: informing, advising and counselling, coaching and assessment, advocacy and feedback. There is also a clear need for improving visibility and coherence rather than an overproliferation of programmes. Insight into the structure of the adult education market is an absolute prerequisite for a well-functioning system. The question of how different variants of learning relate to each other in terms of structure, content, method and time is therefore crucial.

Realizing the importance of guidance in a national strategy of adult education and training, the Dutch government has initiated some experiments that may be worthwhile reviewing for an international audience. Perhaps the best example is that of the Dutch PBVE (Primary Vocational Training for Adults). This institution offers previously poorly educated people, the unemployed, and others who are at a relative disadvantage in the learning society the possibility to participate in education and training programmes aimed at conferring the skills needed in order to get a job or to improve their chances on the labour market. For many poorly educated adults it is not so easy to acquire an insight into the available educational provisions that may suit their needs and expectations. Many unemployed adults lose their way in the overwhelming and incoherent supply of further education and training possibilities. The PBVE has developed a method of case management aimed at offering a person-oriented pathway of training and guiding the individual participant throughout the training activity.

Case management can be particularly relevant for unemployed adults with clearly traceable shortcomings in their qualifications, who can be helped in improving their chances of obtaining a job with a short and focussed training course. Another target group may consist of adults with a short previous education and a weak position on the labour market, who need sustained personal guidance and a pathway of training of comparatively long duration in order for their chances on a job to be improved. Extended personal guidance is necessary especially for the latter group, as this may be effective in lessening frustration, optimalizing learning, and avoiding wastage and dropout.

The PBVE is subsidized by the government. Den Boer (1991) has investigated the external effectiveness of the PBVE by means of a telephone interview among former participants one year after they finished their course. The results of his study were encouraging, although the follow-up may be too short in duration for the whole picture to emerge: the majority of the former participants either had a job or were enrolled in a programme of continuing vocational education. About one of every four participants was still unemployed a year after finishing their studies. Among these, the participants with an immigrant or minority status were overrepresented. The PBVE programme is beset with a high rate of wastage, however. One-third of all students drop out before completing the course. This percentage is even higher for allochthonous participants.

Conclusion

Some implications of the increased knowledge on aspects of adult learning for the practice of adult education were discussed in this chapter. In the international debate on the imperative of investing in adult education, matters of policy and organization have attracted much attention. But the consequences for the practice of adult education have been rather neglected. In order for continuous learning across the lifespan to be realized, new designs, methods, and approaches are needed. These cannot be established only on theories of learning, but make experimentation with powerful learning environments and didactical approaches necessary. Such experiments have to be accompanied by carefully designed evaluation studies, so that insights concerning the effectiveness of the various innovations can be arrived at. Unfortunately, this is hardly the case at present. As public and private investment in adult education is increasing, however, there is also a new demand for accountability in adult education. It can be noted that an increasing number of countries now conducts evaluations of public training programmes as a matter of principle. A similar development may be in store for general and liberal adult education. Programme evaluation in adult education, if systematically carried out and if the appropriate mix of both experimental and nonexperimental methods is applied, can provide information on the factors that make adult learning effective.

References

Bailey, D. (1988). Guidance and counselling in work-based open learning. In N. Paine (Ed.), *Open learning in transition. An agenda for action* (pp. 332-349). London: Kogan Page.

Blais, J., Duquette, A., & Painchaud, G. (1989). Deterrents to women's participation in work-related educational activities. *Adult Education Quarterly, 39*, 224-234.

Brainbridge, L., & Quintanilla, S.A.R. (1989). *Developing skills with information technology*. Chichester: Wiley.

Brookfield, S. (1989). Teacher roles and teaching styles. In C.J. Titmus (Ed.), *Lifelong education for adults: An international handbook* (pp. 208-212). Oxford: Pergamon Press.

Cohen, S.A., Hyman, J.S., Ashcroft, L., & Loveless, D. (1989, March). Comparing effects of metacognition, learning styles, and human attributes with alignment. Paper presented at the Annual Meeting of the American Educational Research Association, San Francisco.

Cross. K.P. (1984). *Adults as learners*. San Fransisco: Jossey-Bass.

Darkenwald, G.G. and Merriam. S.B. (1982). *Adult education: Foundations of practice*. New York: Harper and Row.

Den Boer, P. (1991). Effectiviteit van de scholingsmaatregel PBVE. In J. Koppen, H. Stroomberg and M. Van der Kamp (Eds.), *Hoger onderwijs en volwasseneneducatie* (pp. 185-198). Amsterdam: SCO.

Eraut, M. (Ed.) (1989). *The international encyclopedia of educational technology.* Oxford: Pergamon Press.

Houtkoop, W., & Van der Kamp, M. (1992). Factors influencing participation in continuing education. *International Journal of Educational Research, 17,* 537-548.

Kolb, D.A. (1984). *Experiential learning.* Englewood Cliffs, New Jersey, Prentice-Hall.

Martindale, C.J., & Drake, J.B. (1989). Factor structure of deterrents to participation in off-duty adult education programs. *Adult Education Quarterly, 39* (2), 63-75.

Paine, N. (Ed.) (1988). *Open learning in transition. An agenda for action.* London: Kogan Page.

Peterson, D.A. (1987). *Facilitating education for older learners.* San Francisco: Jossey-Bass.

Rubenson, K. (1987). Participation in recurrent education: A research review. In: H.G. Schütze and D. Istance (Eds.), *Recurrent education revisited. Modes of participation and financing* (pp. 39-67). Stockholm: Almqvist and Wiksell.

Thijssen, J.G.L. (1988). *Bedrijfsopleidingen als werkterrein.* The Hague: VUGA.

Tuijnman, A.C. & Van Der Kamp, M. (1991). *Effective adult learning: Theories and policies.* Paris: OECD-CERI.

Van Der Kamp, M. (1990). Education for older adults in Europe: A common problem, different solutions? In: A. Wellings (Ed.), *Towards 1992. The education of adults in the new Europe.* Sheffield: SCUTREA.

Van Der Zee, H. (1989). Developing the educational potential of public libraries. In F. Goffree and H. Stroomberg (Eds.), *Creating adult learning.* Leiden: SMD.

Wolf, H. de (1990). *Open leren en open leercentra.* Leiden: SMD.

Chapter 13

PARADIGM SHIFTS IN ADULT EDUCATION

ALBERT C. TUIJNMAN
University of Twente, The Netherlands

This chapter deals with the changing policy context of adult education. Some examples are presented that illustrate the argument that, in recent years, there has been a slow but significant shift in emphasis from "adult education" to "adult learning". The factors calling for an emphasis on the adult learner are discussed and some of the implications for policy and research presented. [1]

Means and Ends of Adult Learning

The economies of the industrialized countries have been going through a complex and gradual process of structural adjustment, especially since the early 1980s (OECD, 1987). This is particularly true in Europe, where the traditionally strong hold of national governments on monetary and fiscal policy, industrial policy, and even higher education policy, is weakening and a new political geography emerging. The withering of the "old" and the rise of "new" economic and political structures in Europe and elsewhere poses numerous challenges and opportunities for economic and labour market policy and also sets a new agenda for education (Husén et al., 1992). Indeed, the construction of the new Europe involves by definition the making of decisions about what an appropriate education would be like in relation to the problems and opportunities an integrating Europe is now facing — challenges which evidently derive from changes both within and outside the region.

---

[1] Sections of this chapter are drawn from the CERI-OECD study *Effective Adult Learning: Theories and Policies,* by Albert Tuijnman and Max Van Der Kamp (1991).

Since the school may be seen not only as a place for teaching the glory of national history but also as a means for promoting international under-standing and solidarity for the "larger unit Europe", schools may be required to live up to the task of fostering, in the new generation, a ten-dency to view Europe as a cohesive whole — appreciating communality in the ideas from antiquity, Christianity, humanism and the Enlighten-ment that lie at the basis of the common history, while also acknow-ledging that cultural diversity represents the backbone of any European identity.

Special tasks are emerging for adult education as well. These relate to economic and social objectives, to which adult education and training are expected to contribute. Among the economic objectives are those of improving the efficiency, productivity, and profitability of the work organization and hence raising individual earnings and, of course, national income. Other goals concern the prevention of skills obsolescence and the alleviation of redundancy pressure among the various high-risk groups in an industrial society, especially the initially poorly educated and those with a comparatively weak attachment to the labour market: poorly educated women, older employees, immigrants, and workers employed in labour markets undergoing rationalization. Additional goals are to improve the employability of displaced people or school leavers lacking adequate prospects for an occupational career and, of course, to satisfy the general social demand for adult education. At an individual level, the objectives are not merely economic but also to a large extent social-psychological: the satisfaction of individual demand is not just a matter of meeting material needs or even perceived learning needs, but also concerns higher-order needs in relation to subjective well-being and life satisfaction — something which, in the 1970s, led some economists to hypothesize that adult education was less an investment than a consumption good, a pastime of the already "over-educated" middle-classes.

The second half of the 1970s was characterized by feelings of frustra-tion and even disenchantment with the benefits of education. These years were characterized by stagnating economic growth and mass unemployment, environmental pollution, and the thwarted educational and occupational expectations of students who discovered that they had become "over-educated". These "effects" were not among those usually predicted by human capital models of the relationships between school inputs, educational outcomes and national development. Much theorizing about the nature of the relationship between education and development in the 1960s, when belief in the beneficial outcomes of education was an article of faith among decision makers and research workers, was discredited during the 1970s. Concomitantly with the upturn in world trade during the mid-1980s, confidence in the economic "value" of education returned.

The Changing Context of Adult Education Policy

The policy context of adult education has in several respects changed remarkably since the 1970s. A comparison of the strategies for educational development proposed at that time (for a summary, see Bengtsson, 1989) with the ideas gaining currency at present in some European countries such as France, Germany, and the United Kingdom clearly bears this out (see, e.g., Davis et al., 1991). Some major aspects of change are discussed in the paragraphs below.

The concept of recurrent education, which was introduced by an advisory committee to the Swedish government in the late 1960s, became a cornerstone of the educational philosophy of the OECD during the 1970s. According to one source, the basic principles of recurrent education as proposed by the OECD are, first, that access to post-compulsory education should be guaranteed to the individual at appropriate times over the life cycle, second, that it should be possible to alternate education and work in an intermittent way and, third, that each adult should have a legislated right to study leave (Bengtsson, 1989, p. 44). In considering the situation in most European countries at present, one can note that the tendency during the 1980s has been to strengthen the development of continuing vocational training, especially job training in industry sponsored by employers, rather than postcompulsory, formal education, as was the idea at the outset.

The notion that work ought to be alternated on a recurrent basis with formal education has been replaced by strategies to provide workers with the appropriate learning opportunities while remaining part of the labour force, for example, by offering on-the-job training, distance education and refresher courses of a brief duration financed by firms. The shift in emphasis from time off from work for study to time for learning as an integral part of the occupational task is characteristic of the current situation. Another aspect is that formal arrangements for study leave, as originally envisaged in the 1970s by the International Labour Office and the OECD, have not been legislated in the majority of countries, Sweden being a notable exception. Instead, the tendency has been for governments to rely on collective agreements, partnerships with industry, and the initiative of the individual adult learner.

The reasons why recurrent education has apparently failed to catch on in practice are discussed elsewhere and need not in detail be brought up here (see, e.g., Levin and Schütze, 1983; Tuijnman, 1991). The economic austerity besetting many OECD Member countries from the mid-1970s until the early 1980s has had a significant impact on the perceptions of the role of governments in the financing of further education and training. International competition and problems of structural adjustment and modernization have called for a flexible approach to efficient skills development. In retrospect it seems that employers, but also the governments of many OECD countries, considered that the principle of recurrent education offered neither flexibility nor efficiency, as it was rightly interpreted as calling for an active role of the government in facilitating the expansion of the formal system of education. Such an expansion was seen as expensive and was deemed inefficient (OECD, 1991a). Recognition of the need for flexibility in the provision of adult education was enhanced by demographic change and by uncertainty: it cannot be known precisely what kinds of skill workers will need a decade from now. The tendency of shifting the emphasis from "adult education" to "adult learning", which was mentioned at the outset of this chapter, can be explained as a consequence of widespread concern with this uncertainty and the derived need for flexibility in the skill formation process.

The above discussion provides a background necessary for understanding why the original concept of recurrent education has to an extent become obsolete. There is now less emphasis on the role of the government in finance and provision, and more on the responsibility of the social partners and the individual adult learner. Even though formal adult education and public labour market training are still considered useful as instruments for influencing the elasticity between internal and external labour markets, in recent years the focus has clearly shifted from formal adult education provided by institutions controlled by the State and, in the case of targeted provision, paid for by the State, to often independently managed institutions that compete with one another in order to supply continuing vocational training to the buyers — often industrial firms but also private individuals and the government itself.

Rising trade competition and its possible consequences for economic stability and growth has now become a paramount concern in Europe and North America. This has stimulated a debate on the factors enhancing the competitiveness of industrialized nations. Mostly because of its assumed economic significance, education has reentered the policy arena in a way resembling the situation characterizing the major part of the 1960s — the period during which the belief in the positive outcomes of (school) education was an article of faith among many social scientists and politicians.

Whereas in the 1960s and early 1970s the debate was mainly focussed on the potential benefits of school education, the tendency since the mid-1970s has been to emphasize vocationalism in education. During the 1980s there was a further shift from vocational education offered in schools and through apprenticeship training schemes to further education and training sponsored by companies. The centre of gravity for the financing and provision of adult education has shifted from public educational institutions to both firms and labour market authorities, for example in Germany (Lenske and Zillessen, 1987; Bundesminister, 1990). This interest in human resource development is to no small extent driven by new technology (cf. Levin, 1987).

Overall, participation in adult education and training has increased in many OECD countries during the 1980s. The main force behind this increase is the expansion of investment by the private sector. Today the question is being asked as to whether there is underinvestment in adult education relative to investment in school education. Stimulated by influential studies (e.g., Stern and Ritzen 1991), which on the whole seem to indicate that the private rates of return to training tend to be very high compared with the rate of return to formal schooling, the scales seem to be tipping in favour of the conclusion that there is, indeed, underinvestment in adult education compared to initial education. The idea that some of the problems besetting Europe — examples are not only unemployment, inflation and low productivity growth, but also racism, xenophobia and parochialism — can be reduced by improving the quality of general education and by developing lifelong education, both generally and vocationally oriented, is gaining currency among politicians and decision makers.

The hypothesis guiding the development of adult education markets in Europe at present is that increased investment particularly in continuing vocational education will provide the labour market with the skills required for the revitalization of industry and produce added value boosting the development of the nation and the region. Another crucial assumption is that the individual or microscopic, and the societal or macroscopic, benefits of continuing education are interrelated: if the balance of individual costs and benefits is positive, then there may well also be an aggregate gain for society. This postulate provides the key to most theories and analyses of the relationship between initial and post-initial education, on the one hand, and economic growth and national development, on the other. Indeed, the basic premise guiding the development of both public and private training markets is that the skills and know-how acquired by the adult learner through participation in an educational activity or training programme "add to" the population's "stock" of intellectual and cultural "capital". This increase in the intellectual level of the population, which is "produced" by education and training, may well constitute a major source for improving the conditions determining economic strength and, ultimately, the wealth and happiness of the nation (Tuijnman, 1992a).

The Market Model in Adult Education

Compared with the situation prevailing a decade ago, there would seem to be more appreciation today of the fact that adult learners are inherently different. It is also recognized that the contexts in which adults decide to engage in learning tasks and choose among a variety of learning options are not invariant but change over time. Populations vary from immigrants and unemployed workers to engineers, scientists and older adults. There are many factors that influence the decision of individuals to take part in an educational or training activity. The delivery mechanisms for learning vary as well. These may be classroom-based, using the traditional lecture method, or use self-directed learning in an informal setting, at work or at home.

The notion of the adult education market, which was briefly introduced in the preceding section, is central to an understanding of the new policy context of adult education in many industrialized countries. The following themes or "slogans" are useful in describing the general policy at present: (a) "economism" and "vocationalism", (b) financial austerity and decentralization, (c) individual demand and accountability and (d) politicization and fragmentation. [2]

Economism

"Economism" — or the belief in education as a profitable investment — dominates the debate in many countries at present. The increase in international trade provides a part of the explanation. The current emphasis on European integration, the goals, means and ends of which are spelled out in the Draft Treaty Establishing the European Union and the White Paper on Completing the Internal Market, can be interpreted as an attempt to provide an answer to the challenges posed by industrial competitor countries. The pursuit of the largely economic goals of European integration as set out in the Single European Act may well produce a "knock-on" effect with respect to adult education, as the latter is increasingly regarded as an important means of enhancing the competitive advantage of countries dealing on international markets. The implications of "economism" in education are, firstly, that the interests of firms in training tend to take precedence over public interests in skill development and, secondly, that economic objectives such as achieving competitiveness and profitability are weighted much higher than social goals aimed at, for instance, equity and the maintenance of the "welfare society". In the case of a country such as Germany, but also in many of the countries formerly belonging to the Soviet Union, there are,

---

[2] Some of these themes are used by Halls in discussing the development of school education from 1960 to 1985 (see, e.g., Husén et al., 1992).

moreover, clear implications for adult education caused by the shifting of the various boundaries and allegiances. There is no doubt that the unification of the two Germanies brings a huge task and challenge to adult education. This challenge is equally visible in the formerly socialist countries in transition to market capitalism. However, with respect to the affluent Western European countries the claim that these countries are faced with the harmful effects of underinvestment in adult education and training goes not entirely uncontested.

Vocationalism

"Vocationalism" refers to the tendency at present to assign priority to vocational and technical courses in adult education, supplanting the previous "academic" hallmark and general character of many adult education programmes. There can be no doubt that decision makers now put emphasis on "employable skills" syllabuses, that is, on programmes of continuing education conferring instrumental qualifications either for the present job or a future occupation. Less attention is given to "consumption" education — educational programmes that are seen as lacking a clear investment profile, primarily courses intended for personal development and the enrichment of leisure. The themes of "economism" and "vocationalism" reflect an awareness that there may be underinvestment in certain components of the skill formation process, particularly job training.

Financial austerity

There seems to be a political consensus in many of the European countries that public spending on education cannot at present be increased. However, the poor state of public finance in countries such as Italy, Sweden, and the United Kingdom is in open conflict with the need to invest in skill formation. That the costs of educational provision tend to rise over time makes it even more difficult to accomodate new claims on the public budget for education. Consequently, there is a realization in some countries that firms and individuals should assume a major responsibility for investment, much more than has hitherto been the case. Although time-series data on training expenditures are either not available or of very doubtful quality, there is some indication in countries such as France, Germany, and the Netherlands, and Nordic countries such as Finland, Norway, and Sweden, that firms have indeed perceptibly increased their overall share in the finance of adult education and training since the mid-1980s (OECD, 1991b). In countries where data are available, for example France and Germany, participation seems to have increased concomitantly with the increase in total expenditure.

Decentralization

In many countries, stagnation or even a relative decline in the amount of public resources for education is matched with a diminishing role of government in educational decision making generally. Power seems to have devolved down to the institutional and individual level. This may reflect distrust of the capacity of central authorities in achieving many of the goals sought by firms and also many — but not all — individuals, such as coherence and efficiency in the management of educational change and improving the quality and relevance of education and training. Whereas it was common in the 1960s and 1970s to adhere to a strategy of planning at a central level of government, the trend emerging in the 1980s was to decentralize, that is, to leave the matching of supply and demand to the adult education market. It may be obvious that this new approach to educational planning has important implications for training policy. It implies an increase in the role of third parties, not only in the finance of adult education and training but, by implication, also in decisions about who is to be trained, how much and where. The capacity of governments to intervene in training markets is generally low. Hence the debate at present concerning the possibly negative consequences of decentralization. For example, the question is raised how the learning needs of adults not in employment or otherwise not affected by the development of private markets for adult education can be guaranteed.

Individualism

The notion of "social demand" seems to have been replaced with "individual demand" as a determinant of provision. The primary responsibility for organizing a learning encounter rests with the individual. Hence the problem of access is being considered in relation to the needs of the individual adult learner. This theme is closely linked up with other characteristics of the policy context of adult education at present, namely, a renewed emphasis on freedom of choice, individualism and meritocracy. The market solution is generally seen as an attractive means of making the skill formation process flexible and responsive to changes in demand. This new emphasis on individual instead of social demand may well reflect a tendency of favouring a bounded *laissez-faire* approach to adult education, in which the role of the State seems to be limited to one of passively encouraging participation. In contrast, the notion of social demand would imply a more active role of government, for example selective intervention rather than a mere monitoring of trends.

Accountability

The demand for accountability is a general phenomenon in education. It constitutes a key factor in an explanation of the general tendency in the Western European countries of adopting a market-oriented approach to the development of adult education. Accountability arose in part from the "new consumerism" of the 1980s. The "consumer" of adult education — the individual learner, firms, and local communities — were seen as demanding value for money. Catchwords such as quality control, efficiency and cost-effectiveness began to be bandied about as a result. The "buying" and "selling" of adult education and training on competitive markets are considered essential ingredients in a strategy aimed at ensuring quality control and meeting the demand for accountability. That untapped resources are supplied by the "consumers" of education, the firm and the adult learner, is considered an additional advantage. International organizations such as the OECD, UNESCO and the EC through its FORCE-programme run projects aiming at the development of an international methodology for the collection and reporting of statistics on further education and training (OECD), adult and nonformal education (UNESCO), and continuing vocational education (EC). This may well be seen as a reflection of the widespread demand for accountability in adult education.

Politicization

It is only natural that all stakeholders in the skill formation process demand a say in decision making. The major stakeholders are the central and local government, employers, labour unions and, not least, the individual adult learner. As previously mentioned, the role of the government in training has generally been scaled down. The government has become more of a facilitator and mediator than an initiator and legislator. The importance of collectively negotiated agreements has concomitantly increased. In certain respects the position at present is one of politicization. In many Western European countries there is now a "partial agreement" among the political parties, employers, and labour unions, with respect to the objectives, means and ends of skill formation, but disagreement about how to achieve this. Whereas representatives of the social partners, political groups, and the governments are generally in agreement with respect to the overarching goals of adult education and training, major interpretative differences emerge once the goals of specific educational policies are examined. Differences between the countries in their general approach to adult education, and especially in the way adult education is being financed, can in part be explained by the country-specific history of educational policy making, which is heavily influenced by the dynamic of change created by previous policy commitments.

Fragmentation

The range and variants of learning possibilities have generally increased in the industrialized countries. They now vary from classroom learning to collaborative group learning, open learning networks and support for self-directed learning. New programmes have been added on top of already existing ones. As a consequence of this "fragmentation" in adult education, the choice of the "right" learning strategy is becoming increasingly important but also increasingly difficult. Fragmentation may prevent some adults from knowing where to pursue a certain learning task. Hence the increased attention being given at present to the need for information concerning the availability of learning opportunities for adults.

Skills Shortages

The economic situation at present encourages firms to strengthen their concern with human resource development. There is also an increasing demand for people with "the skills employers want" (for a typology of such skills see Chapter 9 in this volume). This demand, of course, is driven by factors such as the changes in skills and in the organization of work that follow on the deployment of new technologies in the workplace. Computer integrated manufacturing and robotics, expert systems, and office automation systems, profoundly influence the work environment and, accordingly, the skills demanded of the workforce. It is widely recognized at present that skills gaps are at the heart of some of the problems posed by new technology. The obvious implication is that educational systems must prepare people for a life of active learning. This raises the question as to the role of the school in promoting lifelong learning.

Implications for School Education

Schooling tends to be extended to cover an increasing part of the lifespan of the individual. This development has a number of implications for school education. Firstly, the purpose of basic schooling is no longer to provide young people with the knowledge and skills for the rest of their life. As knowledge in advanced societies becomes rapidly obsolete, the goals of schooling are increasingly defined in relation to preparing not only for working life but also for educational and cultural life. Secondly, as schools are sharing their educative responsibility with other agents and institutions, the socialization function of schools must be assumed to change as well. The implication is that ways must be sought to encourage greater participation and meaningfulness in education, for example, by conferring adult responsibilities on young people in the larger societal context.

Here, we are faced with a dilemma. On the one hand, future society will demand a well-educated population. The idea is that the level of educational attainment among the general population should be raised. However, large groups of young people seem not to be interested in staying on at school once attendance is no longer compulsory — usually after 16 or 18 years of age. Is it really desirable to have compulsory schooling until the age of 16 years or above? Should the period of mandatory schooling be lengthened or, perhaps, should the opposite be promoted, which is argued by those who consider that problems of modern schooling could be reduced if children were given more adult responsibility, for example as would be the case if school systems were organized with a recurrent education strategy?

The principal objective of the recurrent education strategy advocated since the late 1960s by the OECD and its Centre for Educational Research and Innovation (CERI, 1973) has been to increase flexibility, efficiency and equity in developing and utilizing human resources. This was to be achieved by alternating education, work, and leisure over the lifespan. The pursuance of alternation between education and work has a practical implication for school systems. Terminal points in the educational system, particularly at the upper secondary level, could be abolished so that all educational programmes could lead on to other programmes. Another implication is that students who have dropped out of the educational system after having completed obligatory schooling only, and who are interested in continuing their educational careers after a period of interruption, should have the right and possibility to reenter the system. This is especially important because the formal education young people receive at an early age is in many ways decisive for their life chances and careers in present-day society, where the level of formal education increasingly determines people's general life chances, occupational career and social status. Shortcomings in school education can only be compensated to a limited extent by means of recurrent adult education, retraining, and staff development programmes in working life.

The results of longitudinal research studies (Tuijnman, 1992b; Van Leeuwen and Dronkers, 1992) consistently indicate that a large portion of individual differences in educational attainments are accounted for by nonscholastic factors. Disparities between social groups have a tendency to continue up the educational ladder, from primary to secondary to post-school levels of education. Education gained in youth influences occupation and the opportunity of acquiring additional educational experience later in life. These results may well be interpreted as showing that a cycle of accumulation is in operation in which education received initially plays a decisive role both in mediating the effects of home background and cognitive ability, and in influencing the likelihood of receiving postinitial education and training.

Longitudinal studies of how the individual's life career and earnings profile have developed over time show that adult education and training play a role in the accumulation of advantages and disadvantages over the lifespan. Those who have used the system of recurrent education later in their lives tend to have reached occupations with higher levels of responsibility, social prestige, and earnings compared to others untouched by the system. But the same studies also show that those who have had a relatively long and qualitatively good formal education in early life are those who make most use of the possibilities for upgrading and retraining offered in a society. It may be anticipated that those who have postponed a phase of their formal education until later in their lives, instead of transferring to higher education immediately after taking the school-leaving examination, cannot compensate for the relative disadvantages they face early in their career by returning to formal education later on. The implication is that the increased provision of postinitial education does not lessen but reinforces the important role of schooling as a determinant of social stratification.

Although the effects of home background on educational and occupational careers are consistently strong, there would seem to be no place for fatalism of the kind espoused during the early 1970s, when the claim that schooling "did not make a difference" was frequently heard in debate on educational policy. The implications are that the differentation of students into qualitatively dissimilar programmes may well have to be delayed, possibly until age 15 at least, and that overspecialized vocational education at the secondary level ought to be avoided. It may be noted in this respect that the mandate of the school in imparting knowledge and skills for a vocation and citizenship is diminishing relative to the influence of other educative agents operating in a society. A high price will have to be paid in the long-term perspective if policy to ensure equity in school education is sacrificed for short-term gains in quality, efficiency, and school effectiveness. Under the impact of changes affecting the precarious balance between equity and efficiency, it may well become necessary to reassess the basic values guiding educational policy and practice. It is possible that children and society may be better served if the content of initial schooling is broad and general rather than narrowly focussed on the specific vocational skills in high demand on the labour market at a given moment.

There are good reasons to assume that, to a certain extent, what is beneficial for the career development of the individual is also good for the development of the nation at large. If the findings of research studies are generally valid, then they must be held to have far-reaching consequences for the structuring and organization of educational systems. This applies also to the criteria that can be employed in selecting students for university admission. One implication is that it may well be beneficial in the long run if children start school at an early age. In those countries where children begin their formal schooling at seven, one could consider whether the entry age can be lowered to six or even five years. As it does not seem to pay off, at least from the viewpoint of the individual, to postpone part of higher education until a mature age, students may be well advised to transfer to higher education immediately after finishing the upper secondary school.

One has begun to realize that the goals of schooling have to be more limited than was believed in the optimistic period of the 1960s. At the same time, though, it is essential to place these goals in a larger framework of interaction with other educative agents, since schools by themselves furnish an incomplete context for maturation. It can be concluded that children are best equipped for life if they are eager to keep on learning after leaving school. One purpose of the school is therefore to foster the idea and desire for lifelong learning. This may be achieved only if the school can be made into a place where children like to go.

Implications for Adult Education

As mentioned previously in this chapter, much has occurred since the theory of recurrent education was developed in the late 1960s. Recurrent education — and varieties going under labels such as continuing education and further education and training — has assumed vastly greater visibility and importance in industrialized countries during the 1980s, mainly on the strength of a new appreciation for its potential economic consequences. Yet, although its importance as an educational and economic activity is generally recognized by governments at present, adult education remains structurally weak. This raises some interesting questions concerning the scenarios for change and development in the 1990s and beyond. These will be considered in the next chapter.

In some countries concern has recently been expressed at an alleged drop in standards in basic literacy and numeracy. If true, this presents a major problem, as these skills are fundamental to all learning. Information-processing skills are also at the very centre of a society, affecting not only economic growth, the distribution of wealth and opportunity, and a country's capacity to attract investment, but also influencing culture and the functioning of a democracy.

Illiteracy in the adult population was, until recently, not perceived as a major problem by decision makers in many industrialized countries. Although perhaps for different reasons, countries routinely reported to international agencies that illiteracy either did not exist or could only be found among a very small portion of the population. The view that illiteracy is a problem affecting only certain marginal groups in a society, particularly immigrants, was widely held for example in the Nordic countries, Germany, the Netherlands, and Switzerland.

Yet, in France, the position changed in the mid-1980s when several surveys established not only that functional illiteracy affected a sizeable proportion of French-born citizens (figures of 12 to 20 per cent have been mentioned, according to the criteria used) but also immigrant workers. The "rapport Migeon" led the Ministry of Education in France to consider new measures for assessing and improving the reading comprehension of adults and encouraging reading practice among the young. These findings corroborated those arrived at in the United Kingdom some years previously and helped to draw public and political attention to the issue. The promotional activities and studies launched by many countries in connection with the United Nations International Literacy Year in 1990 have also called attention to the idea that illiteracy is a much more pervasive and difficult problem than generally anticipated, even in the highly industrialized and affluent countries.

The realization that adult illiteracy in fact constitutes a problem, although one that may vary in degree from country to country, has led to government action and the launching of adult basic education programmes in different countries. This development has reinforced the concern with school quality, as schooling is expected to provide a basis for lifelong literacy, and has prompted an interest in learning on the job, since work is regarded as a part of lifelong learning. The transformation of the work organization into a learning organization has therefore become a recognized objective in many countries. But there are also many unanswered questions. An understanding of how learning in the work place occurs, whether in the form of structured training on or off the job or by means of informal and self-planned learning, may reveal ways of linking work place learning to business needs, determining learning priorities and improving the practice of human resources development, thus improving the cost-effectiveness of the operation.

However, given that the skills employers want and the learning needs of adults are highly diverse, general answers to the question as to what constitutes an effective approach to skill development do not seem to exist. Because the economic significance of skill formation has vastly increased as a consequence of new technology and increased trade competition, answers to questions such as how adults learn and why they prefer one learning option rather than another are urgently needed. Some priorities for research on the adult learner are summarized below.

Implications for Research on the Adult Learner

The OECD, as part of the CERI activity on Technological Change and Human Resources Development, is conducting a study on the adult learner. This may be taken as a strong indication of the renewed interest in the lifelong learner as presenting a focal point in the design of strategies needed to improve the equity, efficiency, and effectiveness of skills formation. Since investment in initial education serves mainly long-term goals, labour markets which face a sudden need for structural adjustment depend for the timely supply of new skills and competences on the willingness and capacity of adults to learn effectively. Adult learners and their learning capacity, needs, and preferences must therefore be taken into account in the design of a strategy for skill formation. Because the economic significance of skill formation has vastly increased as a consequence of new technology and increased trade competition, answers to questions such as how adults learn and why they prefer one learning option rather than another are urgently needed.

The learning routes and options that are open to the adult learner have, in many cases, become unclear as a result of the increased diversity, incohesiveness and apparent unstructuredness of adult education and training markets in the industrialized countries. The role that guidance can play in helping adults in making an informed choice among the various learning possibilities that are available in a society has therefore become an all-important factor in making both provision and learning effective. This inevitably raises the question as to the factors that influence guidance, and how these can be optimalized. Research studies could look into the determinants of effective guidance and the development of support systems for adult students.

Bailey (1988, p. 334-5) suggests a range of activities aimed at assisting adults in becoming aware of learning options and helping them in managing learning: informing, advising, and counselling; coaching and assessment; advocacy and feedback. There also is a clear need for visibility and coherence rather than an overproliferation of programmes. Insight into the structure of the adult education market is a prerequisite for a well-functioning system. The question of how different variants of learning relate to each other in terms of structure, content, method and time is therefore crucial.

The recent shift from institutional adult education to nonformal provision with an emphasis on the training and retraining of workers in internal labour markets has led to an even more diffuse picture of the learning opportunities that are available in a society. This development has led to a concern with the structural weaknesses of adult education provision. The question of why and how adults learn at different moments in the lifespan has come to the fore as a result of this reorientation towards strategies for lifelong learning. A new interest in learning contents as well as in teaching methods for adults can also be noted.

Now that countries such as Japan, Norway, Canada and Australia are targeting lifelong learning as a major goal of educational development, concern with the consequences of unequal school education and unequal opportunity to learn in adult life is returning. Given the implications of the findings alluded to above, a reorientation of policy towards lifelong learning may also necessitate a revival of concern with equality of educational opportunity.

While interest in lifelong learning is slowly gaining momentum, governments have so far opted for a strategy to increase provision by relying on the strength of private initiative. Informal learning at the work place is being given particular attention. However, empirical data showing that such learning takes place and that it is sufficient and effective in responding to the diverse learning needs of adults is generally not available. Hence the emphasis on private provision and informal learning at the work place may also entail certain risks. This situation raises questions concerning the determinants of the nature and distribution of opportunities to learn at the work place. An understanding of how well these learning opportunities correspond to the needs is also required.

Despite the critical note above, it is acknowledged that informal and independent learning may be highly cost-effective in satisfying the diversified learning needs of adults in relation to their work and leisure activities. The contribution of self-directed learning to skills formation is therefore an appropriate question for research. Questions such as what motivates the adult learner, why adults decide to embark on certain learning projects, and how they fulfil their own learning needs through self-directed study or participation in educational programmes, are also worthy of attention.

Underlying all of the above is the desire to help adults learn and to promote effective learning environments. The increased reliance on nonformal and informal approaches to providing learning opportunities for adults raises the question whether and to what extent public policy and intervention by employers can influence the learning process and optimalize its outcomes. These questions are considered in the next chapter.

Conclusion

This chapter has described how the policy context of adult education has changed during the 1970s and 1980s. Amongst the principal changes are a tendency to move from collective solutions to individual approaches. Concomitant with development there is a loosening-up of the formerly sharp division between education and work. It is now more and more accepted that learning forms an integral part of work.

It can be concluded that the imperative of investing in the adult learner is not in doubt in the OECD countries (see also OECD, 1991c). Less certain are the answers to questions such as how to raise the human and financial resources and which strategies to employ in order to facilitate adult learning and increase yield. The law of diminishing returns to investment almost certainly also applies to the adult education market. More money does not necessarily produce the desired results.

References

Bailey, D. (1988). Guidance and counselling in work-based open learning. In N. Paine (Ed.), *Open learning in transition. An agenda for action* (pp. 332-349). London: Kogan Page.

Bengtsson, J. (1989). Recurrent education. In C.J. Titmus (Ed.), *Lifelong education for adults: An international handbook* (pp. 43-51). Oxford: Pergamon Press.

Bundesminister für Bildung und Wissenschaft (1990). *Betriebliche Weiterbildung. Forschungsstand und Forschungsperspektiven: Zwei Gutachten.* Bonn: Bundesminister für Bildung und Wissenschaft.

Centre for Educational Research and Innovation (1973). *Recurrent education: A strategy for lifelong learning.* Paris: OECD.

Davis, N., Ravanel, B., & Walther, R. (1991). Continuing vocational training in companies. A study in comparison: France, United Kingdom, Germany (Working paper). Brussels: Commission of the EC, Technical Assistance Unit, Force.

Husén, T., Tuijnman, A.C, & Halls, W.D. (Eds.) (1992). *Schooling in modern European society: A report of the Academia Europaea.* Oxford: Pergamon Press.

Lenske, W., & Zillessen, R. (1987). *Ergebnisse einer Betriebsbefragung zur beruflichen und schulischen Bildung.* Berichte zur Bildungspolitik 1987/88 des Instituts der Deutschen Wirtschaft. Cologne: U. Göbel und W. Schlaffke.

Levin, H.M. (1987). Improving productivity through education and technology. In G. Burke & R. Rumberger (Eds.), *The future impact of technology on work and education.* London: The Falmer Press.

Levin, H.M., & Schütze, H.G. (Eds.) (1983). *Financing recurrent education: Strategies for increasing employment, job opportunities, and productivity.* London: Sage.

OECD (1987). *Structural adjustment and economic performance.* Paris: OECD.

OECD (1991a). *Intergovernmental conference on further education and training of the labour force: Issues paper.* Paris: OECD.

OECD (1991b). Enterprise-related training. In *Employment Outlook, July 1991* (pp. 135-175). Paris: OECD.

OECD (1991c). *Further education and training of the labour force in OECD countries: Evidence and issues.* Paris: OECD.

Stern, D. & Ritzen, J.M.M. (Eds.) (1991). *Market failure in training? New economic analysis and evidence on training of adult employees*. Berlin: Springer-Verlag.

Tuijnman, A.C. (1991). Emerging systems of recurrent education. *Prospects 21* (1), 17-24.

Tuijnman, A.C. (1992a). Der Beitrag von Schule und Weiterbildung zur individuellen und gesellschaftlichen Entwicklung. *Unterrichtswissenschaft 20* (1), 83-96.

Tuijnman, A.C. (1992b). Continuing education, training, and life chances: A linear structural relations analysis. *International Journal of Educational Research 17*, 593-608.

Tuijnman, A.C., & Van Der Kamp, M. (1991) *Effective adult learning: Theories and policies*. Paris: CERI/OECD.

Van Leeuwen, S., & Dronkers, J. (1992). Effects of continuing education: A study on adult education, social inequality, and labour market position. *International Journal of Educational Research 17* (6), 609-624.

Chapter 14

PUBLIC INTERVENTION IN ADULT EDUCATION

JOHN LOWE
University of Warwick, Coventry, U.K.

This chapter considers the role of governments in the education of adults, whether that role be active, passive, or somewhere in between. The context is the national or federal level but, wherever appropriate, references are also made to the local level. [1]

The chapter describes and discusses the nature and scope of public intervention in adult education and points to the gap, which in many countries is very wide, between expressions of verbal support and practical action. It examines the issues surrounding the notion of intervention and indicates the options available to governments that make a commitment to comprehensive policies.

The Marginal Position of Adult Education

In all OECD countries there has been an increasing public commitment in recent times to continuing and recurrent education and, specifically, to making adequate provision for the training and retraining of national workforces (OECD, 1989). The reason for this may be summarized as follows. The exclusive emphasis on the education of the young generation was understandable when change was a relatively gradual process. It has ceased to become so in the present epoch of economic and technological upheaval. Educational reforms do not take effect in the short term. The investment in youth education is for the long term. On the other hand, an investment in the education and training of

---

[1] This is an abridged version of a study originally commissioned by OECD/CERI as a contribution to its programme on The Adult Learner.

adults, whether inside or outside the labour market, can bring about more
or less instant returns. Besides being as a rule motivated and efficient
learners, adults are able to apply what they learn.

Simultaneously, adults in rapidly expandingly numbers have been
seeking organized learning opportunities in a wide range of programmes
for a variety of reasons. In response, the quantitative growth of public
and private provision has been spectacular and matched in most countries by a steep increase in overall expenditure. What is striking,
however, is that adult education, considered as a whole process and
discrete sector of national education systems, remains curiously marginal
and even fragile, except in a few countries. It does not enjoy the constitutional, administrative and financial underpinning of the formal system
of education. National and regional governments can be said to recognize
the necessity for active adult learning on a large scale but not the
concomitant necessity for ensuring that it is systematically provided and
organized. As many professional adult educators have been protesting for
the past 30 years, public education systems continue to be obdurately
front-loaded.

In reality, systems of adult education scarcely exist (Darkenwald and
Merriam, 1982, p. 177). There are only subsystems with diverse purposes. The current forms of provision originally emerged in response to
spontaneous private demand, or because public authorities identified a
specific economic or social need, such as improvements in farming
methods or literacy classes for immigrants, which might be satisfied
through educational programmes. It is only relatively recently that a
minority of countries has come to perceive adult education as a discrete
entity and to create coherent systems. Thus, the Nordic group now treats
it as a priority within the context of their attachment to lifelong learning.
A Swedish official report declares: "One ought therefore to avoid
excessive preoccupation with youth education and its effects. Measures
for the subsequent and further education of people in the existing labour
force are every bit as interesting, if not more so, in terms of impact on
working life" (Sweden, 1987, p. 9). And a report from Finland (1990)
echoes: "the focus in education policy will move more and more to adult
education. The quantity and time devoted to adult education will
increase". Japan is another country where it is the official policy to break
away from excessive dependence on initial education by expanding and
diversifying lifelong learning facilities (Shiokawa, 1987), and where
employers insist on the continuing training of their employees. A Bureau
of Lifelong Learning has been set up in the Ministry of Education,
Science, and Culture (Japan, 1991).

In most countries, however, adult education services continue to be
fragmentary, understaffed, and underfinanced except in the occupational
training sector. Much of the provision is not linked to public, social,

cultural, and economic concerns. Some of it is dysfunctional. It is not perceived as a necessary appendage of the formal education system. Implicitly, governments consider that some educational sectors are more valuable than others because they serve the national interest. In other words, priority is given to collective or societal rather than individual development.

The marginality of adult education might appear surprising in view of the groundswell of support that had become manifest by the early 1970s. The traditional arguments in its favour propounded by interest groups such as workers' educational associations appeared then to be strengthened by the impact upon public opinion and official thinking of the newly fashionable concepts of lifelong education and recurrent education, since these furnished a persuasive rationale for treating it as the necessary complement of initial education. CERI's own analysis of the policy implications of introducing the principle of recurrence pointed to the conclusion that in all, or at least many of its aspects, adult education should be treated as an integral component of comprehensive and revamped national education systems (CERI/OECD, 1973; Mushkin, 1973).

In the mid-1970s the report *Comprehensive Policies for Adult Education* (OECD, 1977a) was published. It was prepared in collaboration with official representatives of Member countries and took the form of a guide to policy development. Four possible futures were envisaged:

1. to let adult education evolve, as in the past, in a spontaneous and sporadic fashion without reference to any explicit public intervention;
2. to strengthen and coordinate the existing range of activities but not to perceive it as an active instrument of public policy in the social and economic areas;
3. to strengthen and coordinate the existing range of activities while simultaneously pursuing a positive policy of support for specific activities judged to be national priorities, for example secondary education equivalency programmes designed to promote equality;
4. to create a comprehensive service of adult education as an integral element of broadly conceived education systems and to relate its functions to the social, economic, and cultural objectives of the nation.

The report estimated that in 1976 the majority of countries found themselves in the third position though some appeared clearly to be moving in the direction of the fourth as a long-term destination. The logical consequence of its own findings was that countries should adopt gradualist policies, based on a judicious mix of the third and fourth alternatives, tuned to fit national circumstances, on the grounds that in an epoch of unprecedented flux, active learning had become a social and personal imperative as much for the adult as for the child or young person (OECD, 1977b, pp. 80-81).

Fifteen years later, however, little progress has been made, and in certain countries, there has even been regression. Explanations are easy to come by. One is that the report was prepared at the heights of the overall expansion of education after the end of the Second World War and just before the advent of the widespread youth unemployment that was to absorb nearly all the attention and spare resources of national and regional authorities. Another is that the task of reducing adult as well as youth unemployment threw all the emphasis on vocational training as opposed to the other purposes of education and put paid to any notions of strengthening and coordinating the existing range of activities, let alone creating a comprehensive service as recommended in the report. A third is that the relative optimism of the early 1970s was misplaced. There was no inevitability about adult education attaining parity of esteem and constitutional backing with the rest of the education system or, indeed, of ever becoming an authentic system.

Degrees of Intervention

The intervention of governments in adult education falls into four broad categories of intensity reflecting the four futures envisaged in the OECD (1977b) report: (a) there are those that treat it with benign neglect, "benign" being the operative word since there is no evidence anywhere of a positive or calculated rejection; (b) there are those who believe that the provision of adult education should be very largely left to private initiatives on the ground that it is an individual rather than a collective good; (c) there are those who recognize a duty to promote adult education by means of both direct and indirect provision; (d) there are those who recognize a duty to promote and support adult education by means of both direct and indirect provision.

The third and fourth categories share the view that the educational needs of adults are too complex and too costly to be left solely or mainly to the efforts of nongovernmental organizations. In addition to the economic or instrumentalist reasons for supporting adult education enumerated above, they are swayed by equitable, ethical, and social concerns. First, they recognize that if disadvantaged people are to improve their social and economic position and if immigrants are to be assimilated into society, then, among other desiderata, they must have access to opportunities for basic education. Second, in order to help disadvantaged children to profit from their schooling it is necessary to modify the attitudes and to enlist the cooperation of their parents by means of formal and nonformal learning as well as systematic consultation. Third, they are increasingly aware that some of today's social, cultural, ecological, and energy problems can be controlled or eliminated only by raising the level of public consciousness and understanding by means of education. Finally, they are slowly but surely acknowledging that schools cannot be expected to fulfil all the responsibilities that have been thrust upon them by parents and communities and that some educational tasks might more effectively and economically be carried out by developing and diversifying forms of postschool education. At the same time, they believe not only that nongovernmental agencies should have complete freedom to operate but also that they should be given every encouragement, including financial assistance. The differences between the third and fourth categories will now be considered.

The third category comprises those countries in which adult education has evolved in spontaneous fashion under the leadership of enterprising groups and individuals. Its dynamic is voluntary endeavour and its credo is pluralism, diversity, and autonomy. The Nordic study circles exemplify this tradition: in Sweden it is estimated that there are about 2,700,000 participants each year. One may also note the seeming paradox that governments have supported civic education programmes, including those sponsored by trade unions. Little by little, however, governments have become engaged indirectly — first, by financing providing agencies under specified conditions and then by promoting the overall development of adult education in a variety of ways. But the policy is still to let adult education develop spontaneously. Thus, "free civic education work" is a term often used in Finland in speaking of adult education. Particularly significant is the word "free". It indicates that education outside schools, university and vocational schools proper depends mainly on the activity of the citizens themselves. Society plays as small a role as possible in this work and gives adult education maximum internal freedom. The laws and statutes on this usually concern the financial support offered by society, while the work itself is left to those concerned, the State merely keeping a reasonable eye on standards. Many nongovernmental agencies are sustained by long and powerful traditions (Finland, 1990).

Most of those who identify themselves with the field or profession of adult education strongly criticise the persistent shortage of public funding but they are essentially content with the arrangement whereby the public authorities are not direct providers on a major scale and wield limited administrative powers. Their position is comprehensible given their wish to remain autonomous, their unease about public intervention on libertarian grounds and their fear, justified by experience, that as public authorities invest in direct provision they are increasingly tempted to reduce their material support for nongovernmental agencies. One may cite the experience of Quebec where after 1966:

> This large input of government resources into an area (adult education) hitherto dominated by community enterprises was to have significant results. On the one hand, formal academic training, of the type given to young people became the outstanding feature of adult education. On the other hand, the considerable human and material resources pumped into this sector by the government over-shadowed and even upset, whether by design or otherwise, some important adult education networks. (Gouvernement de Québec, 1981, p. 33)

There has also been widespread concern among adult educators that:

> ... there is taking place a shift of power from the local community, however it may be defined, to central authorities, from private initiative to public direction that, in the process, certain qualities traditionally valued by adult education are in danger of disappearing in spite of positive action to preserve them; that the very nature of adult education may be changing and not necessarily for the better. (Titmus, 1980, pp. 136-7)

The trouble is that some nongovernmental agencies may be serving the public interest only partially and that a few may not be serving it at all. Others have become monopolies. It is also arguable that so long as their role is indirect, the public authorities will not commit funds to the development of adult education on a significant scale.

It is the fourth category that constitutes the best arrangement, namely the formulation of policies for the development of adult education and a judicious mixture of direct and indirect support for programmes. Thus, programmes may be offered directly by public authorities using a variety of agencies including schools, short-cycle postsecondary institutions and universities. Simultaneously, they may give financial and other support to nongovernmental agencies. To avoid the danger of selling the latter short, it is sufficient to create constitutional mechanisms for determining both the particular agencies and types of programmes that merit support and appropriate levels of financing. That mechanism can be made free of public interference.

There is potentially a fifth category of public intervention, simply mentioned here for the record, namely support exclusively for public institutions and programmes. This applies in a large number of countries with undemocratic constitutions, above all and paradoxically in those countries where, unlike in the OECD group, the public authorities have declared a national commitment to adult education as a whole system and enacted legislation accordingly.

Responsibility, Administration, Coordination and Control

Countries in the first two categories are by definition not concerned about who is responsible for adult education and how it is to be organized, administered, coordinated, supervised and evaluated. Countries in the third and fourth categories, however, must seek answers to these questions. As they do so, four factors have to be taken into account:

1. integration of public and parapublic services;
2. relationships between publicly provided adult education and the formal system;
3. supervision and coordination of public and nonpublic provision;
4. the State and training at the work place.

Integration of Public and Parapublic Services

Many government ministries, departments, and agencies other than ministries of education now sponsor instruction of one kind or another for members of the public. These chiefly include ministries of agriculture, social welfare, health, and labour. The problems raised by the overlapping responsibilities of ministries of education and labour, including the lack of complementarity between general and vocational education, have become notorious. Occupational training has become almost everywhere a major function of ministries of labour, which often command vast resources for the purpose. Their programmes tend to be heavily decentralized to the local community level where they often overlap or conflict with the programmes of the local adult education authorities and nongovernmental agencies.

Darkenwald and Merriam (1982, p. 179) write that coordination of adult education at all levels of government has two basic and interrelated dimensions: "coordination among different public programmes with similar or complementary objectives; and coordination among different kinds of institutions or delivery systems that provide similar or complementary services".

The case for coordination has fully convinced the Netherlands government. Until 1989, the Ministry of Education and Science was responsible for formal adult education, the Ministry of Culture and Recreation for socio-cultural education and personal development, and the Ministry of Labour for occupational training. Under a new arrangement overall responsibility for determining policies and programmes and administering funds has been entrusted to a cabinet committee within the Prime Minister's office (UNESCO, 1989, p. 312).

Coordination at the community level is a crucial requirement. In practice, the direct public provision of adult education, and much of the public support for nongovernmental agencies, take place within the jurisdictions of communities, municipalities and regional authorities, even though these usually operate largely in response to policies formulated centrally and spend funds also largely allocated from the centre. Adult education is far more a local activity than formal education.

Schools and universities are governed as a rule by national regulations and are generally viewed as part of a national or, at least, *Länder* or State service, even when there is a good deal of local or institutional autonomy. In contrast, adult education is generally viewed as decentralized to communities where adult learners choose for themselves what, when, and where to study. Only professional adult educators tend to stress the nationwide dimension or to speak of national movements.

In Sweden, many municipalities have established adult education councils consisting of representatives of the local education authorities, educational associations, libraries, trade union organizations and sometimes folk high schools. In addition, there are county adult education councils and associations. Norway has local councils to coordinate a broad variety of adult education programmes including formal academic courses and vocational training. In each *nome* or local district in Greece, there is an Adult Education Nomarchy Committee responsible for the control of evening primary schools and adult education centres.

In some countries adult education pressure groups condemn the unevenness of provision from region to region and community to community. This criticism can be countered by national authorities if they choose to adopt legal and financial measures designed to ensure minimum levels of direct public provision and support for nongovernmental agencies. However, critics cannot have it both ways. If they want adult education to remain primarily a voluntary and autonomous activity, they must accept that there are necessary limits to governmental engagement and that the analogy with public responsibility for the even-handed administration and financing of the formal system should not be pushed too far. Moreover, public authorities will not be inclined to invest as heavily in adult as in formal education as long as they directly control only a section of it.

Publicly Provided Adult Education and the Formal System

Should adult education and the regular education system be integrated or separately controlled and administered? Arguments can be advanced in favour of either option, although progress towards systems of recurrent and lifelong education necessitates some machinery for integration. The relationship can be determined in four different ways:
1. to regard all adult education services as quite distinct;
2. to distinguish between formal programmes for adults, which are incorporated in the general service, and out-of-school education programmes, which are administered separately;
3. to embody a comprehensive adult education service within the general service but in practice to finance and administer it separately;

4. effectively to integrate a comprehensive adult education service with the general service.

Complete separation is usually impossible if only because no country can afford to set up free-standing buildings and employ great numbers of full-time teachers of adults. The issue of integration is blurred, moreover, by conflicting interpretations of what public provision should comprise. Evidently, for some countries, it implies neither more nor less than offering adults exactly the same courses and syllabuses, taught by the same methods, as are used in the schools or in higher education institutions. It seems logical, then, to place adult education under the school or higher education branch of the ministry of education. In some countries, however, where programmes and courses are specially tailored for adults, it is arguable that it should be placed under the administration of a special branch of the ministry or an agency independent of the ministry.

Some professional adult educators are opposed to control by ministries of education on the grounds that they are inflexibly preoccupied with primary, secondary and higher education. It is claimed that, in practice, they will always subordinate the needs of adult education to what they consider more pressing scholastic needs. This scepticism would seem to be justified by past experience.

The advantages of adult education being provided independently of the State system of education are that it facilitates the pursuit of broad goals, enables institutions to evolve in response to felt needs and to modify their programmes accordingly, imposes no limits on the numbers of institutions that may operate, encourages democratic participation, preserves the distinctiveness of adult education and reduces the risk of its being a poor relation of the formal education system.

The disadvantages are that it can lead to the neglect of certain types of programmes and duplication of others and thus to the waste of what are always scarce resources. It creates difficulties in awarding certificates with the *imprimatur* of public examining boards and it can inhibit the recruitment of competent full-time staff because posts lack the security of State employment. Above all, the financial advantages of an integrated public and nonpublic system far outweighs the disadvantages. When completely divorced from the public education system, adult education is always likely to be short of funds.

What is clear is that at the level of national or local government, some administrative machinery is required for policy formulation and ordering priorities in the public and societal interest. The size and sophistication or absence of such machinery are an indication of the seriousness of the commitment of governments to adult education.

Coordination of Public and Nonpublic Provision

What should be the relationship between public and private providers? Should the State directly supervise all adult education programmes or rely on an independent or quasi-independent national board or development council? Should statutory regulations be applied requiring coordination of the activities of public and private providers? If so, what should be the appropriate coordinating machinery at the national, regional and local levels? Given the pluralist patterns of adult education, the question also arises how wide or limited should be State regulation and supervision? To a large extent the answer is conditioned by national custom but there are common choices facing all countries.

Virtually all governments now accept at least some responsibility for the supervision and coordination of adult education services. In practice, however, there are widely varying degrees of involvement reflecting the differences among the few categories listed above. In Spain, for example, the coordinating role of the public education service, which is intended to be a large one, is made explicit under the terms of the "Regulation of May 8, 1989, concerning Public Institutions of Continuing Adult Education" issued by the Ministry of Education and Science. In each region there is a network of centres responsible for coordinating all education activities. Every year the regional departments of education and science must draw up a development plan. In each region there is a regional committee with a prescribed list of members, including two student representatives, and prescribed functions (Spain, 1989).

What cannot be disputed is that governments have the right to ensure that public funds are used for the purposes intended and for the general improvement of adult education services. This calls for some form of control, planning and coordination but also the determination not to stifle institutional responsiveness to actual local needs or reasonable competition among institutions. Given the continuing expansion of adult education services, the supervisory and coordinating role of governments seems bound to increase.

The State and Training at the Work Place

What is to be the relationship between adult education and the world of work? To what extent and by what means should vocational training be complemented by general education? Governments do not wish, as a rule, to interfere with the internal affairs of enterprises but, increasingly, they are concerned to ensure that those in the workforce are capable of adapting to changing requirements, undertaking a variety of tasks crossing occupational boundaries, understanding the wider purposes of their enterprises and acquiring new knowledge and skills as the occasion demands. This calls for an efficient pattern of training on a nationwide scale.

As new techniques proliferate, it is often necessary to update the knowledge and skills of the entire workforce in given enterprises. New technologies require fundamental changes in processes as well as production methods. The practice of concentrating on the training of only a few people in key positions no longer suffices. The interest of governments is illustrated by the United States where in 1989 the then Secretary of Education, William J. Bennett, joined the Labour Secretary, Ann McLaughlin and the Commerce Secretary, C. William Verity, at an exceptional joint press conference in order to announce the publication of a booklet entitled *The Bottom Line: Basic Skills in the Work place*. This contained guidelines for enterprises, education and training institutions and local government authorities on how to identify basic education and training requirements at the work place and to develop sound programmes for addressing them. According to Mr Bennett, "It's not that business has a problem and they don't know it ... Education and training does not stop with the schools, and industry must take an active role in training workers for the future". Mrs McLaughlin added that "Many workers are ill-prepared to deal with rapidly-changing technology because they lack adequate basic skills". For his part, Mr Verity stated that "Basic work place literacy is an absolute necessity if we are to increase our productivity, remain competitive in the global economy and continue to be a world leader" (United States, 1989).

Laws, Regulations, and Financing

The most obvious constitutional difference between the initial education of the young and the education of adults is that the former is usually governed by statute and the second is not. Initial education in many industrialized countries is compulsory for eight to 10 years and, increasingly, young people are required to remain in some form of education and training up to the age of 18, at least, if they are to be eligible for social security payments. Beyond that age, those who complete the entire secondary cycle usually have the right to proceed to a postsecondary institution, often with more or less financial support from public funds. In the great majority of countries, adult education is not a right, even if, *de facto,* adults may be admitted to certain educational institutions, such as the universities in Sweden, and programmes under favourable terms. Adult education is rarely mentioned in legislation, at least explicitly, which is scarcely surprising given that it is not regarded as a discrete part of the education system.

The great exception is Norway where the Parliament passed an Act of Adult Education in 1976, which became operative in August 1977. Previously, the Parliament had established two principles: Adult education should be on an equal footing with basic general education for children and young people, and the definition of adult education comprised vocational as well as liberal and general education (Norway, 1985).

The Act is explicit about the relative duties of the State, the countries and the municipalities, contains detailed regulations for financing non-governmental agencies, and covers a very wide range of provision, classified under eight types of programmes.

In Sweden, the Adult Education Act of 1984 issued regulations for direct provision by the municipal authorities:

> Adult basic education at the 6th grade level in the compulsory school system is guaranteed by law. All immigrants are entitled to special programmes in Swedish as a second language. Furthermore, special measures are drawn up for functionally disabled adults. A current policy issue is if this level will be elevated to up to nine years of formal schooling or even some general subjects at the upper secondary level. (Abrahamsson, 1990, p. 9)

It is self-evident that the organized provision of facilities for adult education will only occur if legislation puts obligations on education and other authorities, requires minimum levels of funding and prescribes rights of access to individuals. In Denmark, for example, the law requires that public institutions such as schools and libraries should provide accommodation for adult classes when they are not serving their primary purpose and that any group of 12 adults may participate in classes subsidized by the State up to 80 per cent of the cost. It is equally self-evident that legislation as such may have little effect if it does not spell out ways and means of attaining desired objectives by the use of decrees and regulations.

Legislation alone does not suffice unless complemented by appropriate financial measures. But the issue of financing is complex and many questions arise. To what extent should the State assume responsibility for the financing of a comprehensive service of adult education? How much money should adult education be allocated in relation to the regular education sector? Should finance be provided exclusively by the State or by the State in conjunction with nongovernmental agencies? Should participants pay fees that cover total costs or partial fees or none at all? Should all workers have the right to periodic paid leave or only certain workers? Should paid leave be granted for attendance at all kinds of educational programmes or only for programmes directly related to a worker's particular occupation? Should paid leave be granted to all workers or should priority be given to those who have received the minimum of initial education? Should the State make special allocations to service agencies, such as libraries and to broadcasting companies in order that they may carry out an educational function independently of or in conjunction with adult education agencies?

Innumerable institutions and groups finance education and training programmes for adults. Many private firms offer learning opportunities on a scale as large as publicly maintained institutions. Many agencies are profit-making. The State is not under the same financial duress, therefore, as for initial education. It can justly assume that many providers are able and willing to undertake their own financing wholly or in large part. On the other hand, there are institutions that cannot function without external help and there are neglected groups in society with obvious learning needs that can only be met by positive public action and expenditures. That action depends, however, on the willingness of national, regional, and local authorities to undertake detailed surveys of the present sources, scale, and patterns of financing with a view to filling the prevailing knowledge gap and identifying urgent needs. This is all the more necessary given that public expenditure on adult education is never contained in a single envelope but, on the contrary, is often completely uncoordinated among government departments and agencies so that, for example, there are different regulations concerning subventions to institutions and the payment of tuition fees.

What should be the nature of the financial obligation at the national and the local level? Some argue that the State should allocate a specific percentage of the national education budget or of GDP to adult education, since otherwise it will inevitably be ignored. In other words, permissive or *ad hoc* funding always means that adult education is sold short and that providing agencies cannot plan for long-term development.

The difficulty for the State is that it can scarcely make open-ended commitments either by guaranteeing subventions to institutions in perpetuity, matching the demand for places in programmes, or giving drawing rights to individuals as proposed in OECD reports on recurrent education. It has also to determine the balance of expenditure between public agencies, such as evening colleges and community colleges, and nongovernmental agencies. The temptation is to treat the former as a priority and to give the latter only the crumbs that remain. Thus, in periods of economic austerity it is common to reduce or cut off subventions to nongovernmental agencies.

Even if a State does resolve that all adults should have the right of access to educational opportunities, neither existing nor reallocated nor additional public resources can possibly meet all demands. This implies that the State must determine short-, medium- and long-term priorities. How are these to be selected? There are at least three possible criteria. First, the State may choose to give support only to those aspects of adult education that are directly related to overall social, cultural, and economic policies. For example, it may decide to promote parent and health education as a means of improving the quality of early childhood education. Second, it may decide not to support any adult to participate in any type of programme but rather only certain categories of adults to attend certain categories of programmes. For example, it may elect to finance literacy but not university-level classes, disadvantaged but not advantaged groups, and promising new ventures rather than well-established programmes. Third, it may support programmes that appear to offer the best returns for money, for example distance learning.

A fundamental issue to be faced is whether adult education can ever become a viable service unless the public authorities are prepared to divert resources from the regular education system. For example, it costs a great deal of money to attract the educationally underprivileged into programmes. Are the necessary funds to be derived from new revenue or from present revenues? In the past, that question was unrealistic given the strain on the finances of most governments and ministries of education. With falling school enrolments and renewed interest in the scope for recurrent and lifelong education, however, it is conceivable. What seems certain is that governments will play an increasing role in the financing of adult education and many agencies will be increasingly dependent on public funds for at least part of their expenditures. At the same time, education and other authorities will be anxious to ensure that the programmes they support are cost-effective.

Conclusions

The report on *Comprehensive Policies for Adult Education* (OECD, 1977a) concluded with a statement that remains valid today:

> If adult education is to realize its full potentials as an instrument of public policy, then it is essential to:
> i)   establish a comprehensive and coordinated pluralist service commanding ample public resources;
> ii) relate its functions to such national social concerns as an active manpower policy and the quality of life;
> iii) integrate the formal (academic) and occupational training sector with regular education as part and parcel of a recurrent education system;
> iv) initiate extraordinary measures to identify and satisfy the unmet educational needs, not least those of persons adjudged to be disadvantaged. (OECD, 1977a, pp. 80-81)

The necessity for lifelong learning has been widely proclaimed but not for its implementation, even though instruments for making it realizable have been designed, notably the strategy of recurrent education. It is likely, however, that governments and societies will be obliged to take more positive measures to realize it in future under the impulse of at least three factors: the redistribution of the population owing to the decline in the number of young people; skilled labour shortages; intensifying international economic competition. Countries may therefore be expected increasingly to encourage adults to undertake regular education and training so as to maintain and develop their knowledge and skills, stay in productive employment and pay the taxes required to sustain public expenditures on the social sector.

The adoption of competitive but pragmatic policies will require countries to clarify the exact aims and principles of adult education within the national or regional framework and to develop flexible models for control, administration, the organization of direct provision, and coordination of the total field. A few national and rather more regional education authorities have already undertaken wide-ranging and detailed analyses of the implications for government responsibilities and specific actions. The report on Adult Education in Quebec, cited above, and a report on Adult Education for the 21st Century (California State Department of Education, 1989), are two remarkable examples of penetrating inquiry and incisive recommendations both for addressing urgent problems and identifying what might be achieved in the short, medium, and long term through systematic planning.

As adult education and training expand and become more systematized, mainly to satisfy economic demands, governments will have to tackle the outstanding issue of the equitable distribution of opportunities, so that all adults may have reasonable access to suitable programmes. Will they continue to finance only those programmes and individuals promising an economic return? All but the most altruistic of private enterprises will certainly be impelled mainly by the profit motive. Or will governments be prepared to finance on a generous scale programmes for the disadvantaged, the rapidly expanding underclass in many Western societies? The disadvantaged are hard to reach and expensive to provide for. In affording them opportunities to learn there is no guarantee of a visible or at least quick return on the investment. It is probable that only those governments that are actuated by enlightened self-interest will allocate generous funds to programmes intended for the disadvantaged.

References

Abrahamsson, K. (1990). Learning rights for the next century: Improving learning options by a new deal between the public and private interests in adult learning. Discussion paper. Stockholm: Swedish National Board of Education.

California State Department of Education. (1989). *Adult education for the 21st century: Strategic plan to meet California's long-term adult education needs.* Sacramento: California State Department of Education.

CERI/OECD (1973). *Recurrent education. A strategy for lifelong learning.* Paris. OECD.

Darkenwald, G.G., & Merriam, S.B. (1982). *Adult education: Foundations of practice.* New York: Harper and Row.

Finland, Ministry of Education (1990). *Developments in education 1988-1990 in Finland* (Report to the 42nd Session of the International Conference on Education in Geneva). Reference publications 1990:15. Helsinki: Ministry of Education.

Gouvernement de Québec (1981). *Adult education in Québec: Possible solutions.* Québec: Gouvernement.

Japan, National Council on Educational Reform (1991). *Further education and training of the labour force. A report to the OECD.* Tokyo: Government of Japan.

Mushkin, S.I. (Ed.) (1973). *Recurrent Education.* Washington, D.C.: National Institute of Education, U.S. Department of Health, Education and Welfare.

Netherlands (1987). Submission to the OECD Conference of High-level Experts on Education, Kyoto, January 1987.

Norway (1985). *Adult education in Norway.* Oslo: The Norwegian Association of Adult Education Associations.

OECD (1977a). *Comprehensive policies for adult education.* Paris: OECD.

OECD (1977b). *Learning opportunities for adults: General report.* Paris: OECD.

OECD (1989). *Education and the economy in a changing society.* Paris: OECD.

Shiokawa, M. (1987). Minister of Education, Science and Culture, in *Proceedings of the Conference of High-level Experts on Education,* Kyoto, January 1987.

Spain, Ministry of Education and Science (1989). *Regulation of May 8, 1991 concerning public institutions of adult education under the auspices of the Ministry of Education and Science.* Madrid: Ministry of Education and Science.

Sweden (1987). Submission to the OECD Conference of High-level Experts on Education, Kyoto, January 1987.

Titmus, C.J. (1980). Local decision-making, private provision and the role of the State. In J.H. Knoll (Ed.), *Internationales Jahrbuch der Erwachsenenbildung, No. 8* (pp. 133-158). Cologne: Böhlau.

UNESCO (1989). *Adult education legislation and administrative measures.* Paris: UNESCO.

United States Department of Education (1989). *The bottom line: Basic skills in the work place.* Washington, D.C.: United States Department of Education.

Chapter 15

LEARNING FOR LIFE: POLICY CONCLUSIONS

WILLEM HOUTKOOP
Dutch Advisory Council for Adult Education and Training,
RVE, Bunnik, The Netherlands

PETER VAN DEN DOOL
Ministry of Education and Science,
Zoetermeer, The Netherlands

The fact that the Dutch Ministry of Education and Science took an active interest in the conference "learning across the lifespan" is no coincidence. Dutch policy with regard to adult education and continuing vocational training has gained momentum, and the conference themes that are addressed in this volume are directly relevant for the policy issues confronting policy-makers, the social partners and the education community in this country.

In general the Dutch government strives for the quantitative expansion and the qualitative improvement of the system of adult and continuing education, albeit within a climate characterized by serious budgetary constraints (Ritzen, 1991). Efforts are being made at present to design a comprehensive policy for adult education and training, which involves defining the financial and legal roles of the different actors. In line with a tendency of functional decentralization, the broad policy goals must be implemented by the regional and local authorities, the social partners, and educational and labour market institutions. Since the policy programme is quite ambitious, the process of actual implementation often has turned out to be laborious and difficult.

The new structural framework for postinitial education will affect the adult learners in many ways. However, they should not be the passive receivers of political and institutional developments, but be the active and conscious users of the system for adult and continuing education, according to their own needs. For the adult learner, but also for teachers, trainers and other resource persons responsible for the operation of

239

student support systems in adult education, this implies that the structural framework must be "translated" into practical programmes and instruments.

The contributions in this volume are about the ways in which these different actors can be empowered to take on this role. In this concluding chapter, the broad outlines of a new, innovative policy for the development of adult and continuing education in the Netherlands are presented, and the consequences of this plan for the adult learner are discussed. It is hoped that this discussion will be of relevance to decision makers and adult educators in other countries of the European Community and the OECD countries more generally.

The Development of Adult and Continuing Education

In the Netherlands, as in other OECD Member countries, participation in adult education has considerably increased during recent years. Two million participants were counted in 1988, amounting to 20 per cent of the adult population. This may well be an underestimate of the size of the adult education market, since the noninstitutionalized forms of adult education such as informal learning and on-the-job training are not taken into account in this estimate. Two-thirds of the activities take place in the private sector, and one-third in the public sector. Whereas the public sector is wholly or partly funded by the government, the private sector relies mostly on its own resources. The demarcation line between these sectors is becoming increasingly blurred — public institutions operate to an increasing extent on the private market, and private institutions render services for public authorities. The profile of the "typical" participant is, as usual, one-sided — they are usually young, male, have a high-quality initial education, are employed, and have high-prestige, well-paid jobs that moreover also offer opportunities for learning on the job.

Funding and Regulations

Public involvement with adult education and continuing vocational training in terms of funding and the setting of regulations has become more prominent in recent years. This involvement concerns, first and foremost, the public educational infrastructure, but also extends to the private sector. The role of the Dutch Ministry of Education is primarily a co-ordinating one.

This public role has grown in an incremental way, usually unplanned, and building on the foundations of a variety of private initiatives. However, recently policy with regard to adult and continuing vocational education has entered into a new phase. The Government strives for a quantitative and qualitative expansion of provision for adult and continuing education. It is supposed that this will lead to certain benefits for society. Economic growth, participation in the labour market and in social and cultural activities in society at large, as well as the more equal distribution of learning opportunities, are mentioned as policy objectives to which adult education can contribute. However, public resources cannot possibly meet all demands. The intended expansion of the adult education sector must occur within the constraints of a constant or, at best, a slightly increased budget. This requires, on the one hand, a sharpening of the definition of public responsibilities and, on the other hand, the effective and efficient use of means and instruments for reaching the stated policy objectives.

Redefinition of Public Responsibility for Adult Education

The redefinition of public responsibilities with respect to adult and continuing vocational education is the key policy issue facing decision makers at present. In general, the safeguarding and promotion of equality of educational opportunity is a major commitment. Public means must by preference go to those citizens who have had the least (educational) chances and who, in the present situation, profit the least from the public supply of educational opportunities. Beyond that adult education becomes the (financial) responsibility of the social partners and the individual learner. This principle is behind the policy being pursued at present by both the Ministry of Education and the Ministry of Labour. The exact boundaries of public responsibility, however, are still being debated. Possible criteria are age, the amount of educational credits already consumed, and the initial level of key qualifications one has reached in the formal educational system, before embarking on an occupational career. Since the Government, together with the social partners, may be considered to be responsible for the training of the unemployed, the labour market position of prospective trainees is also an important criterion. Specific target groups, such as immigrants, ethnic and linguistic minorities, and women seeking to enter or return to the labour market, mostly fall within the criteria mentioned, with the possible exception of the age-criterion.

In the Netherlands, there is a consensus at present that the government is not principally responsible for the training of the employed. This is a responsibility of public and private employers. Marginal public support may be allocated to certain unprofitable sectors of the labour market that are in need of restructuring but lack the resources for achieving this on their own. In general the effort should be focussed on employees who find themselves in vulnerable positions.

Up to now "government" has been used as a container concept for delineating the responsibilities for adult education of the public authorities, private industry, and the individual adult learner. However, between the different ministries a sharper demarcation of responsibilities is also needed. Regularly there is overlap and competition between policy objectives, target groups and institutions residing under different ministries. An example is labour market training for the unemployed. Depending on the level and generality of the qualifications concerned, it can be seen as a responsibility of the Ministry of Education or as that of the Ministry of Labour. The relationship between central, regional and local authorities is also in need of clarification.

Implementation of Public Policy for Adult Education

The definition and demarcation of public responsibility for adult and continuing vocational education is the first major policy issue discussed in this chapter. The second is the question as to how this responsibility can be implemented.

On the one hand, the Government strives for an expansion of the adult education sector; on the other hand there are limits to the public budget for education. This means that, in principle, a large segment of the adult education sector will have to operate under market conditions. Traditionally this is the realm of private institutions. However, public providers will also be required to offer an increasing part of their programmes cost-effectively. Under market conditions, the role of the central-level public authorities is limited to the creation of conditions (certification, quality control, information) that will make the market transparant. This is expected to facilitate the optimal matching of the demand and supply of learning opportunities for adults.

Deregulation and decentralization are two keywords describing the position at present. The satisfaction of public demand for education will mainly be the responsibility of the agencies that know the local situation well (e.g., the regional authorities, communities, and the local labour market agencies). Provision can be organized by large educational institutions that operate relatively autonomously, within the constraints of budgetary and quality parameters agreed upon at a central level of authority. Several adult education institutions (e.g., adult basic education, general secondary adult education, and part-time secondary vocational education) may well be expected to merge with institutions providing secondary vocational education for youth, thus creating new, large establishments. Institutions for youth and adult education may thus become part of large, regional educational centres that can operate fairly autonomously. The expectation is that these institutions will provide a flexible and varied provision for multiple audiences and target groups. They will also offer cost-effective programs for the adult education market.

A crucial question is whether the separate institutions, which are characterized by different organizational cultures and target groups, can be merged in such a way that added value is realised. In theory this is possible because effective use can be made of the experiences gained so far in the provision of adult basic education, in reaching out to "difficult" target groups, in experiments with educational technology and open learning in adult secondary general education, as well as in secondary vocational education programmes with a strong labour market orientation. The difficult task is to strike a balance between these approaches — a balance that will lead to an "adult" provision instead of a copy of regular youth education.

The new conditions demand that the local public authorities be given increased scope for decision making, for example, in deciding on the ways and means of articulating educational needs with respect to adult basic education, general secondary adult education, and part-time secondary vocational education. However, the question is also whether the local authorities are at present adequately equipped to fulfil this role. Another question is how the decision making power of local authorities can be balanced with the relative autonomy of the regional educational centres that are currently envisaged in the Netherlands. This will make it necessary to integrate, on a local level, educational policy with communal policy in fields such as social security and employment policy.

At the regional level, the social partners and local public authorities are responsible for the organization and provision of labour market training for the unemployed. In organizing these training programmes they make use of needs assessment procedures. Their target groups are the people with vulnerable positions on the labour market. Training must be a part of the overall job matching process. The actual training should therefore take place in specialized training centres or alternatively may be bought from private or public educational institutions.

Consequences for Adult Learners and Educational Environments

In this vision of structures and procedures for adult education, the individual learner seems almost a neglected species. To a certain extent this is typical for adult learners who, as a group, often tend to be invisible. When they enter adult education institutions or engage in self-directed learning activities, the most important step — the decision to undertake a learning project — has already been taken. Moreover, since they are mostly voluntary learners, it is very easy to leave the institutions. Under these conditions, and in contrast to the situation prevailing in compulsory education, educational policy can only be expected to have a limited influence on the learning strategies which adults opt for. However, as has been argued in preceding chapters, there is an urgent need for the adult learning effort to be expanded. The contributions to this volume offer some insights that may help to realize this objective. The policy conclusions that can be drawn from the work presented in this volume are mainly of three kinds.

Motivation and Capacity to Learn

Participation and perseverance in learning depend first and foremost on motivation and on key competences such as the capacity to learn (Houtkoop and Van Der Kamp, 1992). Without a positive attitude to education and self-confidence, adults are not likely to actively engage in the learning society. Initial education must therefore prepare people for a life of conscious, continuous learning. This means that initial education should foster a positive attitude towards learning in and beyond initial education, and must confer upon the students the skills and competences that enable them to continue learning in a self-directed way. Until now the systems of initial and post-initial education have gone their separate ways, and students in initial education are seldom made aware of the fact that all learning is "unfinished business". Although they are mainly oriented towards adult learners, the chapters concerned with the capacity to learn in the lifespan provide some insights that are also relevant to initial education. These chapters show that much still needs to be done in terms of developing adequate theory and practice of lifelong learning.

The institutional integration of secondary vocational youth education and adult education, as intended in Dutch policy, will bring young and adult students together in new, large educational establishments. This will offer new possibilities for the creation of a favourable attitude to lifelong and recurrent education. The cross-over of "adult" approaches to learning may further this prospect. Eventually, it may also have consequences for the curriculum, which will increasingly be required to become oriented towards lifelong learning objectives.

Equality of Educational Opportunity

Equality of educational opportunity is a major policy intention with respect to adult and continuing education. It is envisaged that public means must by preference go to those citizens who have had the least (educational) chances. Beyond this, adult education will mainly become the (financial) responsibility of the social partners and the individual adult learner.

This means that in allocating public resources, priority is given to programmes for the disadvantaged — the rapidly expanding educational underclass, as Coleman and Husén (1985) call them. Early school leavers, the long-term unemployed, people reentering the labour market, and the increasing number of sometimes poorly educated migrants, are considered special constituencies for Dutch adult education. The Government takes the view that these groups must be supported in reaching an educational level (start qualification) that will enable them to enter and stay in the labour market. Basic literacy and numeracy, and basic vocational skills, are part of the start qualifications necessary for reaching that level (cf. Benton and Noyelle, 1992). To an increasing extent, these educational activities are part of broader social programmes that are managed on a local level and that are intended to increase social and cultural participation, and strengthen employment. The skills and competences that are transferred during the learning process should not have a narrow skill orientation, but lead to broad transferable vocational competences. The learning should prepare people for other life roles as well.

Adult learners who do not belong to the risk groups mentioned above can be expected to participate in adult education and continuing vocational training in two major capacities, namely as employees in a work organization, or as autonomous, individual consumers of education. In the former case the decision to engage in learning on the job and the nature of the learning experience will be largely determined by the interest of the work organization.

Learning Opportunities in the Work Place

As mentioned by Tuijnman and Van Der Kamp in Chapter 1, recent theories of economic growth take knowledge into account as a primary production factor. The implication of these theories is that work organizations must be transformed into learning organizations. Informal learning on-the-job and on-the-job training may well take precedence over formal training activities. However, little is known about the determinants of the nature and distribution of opportunities to learn at the work place, the optimal organization and the didactic structure of these learning efforts, and the actual results. The chapters on skills formation in the work place offer a warning in this respect. Since informal learning on the job is highly dependent on the division of labour in firm-internal labour markets, the characteristics of the work organization, and the learning opportunities that go with different jobs, the government may be called upon to monitor the developments in this sector. It is clear from several chapters in this volume that monotonous, low skill-intensive jobs give few possibilities for informal learning, and tend to widen the gap between different job levels and educational and career possibilities.

The social partners are principally responsible for the training of employees. The labour unions can accordingly play an important role in safeguarding the interests of workers at lower job levels by advocating, in the context of collective bargaining agreements, that educational opportunities need to be fairly distributed. Hence, in this domain the role of public policy is by definition a modest one. Yet as the quality of the work force has important external effects on society at large, the Government seeks to stimulate the training of employees by means such as the dissemination of relevant information, the allocation of funds for research, development, and experimentation, and the selective provision of incentives such as allowing tax reductions in order to compensate for the cost of training activities. The studies on learning in the work place, presented in this volume, can be seen as an example of the role of the government in funding and disseminating research studies.

Concluding Observations

The individual adult learner will, to an increasing extent, be expected to function as a consumer in the educational "market place". It is envisaged in Dutch policy that the provision of adult education will become more varied with respect to content, level, teaching methods, and organization. Information technology and multi-media systems of education offer great potential for customized, individualized educational programmes. A further step is the concept of self-directed learning, where learners do not follow formal educational courses but design their own learning environments according to their own needs.

The other side of the market metaphor is that individual learners must be capable of analyzing and articulating their needs, making a realistic assessment of their own possibilities and choosing from among the different learning options available to them. The chapters on lifespan development and education illustrate the variety of these needs as people pass through the different stages of life. Whether people will participate in adult education and continuing vocational training is not so much determined by properties such as "innate" intelligence, but by the learners' motivation and attitudes to education. Thus the perceived relevance of educational provisions is a key determinant of lifelong learning.

Public authorities can play two major roles in this "market model". They can seek to empower individual adult learners to make adequate decisions concerning their educational and occupational careers. Second, public authorities can implement measures to improve the transparancy of the educational market. The assessment of learners' abilities and their prior educational and work-related experiences, the supply of information needed for an understanding of the functioning of the market, and the provision of guidance and counselling services for potential learners, are important instruments in this respect. The transparancy of the educational market can also be improved by independent mechanisms for quality control, certification, and monitoring. Several of these initiatives are part of the new Dutch policy for adult education.

However, the formulation of policy intentions, implementation, and the monitoring of short- and long-term outcomes must be based on sound theory and high-quality statistical data. The development of both national and international indicators of the adult education market is a necessary step in this respect. In order for this to be achieved both basic and applied research studies are needed, as well as close international cooperation in data collection and reporting. The Government can play an important role in furthering this effort. Given the fact that adult education and continuing vocational training are a necessary condition for balanced economic and social development, an investment in the system for educational research and development may be expected to yield beneficial results. Major themes for further research are attitudes to education, learning to learn, informal learning in the work place, and educational technology. The chapters in this volume are a valuable contribution towards the effort of improving policy and practice in adult education and training.

References

Benton, L. & Noyelle, T. (1992). *Adult illiteracy and economic performance*. Paris: Centre for Educational Research and Innovation, OECD.

Coleman, J. & Husén, T. (1985). *Becoming adult in modern society*. Paris: Centre for Educational Research and Innovation, OECD.

Houtkoop, W., & Van Der Kamp, M. (1992). Factors influencing participation in continuing education. *International Journal of Educational Research* 17 (6), 537-548.

Ritzen, J.J.M. (1991). Adult education and training as an economic spearpoint. In *Investing in human resources — adult education and training in the Netherlands* (pp. 13-18). Utrecht: RVE, Dutch Advisory Council for Adult Education and Training.

NOTES ON THE CONTRIBUTORS

Erik De Corte studied education at the University of Leuven, after obtaining his certificate as a primary school teacher. He obtained his doctorate in educational sciences in 1970. He is Professor of Educational Psychology at the Faculty of Psychology and Education, and is also Director of the Leuven Language Centre at the University of Leuven. His research interests are arithmetic problem solving in primary school children and the cognitive effects of educational software on children's thinking and problem solving skills. He is chief editor of the journal *Learning and Instruction*, and president-elect of the Division on Educational, Instructional, and School Psychology of the International Association of Applied Psychology.

Correspondence: Faculty of Psychology and Education, Centre for Instructional Psychology and Technology, University of Leuven, Vesaliusstraat 2, 3000 Leuven, Belgium.

Peter G. Heymans was trained as a mathematical psychologist before turning to developmental psychology in 1973. He was associated with the University of Nijmegen until 1984 and has occupied the Chair for Life-span Development at the University of Utrecht since 1984. His research interests include moral development and the modelling of developmental processes and their (social) determinants.

Correspondence: Faculty of Social Sciences, Department of Developmental Psychology, University of Utrecht, P.O. Box 80140, 3508 TC Utrecht, The Netherlands.

Roger Hiemstra is Professor of Adult Education at the School of Education, Syracuse University, New York. He was also Codirector of the Kellog Project designed for the international dissemination of adult education materials. His research has focussed on several topics, including teaching methods for adults; the identification of older adults' learning needs, activities, and potential; and historical research involving adult education. He has an interest in developing ways to help educators in promoting learning by utilizing community resources and technology.

Correspondence: School of Education, Department of Adult Education, Syracuse University, 350 Huntington Hall, Syracuse, New York 13244-2340, U.S.A.

Willem Houtkoop studied sociology in The Netherlands and worked as a researcher in the field of adult and continuing education at the Centre for Educational Research, University of Amsterdam. At present he is Secretary of the Council for Adult and Continuing Education, and senior advisor at the Adviescentrum Opleidingsvraagstukken.

Correspondence: A&O Adviescentrum Opleidingsvraagstukken, P.O. Box 138, 3980 CC Bunnik, The Netherlands.

David F. Lohman is Associate Professor at the Division of Psychological and Quantitative Foundations, College of Education, the University of Iowa. He was visiting professor at the University of Leiden in 1988 and 1989. His recent publications concern human intelligence, cognitive psychology and educational measurement.

Correspondence: College of Education, The University of Iowa, Iowa City, Iowa 52242, U.S.A.

John Lowe is an honourary Professor of Education at the University of Warwick. He retired in 1987 from the OECD where he was responsible for the reviews of national educational policies in Member countries. Previously he had been Head of the Department of Educational Studies at the University of Edinburgh and the first Director of Extramural Studies at the University of Singapore. He is the author of *Education of Adults: A World Perspective* (UNESCO and OISE Press, 1982) and editor of the OECD series of publications on *Learning Opportunities for Adults*.

Correspondence: 3 Rue Ribera, 75016 Paris, France.

Jeroen H. Onstenk works as a researcher at the Centre for Educational Research of the University of Amsterdam (SCO). His research topics include: learning during apprenticeships; (informal) learning in the work place; in-company training for initially poorly educated workers; analysis of broadly applicable skills and job analysis for curriculum development.

Correspondence: Centre for Educational Research, University of Amsterdam, Grote Bickersstraat 72, 1013 KS Amsterdam, The Netherlands.

Geoffrey Scheurman is a doctoral student in educational psychology at the University of Iowa. He hails from Wyoming, where he taught political science to high school students. His primary interests are in the influence of cognitive functions on the development of critical thinking abilities in adolescents and young adults.

Correspondence: College of Education, The University of Iowa, Iowa City, Iowa 52242, U.S.A.

Tom Schuller has worked at the OECD, and at the University of Glasgow and the University of Edinburgh, where he is currently the Director of the Centre for Continuing Education. He is secretary of the journal *Time and Society*. His most recent book is *Life After Work: The Arrival of the Ageless Society* (with Michael Young, published by Harper Collins).

Correspondence: Centre for Continuing Education, The University of Edinburgh, 11 Buccleuch Place, Edinburgh EH8 9LW, Scotland.

P. Robert-Jan Simons studied psychology in Utrecht and Amsterdam from 1967 to 1973. He received a Ph.D. from Tilburg University in 1981. His dissertation examined the role of analogies in learning. He was a senior lecturer at Tilburg University until 1990 and is now Professor of Education at the University of Nijmegen. His main fields of interest are technology in education and human resources development, learning to learn, learning styles, and organizational learning.

Correspondence: Department of Education, University of Nijmegen, P.O. Box 9103, 6500 HD Nijmegen, The Netherlands.

Robert M. Smith has taught adult education theory at several universities in North America. He served for four years as adult education advisor to three African countries and as a senior administrator in university continuing education. Since 1975 his professional activities have focussed on the concept of learning to learn. He dealt with this topic in publications such as: *Learning How to Learn: Applied Theory for Adults* (Cambridge University Press, 1982); and *Learning to Learn Across the Lifespan* (Jossey-Bass, 1990).

Correspondence: Department of Leadership and Educational Policy Studies, Faculty in Adult Continuing Education, Northern Illinois University, DeKalb, Illinois 60115-2866, U.S.A.

Albert C. Tuijnman received a Ph.D. in international education from Stockholm University in 1989. His specializations are adult education, comparative education and research methodology. He is author and (co)editor of several publications: *Recurrent Education, Earnings, and Wellbeing* (Almqvist & Wiksell, 1989); *The Social Sciences in Sweden* (Royal Swedish Academy of Sciences, 1990); *Schooling in Modern European Society: A Report of the Academia Europaea* (Pergamon Press, 1992); and *Effectiveness Research into Continuing Education* (Pergamon Press, 1992). He is a member of the editorial board of the *International Encyclopedia of Education, Second Edition* (Pergamon Press).

Correspondence: Department of Education, University of Twente, P.O. Box 217, 7500 AE Enschede, The Netherlands.

Peter C. Van Den Dool was trained as an educational psychologist. At present he works at the Ministry of Education and Science in the Directorate for Vocational and Adult Education as Head of the Information and Evaluation Division. Until 1989 he worked at the Centre for Educational Research at the University of Amsterdam. His research has focussed on work experience learning, design of curricula and learning processes for adults, and on policy issues related to vocational and adult education.

Correspondence: Ministry of Education and Science, P.O. Box 25000, 2700 LZ Zoetermeer, The Netherlands.

Max Van Der Kamp is full Professor in Adult Education and Head of the Department of Pedagogy, Andragogy and Education, University of Groningen. He is the (co)author of a large number of publications on adult education. He studied psychology and wrote a dissertation on art education at the University of Amsterdam. He is involved in research on adult education and has formulated a nationwide research programme on adult education for the Dutch Institute for Educational Research. He is also a consultant to OECD and UNESCO.

Correspondence: Department of Pedagogy, Andragogy and Education, University of Groningen, Grote Rozenstraat 38, 9712 TJ Groningen, The Netherlands.

Ben Van Onna studied philosophy, theology and sociology in The Netherlands and Germany, and received a doctorate in 1975. From 1972 he was affiliated with institutes for sociological research in Dortmund and Cologne. Since 1979 he has been Professor of Pedagogy and Adult Education at the University of Nijmegen. He is also a scientific manager of the Institute for Applied Social Sciences (ITS) in Nijmegen. His recent work has focussed on the relationship between new technology, work, and education; key-qualifications; and professional learning in work organizations.

Correspondence: Department of General Pedagogics, University of Nijmegen, P.O. Box 9103, 6500 HD Nijmegen, The Netherlands.

Richard K. Wagner received his Ph.D. in cognitive psychology from Yale University in 1985. He is an associate Professor of Psychology at Florida State University. His research interests include theories of intelligence in general and practical intelligence in particular. Research on practical intelligence has been summarized in a book co-edited with Robert Sternberg: *Practical Intelligence: Nature and Origins of Competence in the Everyday World* (Cambridge University Press, 1986).

Correspondence: Department of Psychology, Florida State University, Tallahassee, Florida 32306-1051, U.S.A.

INDEX